Philosophy and Public Policy

By Sidney Hook

Southern Illinois University Press
Carbondale & Edwardsville

Feffer & Simons, Inc.
London & Amsterdam

Library of Congress Cataloging in Publication Data

Hook, Sidney, 1902–
    Philosophy and public policy.

    Includes index.
    1. Liberty—Addresses, essays, lectures.
2. Civil rights—Addresses, essays, lectures.
3. Heroes—Addresses, essays, lectures.
4. Political science—Addresses, essays, lectures.
I. Title.
JC571.H643   323.4   79-16825
ISBN 0-8093-0937-8

To Morris and Rena

Contents

Preface

The essays in this volume were written over a considerable span of years and represent a selection from a vastly greater number that found their way to publication. They illustrate the application of a philosophical standpoint commonly called pragmatism, but which, with less risk of misunderstanding, should be called experimental naturalism, to a series of questions of continuing importance to a free society. Indeed, a striking feature of the large intellectual and cultural issues of our time is the extent to which, despite their topicality, they involve perennial social and political problems. Each generation approaches them with a different idiom and with its own specificities of feeling. But just as soon as thinking about these problems begins, the lines of division reform along familiar patterns.

Who would have thought a generation or two ago that there would be something of a revival of a religious interpretation of culture or that we would be hearing again that without commitment to some transcendent religious principle there could be neither a just social order nor genuine social peace and progress? Yet it would not be difficult to show that *au fond* the challenging views of Alexandr Solzhenitsyn on religion, secular humanism, and morals are not essentially different from those of T. S. Eliot or Jacques Maritain. Who would have anticipated during the days when there seemed to be universal support in the West for the "four freedoms" and their welfare corollaries that the social philosophy of conservatism would blossom once more, that views in some ways reminiscent of Herbert Spencer would win converts in quarters that had been impeccably liberal? Under the shibboleth of "libertarianism" the economic and social positions of the Liberty League of the thirties have been restated in more sophisticated form. They have not yet received an adequate response.

Although social problems are perennial in form, history, of course, always makes a difference to the particular way in which they emerge and are approached. The principled answers to questions that arise about freedom of expression are as old as Plato and as recent and different as J. S. Mill and Justice Holmes. But in an age that has experienced the Nazi holocaust and the Communist Gulag Archipelago, the questions are sensed quite differently, as if they had nothing in common with the issues of the past. Believing as I do that general principles by themselves do not solve specific cases, I am as firmly convinced that without some general principles we cannot adequately understand and satisfactorily settle specific cases. That is why the analysis of perennial problems has a continuing relevance to the problems of humankind.

Some chapters concern themselves with issues that are far from possessing perennial importance like those deriving from the Cold War and the guilt or innocence of Alger Hiss. They nonetheless remain of continuing interest and still polarize American liberal opinion. I do not claim to have finally resolved them but believe that my analyses offer evidence and argument that reflective readers whose minds are not closed will find helpful in reaching their own conclusions.

Another reason for selecting these essays for publication in book form is that most of them originally appeared in periodicals not easily accessible to the general reader. They are reproduced here substantially as they were written. I am indebted to the editorial good judgment of Professor Jo Ann Boydston of Southern Illinois University who suggested the order of the chapters of the book and whose keen eye enabled me to remove some needless repetitions.

South Wardsboro, Vermont
July 1, 1979

Acknowledgments

Most of the chapters in this volume have been previously published and appear here substantially as written.

"Are There Limits to Freedom of Expression?" is reprinted from *Book Week* (6 November 1966).

"The Autonomy of the Democratic Faith" was originally published as "The Autonomy of Democratic Faith" in *The American Scholar* 15, no. 1 (7 December 1945).

"The Ethics of Controversy" is reprinted with permission from *The New Leader* 37 (1 February 1954): 12–14; "Leon Trotsky and the Cunning of History," originally published as "The Cunning of History," is reprinted with permission from *The New Leader* 47 (11 May 1964): 15–18; "A Talk with Vinoba Bhave," originally published as "A Talk with Bhave," is reprinted with permission from *The New Leader* 42 (4 May 1959): 10–13; "Bertrand Russell and Crimes Against Humanity" is reprinted with permission from *The New Leader* 49 (24 October 1966): 6–11. All copyright © The American Labor Conference on International Affairs, Inc.

"Reverse Discrimination" was originally published in part in *Bell Telephone Magazine* (Fall 1978) and is reprinted with permission. This chapter is also based in part on "Triumph of Racism," *Freedom at Issue*, no. 47 (September–October 1978): 3–6, and is reprinted by permission, copyright 1978 by Freedom House, Inc.

"Religion and Culture: The Dilemma of T. S. Eliot," originally published as "The Dilemma of T. S. Eliot," *The Nation* 160 (20 January 1945): 69–71, and "Religion and Culture: A Reply by Jacques Maritain," originally published as "The Foundation of Democracy," by Jacques Maritain, *The Nation* 160 (21 April 1945): 440–

42, are both reprinted by permission, copyright 1945 The Nation Associates.

"The Scoundrel in the Looking Glass," originally published as "Lillian Hellman's Scoundrel Time," *Encounter* 48, no. 2 (February 1977): 82–91, and "The Case of Alger Hiss," *Encounter* 51, no. 2 (August 1978): 48–55, are both reprinted by permission.

"Philosophy and Public Policy," an extension of an essay with the same title that appeared in *The Journal of Philosophy* 67, no. 14 (23 July 1970): 461–70, is reprinted with permission.

"Law and Anarchy" is reprinted with permission from *University of Richmond Law Review* 5 (1970): 47–69.

"Intelligence, Morality, and Foreign Policy" is reprinted by permission from *Freedom at Issue*, no. 35 (March–April 1976): 3–6, copyright 1976 by Freedom House, Inc.

"Reflections on Human Rights" is reprinted from *Ethics and Social Justice*, Howard E. Kiefer and Milton K. Munitz, eds., volume 4 of Contemporary Philosophic Thought, The International Philosophy Year Conferences at Brockport, by permission of the State University of New York Press. © 1968, 1970 by State University of New York, Albany, New York, all rights reserved.

"The Social Democratic Prospect," originally published as "The Social Democratic Challenge," is reprinted by permission from *New America* 13 (August–September 1976): 8–9.

"Capitalism, Socialism, and Freedom," originally published as part of the symposium "Capitalism, Socialism, and Democracy," is reprinted by permission from *Commentary* 65 (April 1978): 48–50, copyright © 1978 by the American Jewish Committee.

"The Hero in History: Myth, Power, or Moral Ideal?" is reprinted with permission of the publishers, Hoover Institution Press, copyright © 1978 by the Board of Trustees of the Leland Stanford Junior University.

"The Relevance of John Dewey's Thought" is reprinted by permission from *The Chief Glory of Every People: Essays on Classic American Writers*, Matthew J. Bruccoli, ed. (Carbondale: Southern Illinois University Press, 1973), pp. 53–75, copyright © 1973 by Southern Illinois University Press.

"Toynbee's City of God," originally published as "Mr. Toynbee's City of God," is reprinted by permission from *Partisan Review* 15 (June 1948): 691–99, copyright © June 1948, by *Partisan Review*.

Part One:
Philosophy and
Public Policy

Chapter 1
Philosophy and Public Policy

To anyone who believes that there is a body of philosophical knowledge comparable to the bodies of knowledge acquired in other disciplines the very title of this collection of essays must seem anomalous. A series of essays entitled *The Nature of Chemistry* or *The Nature of Mathematics* would strike the reader as rather bizarre if they expressed different conceptions of what the subject matter of chemistry or mathematics was. To be sure there could legitimately be different analyses of the subject matter, different metascientific and metamathematical interpretations, but in every case this would presuppose the existence of, and agreement upon, certain truths whose cumulative development constituted the subject matter being discoursed about. Scientists do not disagree about the validity of specific laws that have been established, nor do mathematicians disagree about the validity of specific theorems. But there is not a single piece of philosophical knowledge, not a single philosophical proposition, on which philosophers are all agreed.

It was Arthur O. Lovejoy who many years ago called attention to this skeleton rattling in the philosophical cupboard. And although he proposed that philosophy become empirical in order to reach conclusions that could be universally agreed upon by all qualified investigators, he never showed how it could be done. Since his time the scandal of philosophical disagreement has, if anything, become more pronounced. When he wrote, there seemed to be rather general agreement among philosophers that what G. E. Moore called "the naturalistic fallacy" was a fallacy and that J. S. Mill had committed it, that there was a sharp distinction between analytic and synthetic judgments, that there were no *a priori* synthetic judgments (including that assertion), and that the truths of logic and mathematics were valid no matter what. Today every one of these positions has been controverted by highly qualified professional philosophers. Every traditional philosophical position is just as much in dispute, when it emerges into the focus of attention, as in the past.

Does this mean that there has been no progress in philosophy? If progress is measured in the same way as it is in fields like medicine or physics, by increase in systematized knowledge and control, then we must acknowledge that there has been no progress. But if the index of progress is depth, complexity, and subtlety of analysis or the level and rigor of argument, then undoubtedly there has been progress. Nonetheless such progress, instead of diminishing disagreement, preserves it and sometimes intensifies it. It has not led to any body of philosophic truths that would warrant reference to philosophic knowledge. Only the style of thinking has changed. It has become more scientific without the fruits of science.

It is at this point that philosophers are tempted to abandon the claim to be in the possession of any knowledge, and to surrender the quest for knowledge to ordinary commonsense experience and the sciences which have developed from it. Philosophy is then defined as an activity, an activity of conceptual or categorical analysis which results not in knowledge but in clarification. There are some difficulties with this view, too. This kind of analysis is not restricted to philosophers. At some point every scientist raises questions about his fundamental organizing terms. But more important, there is no more agreement about the upshot of this analysis than about substantive conclusions. The conceptual or categorical analyses of scientists seem to be controlled by the state of scientific knowledge or by the bearing they have on integrating what is known and furthering more fruitful inquiries. Thus Einstein's analysis of the concept of simultaneity and his contention that the simultaneity of events is relative, not absolute, recommended itself in terms of the consequences of its use. But there does not seem to be any comparable way of determining the relative validity of different philosophic analyses of the concepts of "matter," "self," "consciousness," "individual."

At the present juncture of philosophical thought it seems appropriate, therefore, to present one's conception of philosophy as a *proposal* in the light of the state of affairs described above. To the extent that the proposal is accepted, cooperative inquiry may result in common findings and agreement comparable to some extent to the

universally agreed-upon conclusions of scientific inquiry. But even
if the scandal of philosophical disagreement persists, this would
not be fatal either to professional activity or popular interest in
what goes by the name of philosophy, but only to pretentious claims
to be in possession of genuine knowledge. It may be that philosophy can continue as an autonomous intellectual activity regardless
of whether there is anything like philosophic knowledge or truth,
just as artistic and religious activities are enjoyed regardless of
whether or not there are any such things as universally agreed-upon
"artistic truths" or "religious truths"—about which I myself am
very skeptical.

Together with a few other American philosophers who have studied with or been influenced by John Dewey, I have always believed
that philosophy is legitimately concerned with large problems of
human affairs, that philosophers should have something to say to
their fellow citizens and not only to their professional colleagues.
To those of us who have held this point of view, there is something
ironical about the mounting surge of impassioned interest in public
policy that has suddenly developed among those hitherto indifferent
to its themes. When this is accompanied by zealous and sometimes
self-righteous demands that philosophers *do* something about the
state of the world, that they offer programs and solutions to the per-
plexing problems from which the community suffers, the situation
becomes not so much ironical as one of dramatic parody. I am referring particularly to the actions of some professional organizations of
philosophers which have adopted resolutions by a majority vote at
sparsely attended business meetings or by mail ballot on controversial problems of social and political interest not directly related to
their legitimate professional concerns.

I say "dramatic parody" because it sometimes sounds as if philosophers were being urged to become merely social reformers, to play
the role that we were falsely taxed with advocating by influential
critics among an earlier generaion of philosophers. We were condemned for conceiving of philosophy in a way that betrayed its true
vocation, for reducing it from a position of proud autonomy to that
of handmaiden to the progressive politics of the age.

The charge was false. It is true that John Dewey as a *citizen* was
a great social reformer. And it is true that he believed that the central and continuing concern of philosophy involved problems of
moral choice and policy on which all reflective human beings must
act. But this does not entail the view that *philosophy* is social-re-
formist or revolutionary or counterrevolutionary. And still less does
it justify any demand that philosophers, organized as a *professional*
association to further the interests of philosophic study and the

teaching of philosophy, take stands on specific political issues or programs except those that bear on their freedom to pursue their professional activity.

I propose to consider afresh the relation between philosophy and public affairs and draw some conclusions on how philosophers should conceive their role with respect to its problems. The easiest and least rewarding approach to the issues is the question-begging procedure of defining philosophy in terms of one's own partisan philosophical standpoint, and then reading off what is included or excluded from the circle of its implications. Surely a more fruitful and less partisan approach is the denotative, historical one. Let us ask: What are the criteria by which until now thinkers have been included in a history of philosophy as distinct from a history of physics or mathematics or psychology? Why do we include Descartes, Leibniz, Hobbes, and Spinoza in a history of philosophy, and not merely as figures in chapters of the histories of physics, mathematics, or psychology? I believe the reason is that all of them are concerned at some point with the nature of value, with the nature of the good in man or society or history. The most comprehensive as well as the most adequate conception of philosophy that emerges from the history of philosophy is that it is *the normative consideration of human values*. Another way of putting this is that philosophy is a study of existence and possibility from the standpoint of value and its bearing on human conduct. Thus, it seems to me, is the central thread of continuity in the history of philosophy from Socrates to John Dewey. It envelops even those who, on skeptical or meta-ethical grounds, have concluded that philosophy has nothing cognitively meaningful to say about human values.

If this is what philosophy has been, or even if it is taken only as a proposal of what it should be, it is altogether natural for the community to turn to the philosopher in expectation of finding some wise guidance or some integrated outlook on life. For whatever else wisdom is, it is insight into the nature, interrelation, and career of values in human experience. If philosophers can provide no wisdom, the community turns to others for guidance and enlightenment— traditionally to its priests and prophets, to its poets and dramatists, and in periods of crisis to faith healers, confidence men, and other creatures of the intellectual underworld.

Obviously the philosopher is not unique in his concern with values and with the rational grounds for value-decisions. All men are concerned with problems of human conduct, but what others do episodically the professional philosopher does systematically.

The great difficulty with this conception of philosophy is that it seems unrelated to so many other philosophical concerns—epistemological, ontological, and logical—which for many, if not most, philosophers constitute the very heart of their discipline. How are these technical philosophical problems and questions, like the theory of universals or the knowledge of other people's minds or the analysis of analyticity, encompassed in this view of philosophy?

Two possible answers to this question have a bearing on our theme. One answer is that the perennial problems of philosophy are directly or indirectly bound up with problems of human value, with the quest for wisdom or a satisfactory way of life. The proper ordering of human conduct depends upon knowledge of self and mind, and this in turn upon knowledge of society and history, of the world and its environing cosmos; and both kinds of knowledge, insofar as they differ from opinion, guesswork, or hearsay, are assured by the tested methods of critical inquiry.

This is no new conception of man in the universe. Nor it is an expression of scientism. From time immemorial the pursuit of wisdom or the definition and achievement of the good life has been related to other things. This holds true not only for Western culture, but for all cultures known to man. A simple and amusing illustration of this is provided in a text from Confucius in the sixth century before our era.

The ancients who desired to cast light on illustrious virtues throughout the kingdom, first ordered well their own states. Wishing to order well their states, they first regulated their families. Wishing to regulate their families, they first cultivated their persons. Wishing to cultivate their persons, they first rectified their hearts. Wishing to rectify their hearts, they first sought to be sincere in their thoughts. Wishing to be sincere in their thoughts, they first extended to the utmost their knowledge; such extension of knowledge lay in the investigation of things.

Things being investigated, knowledge became complete. Their knowledge being complete, their thoughts were sincere. Their thoughts being sincere, their hearts were then rectified. Their hearts being rectified, their persons were cultivated. Their persons being cultivated, their families were regulated. Their families being regulated, their states were rightly governed. Their states being rightly governed, the whole kingdom was made tranquil and happy.

Introduction to *The Great Learning*

A more complex illustration is provided by John Dewey, who contends that the connection between philosophy and civilization is intrinsic. Whenever a civilization develops beyond the level of the merely customary and seeks to develop a reflective morality, it asks three questions. First, "What are the place and role of knowledge and reason in the conduct of life?" Second, "What are the constitution and structure of knowledge and reason in virtue of which they can perform the assigned function?" And growing out of this question, third, "What is the constitution of nature, of the universe, which renders possible and guarantees the conceptions of knowledge and of good that are reached?" On this view the quest for wisdom and for understanding the nature of reflective conduct provides the principle of relevance to philosophical inquiry as distinct from purely scientific inquiry. The discussion of public policy and of the value-decisions involved is an appropriate concern for philosophers, and one not unrelated to the ontological and epistemological questions, no matter how recondite and technical, with which professional philosophers deal.

There is an obvious objection to this first answer. It can be argued that the relationship between the quest for wisdom or the ideals of rational conduct, on the one hand, and the many problems in the different fields in which professional philosophers are engaged, on the other, is historical and accidental, not logical or necessary. Chesterton's landlady, who is rightfully, from the point of view of a landlady, more interested in the philosophy of her boarder than in the contents of his trunk, doesn't care a tinker's damn about her boarder's views on universals, the mind-body problems, induction, or the status of theoretical constructs and intervening variables. Whether he will pay his rent or skip may be more reliably inferred from his views on whether promises are *prima facie* binding or the justice of piecemeal appropriation of those who live on unearned income and allied ethical considerations than from his views on ontology or epistemology. A professional philosopher could support her indifference to these latter questions by defending with complex arguments the complete autonomy of moral judgment. The relationships among the various philosophical disciplines is a metaphilosophical problem, and still open.

Further, to the extent that this first answer presupposes that all knowledge either originally or ultimately arises from some practical interest or that thinking exists for the sake of action or application, one can challenge this with the contention that man has a natural curiosity to know for its own sake, and that this desire or drive, and not the practical necessities of living, feeds his metaphysical hunger. It also accounts for his absorption with the minutiae of the technical philosophical disciplines.

We are dealing with a highly tangled question posed by this first answer. It would require a volume to unravel it. But in a tentative way I believe it is justified to bring in a Scotch verdict: "Not proven." Although I believe that Peirce and Dewey are right in their claim that some activity or experiment ultimately enters into all scientific knowledge of fact, I do not believe that all scientific knowledge is acquired for some practical end or purpose. Aristotle's insights in the first paragraph of his *Metaphysics* seem to me to be valid. Even Dewey admits that the division between what is considered philosophical and scientific in the history of natural science is "often arbitrary." The speculative and broadly hypothetical phases of scientific thought can be considered philosophical independently of their bearing on the pursuit of wisdom or human values. But we must be clear that philosophy so conceived is ancillary to or anticipatory of specific scientific views especially in cosmogony and cosmology. Aristotle's view about the role of the heart, Kant's conception of the origin of the world—his acceptance of the nebular hypothesis—and Peirce's notions about the spontaneous generation of life are hardly of any concern to their philosophical successors.

Spin off, then, this kind of scientifically oriented philosophy from the traditional conceptions. Is what is now left essentially related to questions of normative analysis of values that ultimately affect, even when they are not directly affiliated with, issues of social and public policy?

I do not think so. Nor did Dewey, despite some occasional words to the contrary. There is something that Dewey himself recognizes as "a kind of music of ideas that appeals, apart from any question of empirical verification, to the minds of thinkers, who derive an emotional satisfaction from an imaginative play synthesis of ideas obtainable by them in no other way." * This is the aesthetic dimension of philosophy, philosophy for the fun of it, irrelevant to any social use and application.

We turn away, then, from the first answer to the question of how the phiosopher's concern with public policy can be justified as untenable.

This first answer was unnecessarily strong. For there is a second and less controversial answer that justifies concern with issues of public policy not as *the* philosopher's task, but as *one* of them. It makes problems of social and public policy a legitimate field of interest among others. This is a relatively humble view. It does not impose a duty or obligation on all philosophers to busy themselves with questions of this sort, but defends their right to do so against certain methodological purists, and against those whose conception of the subject matter of philosophical inquiry would exclude questions of public policy as improper themes of professional exploration and inquiry. Such purism is simply a form of intolerance, which

---

* John Dewey, "Philosophy," in *Encyclopaedia of the Social Sciences*, ed. Edwin R. A. Seligman (New York: Macmillan Co., 1934), 12:118.

would outlaw from the scope and sphere of philosophy important contributions to the discussion of human affairs by thinkers as disparate as Plato, Hegel, and John Stuart Mill. Such taboos are captious and arbitrary. But just as captious and arbitrary are those who would impose on all philosophers the necessity of taking a position as *philosophers* on those questions which as citizens they cannot escape. Questions of public policy should be the primary concern of those philosophers only who have a strong bent and special capacity for them.

The really important question for our purpose is, How should the philosopher *as* a philosopher proceed in his discussion of public affairs in contradistinction to others? Or, put differently, what can we expect from the contributions of the philosopher that would differentiate them from the contributions of the hosts of unphilosophical laymen already at work in the field?

First of all, we must expect of him a thorough familiarity with the subject matter—the facts in the case—with respect to which policy decisions are to be taken. This means that as a rule the philosopher is initially out of his field when he discusses questions of public policy. His training does not uniquely qualify him to master them. This mastery is a *sine qua non,* and not all the moral principles or sensitivities of conscience can compensate for its lack. Although no policy can be logically derived from any aggregation of facts, there are some facts that are sufficient in some problematic situations to invalidate policy proposals.

Not all philosophers who have suddenly turned to public affairs have shown that degree of familiarity with what they are talking about that we have a right to expect. For example, some philosophers have seriously asserted that United States economic involvement in various parts of the world is motivated primarily by the desire merely to exploit the peoples of those countries and that its only effect is to frustrate their economic plans, apparently unaware that the cessation of that involvement would spell death by starvation to tens of thousands in India, and great hardships to the peoples of Israel, Taiwan, and South Korea, to mention only a few countries. Problems of economic aid and kinds of aid are of tremendous complexity, and cannot be solved by outbursts of moral indignation.

Some philosophers have recently declared that repression in the United States is almost as bad today as it was in Hitler's Germany, thus convicting themselves not only of gross ignorance of what life was like under Hitler and of the unparalleled freedom of dissent in the United States today, but disarming themselves and others by this newly minted version of the theory of social fascism in the struggle against the dangers of a social backlash in the future.

The second thing we must expect from philosophers is a kind of methodological sophistication that either sharpens the issues at point in public controversy or discloses the absence of real or genuine issues, thus clarifying the options open for decision. For example, the confusion that attends the discussion of the self-incrimination clause of the Fifth Amendment is an intellectual scandal and contributes to the mischievous consequences of its abuse in every jurisdiction of the land. Philosophers could render a needed service in dissecting the tortured and tortuous reasoning of the courts. The problem of action, or what to do about the Fifth Amendment, is something else again. This involves a strategy for legislators beyond the competence of philosophical analysts.

The third kind of contribution a philosopher can make to the study and analysis of public policy is philosophical perspective. By this I mean, wherever it is relevant, the disentangling of ideological issues from factual ones. This is particularly important in discussions of birth control, abortion, suicide, and, in general, questions of church and state.

Perhaps the most important contribution the philosopher can make to the discussion of public affairs is to make explicit the ethical issues behind conflicting public policies and to relate them to the kind of society in which we want to live and to the kind of men and women we wish to see nurtured in such a society. It is here that the philosopher's professional interest in systematic moral evaluation, or his vocation as amoralist, should sensitize him to the presence of moral issues in what is sometimes regarded as a purely factual inquiry. The furious controversy over the implications of inquiries concerning genetic group differences is a case in point. Nothing significant in the way of civil rights and equal opportunities follows from any of the reported findings of differences in native capacities of different groups. Suppose in an individual family the IQs of the children range between upper and lower limits of 15 or 20 or even 30 points. Would anyone in his moral senses conclude that therefore this difference justified discrimination against any of the children with respect to their food, clothing, shelter, recreation, health care, and dignified treatment as human beings? There is a distinction between not having the relevant knowledge that would make a difference to our treatment of individuals and not knowing what difference any specific piece of relevant knowledge would make. The crucial questions in the treatment of religious, ethnic, and racial minorities are moral, and those who have thrown obscurantist blocks in the path of inquiry into questions of differential genetic capacities out of fear of the social consequences are fundamentally confused.

This confusion is not the monopoly of any one group whether "conservative" or "liberal"—terms that have become epithets of praise or abuse, not of reliable description. It is illustrated in some of the ways in which "the program of affirmative action" has been implemented. Designed to prevent discrimination in employment on the basis of irrelevant criteria of race, religion, sex, or national origin, in case after case it has resulted in forms of *reverse* discrimination in consequence of both logical and ethical error. The program recognizes that whenever there is unjust discrimination, sharp disproportions in the number of women and members of minorities result. It then infers from the existence of sharp disproportions in the sex and minority membership of the number of persons employed, evidence of invidious and unjust discrimination, thus overlooking the presence of other factors at work, like social stereotypes, that account for the disproportions. Condemning "quota" systems and efforts to achieve them, it imposes on universities "numerical goals" to be achieved within certain time schedules, overlooking the fact that "quotas" are "numerical goals," and that there is no difference in cognitive meaning between the commitment to "good faith" efforts to achieve quotas and the commitment to "good faith" efforts to achieve numerical goals. Finally, when partisans of the affirmative action program realize they are espousing a quota system, they justify reverse discrimination on the ground that it is a form of compensatory justice, as if the fact of injustices against the innocent victims of the past can absolve us from the odium of injustices against innocent victims in the present.

Finally, the philosopher must bring to his analysis of public affairs, no matter how passionate his moral concern, a kind of intellectual disengagement as a safeguard against one-sidedness, bias, and *parti pris*. We have plenty of fanatics and partisans at hand. There is no need for the philosopher to reinforce their shrill voices. In a world of widespread commitment to fixed causes and antecedently held conclusions, the philosopher must never surrender his objectivity. He must be prepared to recognize the truth when it is uttered even by those who are hated or condemned. This is extremely difficult, especially in the field of foreign policy, where a great deal of guesswork is involved. More important, it is a field in which errors are difficult to retrieve because even when they are acknowledged, the consequences of the original mistakes may alter the position to a point where what would have originally been the best alternative to begin with is no longer possible. To say that the foreign policy of the United States is not wise or sensible is not to say, as some philosophers have said, that it is all morally outrageous. And to deny that its policy is all morally outrageous is not to say that all of it is wise or sensible.

Listening to some philosophers indict the foreign policy of the United States since the Second World War, we hear merely a litany of horrors. There are horrible enough errors in the record to give all of us pause; but anyone who can mention that record without mentioning the fact that the United States withdrew its major forces from Europe while the Red Army was astride Europe, that it not only offered the Marshall Plan for the reconstruction of Europe but extended the offer to countries in the Communist orbit, that when the United States had the monopoly of atomic weapons and could have imposed its will on any nation of the world it offered to surrender that monopoly to an international authority—a concrete proposal for international socialism!—that it encouraged an agricultural and political revolution in Japan that restored it to greater heights of prosperity and with greater freedom than it ever enjoyed, that it has not ideologically interfered with its economic aid to Yugoslavia and other socialist and semisocialist regimes in Asia and Africa—anyone who fails to weigh these things and many others like them together with the errors in the balance of judgment is simply a propagandist.

The plain truth of the matter is that philosophers who have concerned themselves with public affairs in the past have not distinguished themselves by the cogency of their analysis or the accuracy of their predictions. For example, every one of the philosophers who ventured a judgment on the Munich settlement of 1938—Whitehead, Russell, Dewey, Santayana according to report—hailed it and urged its approval as the best insurance of peace. It turned out to be the worst.

Indeed, when one looks at the historical record of philosophical involvement in public affairs from Plato to the present, it can only inspire intellectual humility among those of us who are concerned with current issues. To speak only of our own century, we need only refer to Santayana's apologias for Mussolini and Stalin, Heidegger's support of Hitler, Sartre's and Merleau-Ponty's refusal to condemn the concentration-camp economy of the Soviet Union. Of course this is not the whole story. Although the record of Anglo-American philosophy is much better, Dewey's endorsement of the First World War and Russell's proposal for preventive nuclear war against the Soviet Union are evidence that philosophers can go as far astray as their unphilosophical colleagues and fellow citizens.

Seen in perspective, the faults of most philosophic treatments of public affairs flow not so much from defects of analysis as from mistakes of advocacy. This is brought out very well by John Stuart Mill in his analysis of the ethics of nonintervention, which still makes illuminating reading for our time. Although a position may be morally principled like "intervention to enforce non-intervention" when a people is struggling to defend its freedom and independence against despotism, it may not be prudent because of the likely consequences of the action. Mill makes one understand when we read his analysis how men of good will and intelligence can differ with each other. This makes his own conclusions far more weighty and persuasived than those by writers who arrogantly imply that none but fools or knaves can disagree with them. Much of politics is a choice of lesser evils in which the actual upshot of affairs depends upon contingent events. It is well to bear in mind that successful political action often depends upon timing and a discounting or reckoning in advance of what the other side will do.

There are some matters on which practical experience may be a better guide than pure theory. The very virtues of the thinker and man of vision—prolonged reflection, skepticism of one's own first principles, the long view, the attempt to see the situation from the standpoint of the other—may prove to be drawbacks in critical situations, when the fate of a people or a nation or a culture hangs in the balance. They may be sources of weakness when time is of the essence and action must be taken without the benefit of confirmed evidence. That is why as a rule philosophers *as* philosophers are not likely to make good public officials—the careers of John Stuart Mill and de Tocqueville as legislators were quite undistinguished—although in their capacity as citizens or even as party members they may be as good as their neighbors. Philosophers are better as critics than as intellectual laureates of the *status quo*. And this for several reasons. They have a keen sense of alternatives. They are likely to be more aware than others of the disparities between the ideal and the actual. And above all they cannot without stultification give their primary intellectual loyalty to any nation, cause, party, or organization, but only to the truth as they see it. That very commitment to truth should prevent them from using lies and certain selected truths that function as lies, to further what they are convinced is a higher good or a holy cause.

As great and as important as the philosopher's insights may be for the illumination of public affairs of his own time, let us not deny that the outstanding philosophers of the past speak to us for other reasons. Their meaning for us today is found in some moral insight or vision that transcends the events of their own times. Public affairs and public policy do not exhaust the field of normative values. We read Hobbes and Hume, Spinoza and Kant, not because of their commentary upon and analysis of the public affairs of their day, but because of their visions of human excellence, their grasp of recurrent if not perennial problems of social life, and their insights into the condition of man. The great philosophers are not men of one note, or of one season, or of one mood. When they are in their time, they are not merely of their time. That is why Socrates, Plato, and Aristotle do not date in their central concerns, and still possess a freshness for sensitive and inquiring minds that have discounted their parochial setting.

The philosopher is uniquely a moral seer, a moralist, if you will, but not a moralizer or a priest or prophet. He is a lover and pursuer of wisdom wherever he finds himself, in any clime and in any culture. In the words of one whose soaring thought was much more impressive than his petty and uneventful life (Santayana): "It is not easy for him [the philosopher] to shout or address a crowd; he must be silent for long periods, for he is watching stars that move slowly and in courses that it is possible though difficult to foresee and he is crushing all things in his heart as in a winepress until his life and their secret flow out together."

1970

Chapter 2

Law and Anarchy

That the United States is going through a crisis of law enforcement today goes without saying. The mass media in all their forms say it loud and clear. A few months ago Chicago was the eye of the storm. Some weeks later it was New York. Then came eruptions at Santa Barbara and elsewhere. Tomorrow mass violence may boil over almost anywhere. This crisis extends not merely to trust in, and acceptance of, the normal activities of agencies of law enforcement but to the authority of law and government as such. The planned and systematic degradation of the academy has been extended to the courts. Just as in the case of the universities, the efforts made to *prevent* disruption have produced as much criticism and, in some editorial quarters, even more criticism than the original violence that inspired the counter measures.

I wish to consider certain views and attitudes about law and government that seem widely held today, that encourage contempt for law and at least indirectly bear on current political behavior.

Does it really make a difference—one may ask—what human beings think about such abstruse matters as the nature of law, the state, and the source and justification of political authority? John Maynard Keynes asserted that the most important determinant of social and historical affairs is the ideas men carry around in their heads. Certainly the ideas that sported in Keynes's head exerted profound influence. If we look at economic life today, it would require considerable courage to believe that the marketplace is free and that the consumer is king. The decisions of the Federal Reserve Board concerning interest rates—decisions that clearly flow from some large theoretical assumptions—seem to confirm the importance of ideas, even of very abstract ideas. Whether this holds to the same *degree* in other fields is an open question. What is not open to question, regardless of whether we try to explain human action in terms of causes or reasons, and of whether we distinguish between good reasons, real reasons, and mere rationalizations, is the fact that what people believe, or think they believe, makes some difference in their conduct. Otherwise they would not cling to their beliefs in the face of so much evidence to the contrary.

The ideas people carry around in their heads have various sources. Some are traditional and customary, acquired almost in the same effortless way as we acquire speech. Some are the result of schooling. In these days of exposure to the conditioning of mass media, they are absorbed from the professional commentators who are *makers* of opinion even when they pretend only to be *reporters* of opinions. Ideas and attitudes are sometimes transmitted through a kind of osmosis and contagion by ideological groups which are skillful in their capacity to command a hearing on any issue anywhere and to exploit the limelight of mass media publicity without cost. It used to be said that disparities in the ownership of the means of publication and communication gave an undue and uncompensated advantage to those who owned and controlled them, that points of view hostile to, or even different from, those of the so-called Establishment could get no hearing. A sober survey of the facts requires us to qualify and perhaps to reject this easy generalization. The nature of the mass media today, their intense competition for high ratings, and their consequent desire for scoops and spectaculars on radio and television, reinforce the tendency to exploit the sensational, the bizarre, and the extreme. This opens up vast possibilities to reach multiple audiences to those who, on the basis of the intellectual or social importance of what they have to say, could hardly command a single audience.

Whether highbrow or lowbrow, strident or nuanced, ideas and attitudes so acquired have implications and ultimate effects not always understood by those who express them. For example, the impassioned groups that shout in our New York courtrooms today, "All power to the people" are unaware that they are calling for mob rule to which many of their forbears were victims. After all, how can we distinguish between the mob and the people, particularly when every mob speaks in the name of the people, except in terms of the rule of law—a rule of law by which the people themselves, even when they are the ultimate source of the rule, must be bound until the rule can be changed by procedures that also function according to rules. Without the rule of law, "the people" is a mob swayed by gusts of anger and passion that, as often as not, are contrived by shrewd and skillful demagogues. Probably that is what Alexander Hamilton meant when he exclaimed, in a passage attributed to him but which no one has ever found in his writings, "The People, Sir, the People is a Beast." It is the "People" as "King Mob" that is a "Beast."

One cannot expect sophistication on the part of those who mouth slogans. But what shall we say of the new crop of radical activists who justify their desperate organized resistance to the present social order in the name of the classless society of the future in which the state—its armies, police, courts, and all separate bodies of armed men—will have disappeared? When asked how in such a society they would deal with a person who brutally assaulted another or who committed some monstrous or outrageous action or was so charged, what reply do they make, these sincere idealists praised by some admirers of the New Left as the brightest students of our century? They either blandly deny that such behavior will be possible in the classless society—presumably it will be a secular version of the Kingdom of Heaven on earth!—or they fall back on Lenin's answer in his *State and Revolution*: that in the event of what we today call a criminal assault by one person against another, justice will in effect be done on the spot without police, court, or trial.[1] In their revolutionary innocence, they seem sublimely unaware that this is precisely what is meant by "lynch law."

It may seem odd to give attention to ideas and assumptions that at first sound strike the ear as unfamiliar and crude. But if the importance of ideas is gauged by their impact on events, by the growing number of their adherents, and the intensity with which they are held, and if the force of ideas in human affairs is measured not by their truth but by the *belief* that they are true and by the readiness to act upon that belief, then it would be folly to ignore them, however unfamiliar and crude they sound. These ideas are not localized in any one area of the country. As I have indicated, they flourish among the most articulate of our students and also among some of their younger teachers.

In the literature of the philosophers and apologists of the so-called New Left and even more expressly in the justification of their attitudes, criticisms of the law are made on two grounds. The first regards the law as inherently hostile to human freedom, as merely a set of restraints which may justifiably be violated in behalf of one or another variety of personal freedom. The second regards the law as

1. V. I. Lenin, *Selected Works* (New York: International Publishers, 1943), 7:83.

basically a command whose ultimate authority rests exclusively on force. It is asserted that no authority can morally or politically justify itself or acquire legitimacy by power alone. Legitimacy can be rooted only in ideas of justice and reason of which the individual is the sole judge. Consequently no law, regardless of how it came into existence, whether by decree of a tyrant or decision of a democratic assembly after a free and open discussion, is binding on any individual unless *he* voluntarily approves of it. Every individual on this view has a moral right not only to disapprove of laws unacceptable to his sense of justice and reason but to disobey such laws without suffering any punishment. This is the logic of anarchy. Although few people are prepared to call themselves anarchists, all who subscribe to these and similar views are committed to anarchy. And if we listen, we shall hear an over-swelling chorus today, especially among the young, but not restricted to them, who echo these beliefs albeit in an inchoate form.

Let us consider the first of these views, namely, that law and freedom, where "freedom" means the power to effect one's wishes without let or hindrance by others, are intrinsically opposed; that law is always a curb or restraint on one's freedom, so that even when law is necessary, it is a necessary evil.

If it were true that law and freedom are necessarily opposed, it would follow that in the absence of law, men would be free, and that the fewer the laws, the greater would human freedom be. A moment's reflection will reveal the inadequacy of such a view. To be sure, Bentham in his classic analysis of legislation proclaimed that "every law is contrary to [someone's] liberty,"[2] that is, it is contrary to the liberty or freedom of those who would do what the law forbids them to do, and who would interfere with us in the enjoyment of our rights. It was Bentham who called attention to the fact that unless we place restraints upon the freedom of others to do what they please, especially their freedom to interfere with us, we cannot begin to exercise or enjoy our own freedom of speech, press, assembly, property, or life itself—the very substance of our Bill of Rights.

Because every law imposes some specific restraints on some freedoms of action of members of the community, it does not follow in the least that a polar opposition between law and freedom in the abstract can be drawn. Professor Morris R. Cohen, who supports Bentham on this point, says about legislation: "If it takes away the liberties of some, it thereby creates liberties for others."[3] Were any-

2. Jeremy Bentham, *Theory of Legislation*, ed. C. K. Ogden (New York: Harcourt, Brace and Co., 1931), p. 94.
3. Morris R. Cohen, *Reason and Law* (Glencoe, IL: Free Press, 1950), p. 5.

one to doubt this, let him ask himself whether it would be true to say that the fewer the traffic laws, the greater the freedom motorists would enjoy in our crowded metropolitan centers to get to their destinations quickly and safely.

This conclusion seems to me to be strengthened when we recognize that every legal system contains not only commands and prohibitions but allows for choices and conditional actions. One need not make a will. The law does not compel one to do so. But if one decides to do so, a certain procedure is indicated if the will is to be valid. But every free choice that one possesses in a legal system is dependent upon the protection the law gives us against those who would coerce us into making one or another choice, in effect denying our freedom of choice. We cannot be free unless others are unfree to interfere with our freedom.

All this goes to show that things and affairs in society cannot settle themselves. Laws are unavoidable if we are to determine some priorities in the order and range of human freedom, and avoid the chaos that would result if everyone were free to do what he pleased —what *his* reason or *his* sense of justice or *his* conscience dictated to him. Behind the assumption that governments and laws are not necessary in human society, except as the institutional means by which one class oppresses another, is the view that the necessity for legislation arises only out of conflicts of material interests, and that if society were properly arranged or ordered in behalf of the common good, in which conflicting material interests presumably would be transcended, the state would be unnecessary.

Both James Madison and Karl Marx were aware of the complex relationship between property and power, and between power and law. Madison was more realistic than Marx in recognizing that conflicts of interest under *any* social system might give rise to tyrannies of faction—even tyrannies of the majority—whereas Marx assumed that once economic class conflicts were removed by socialization, there would remain only problems of technology, accountancy, and administration. If Marx and Engels were right, once an economy was socialized, the computer would in principle solve all problems. The administration of things would replace the administration of men. The state and the need for sanctions to enforce laws would disappear, and with it politics as the exercise of power by men over other men.

But no economy, however organized, can ever solve or eliminate all conflicts of material interests, although it may moderate their expression and reduce the frequency of their occasion. In no society, whatever its productive potential, can more than enough of everything desired by men be produced at once. In consequence, there will always be problems of distribution—created by shifting distinctions between necessities and luxuries and by the tyranny of time that compels us to differentiate between those who get what they need *now* and those who get what they need, just as urgently as the others, *later* and *much later*. Even in the best run of communities there are problems of material distribution, such as whether one is to acquire his guaranteed housing now or some time before one dies, or whether one is to occupy the apartment with a pleasing view or one overlooking a parking lot or a river of noisy traffic. These are problems of potential conflict.

It is sometimes said that all this requires is the recognition of the necessity of rules, not of laws having the awful majesty of sanctions behind them. But there is a difference between rules and laws—and in matters of politics and social life we are dealing not with rules simply but with laws. We can draw up rules for *games* knowing that they have only conditional and not coercive force. Most games can be abandoned without suffering pains and penalties if we do not fancy the rules governing them. But to speak of the laws governing distribution of rights, goods, or services simply as *rules* is extremely misleading, because we cannot opt out of life and society as we do out of a game. "Rules of distribution" concerning property, or of who gets what when, are emphatically *not* rules of a game. It is even misleading in a society in which one must use his car in order to live and to make a living to refer to "traffic laws" as if they were merely rules—rules of a game.

Madison and his colleagues, I have said, were more realistic about the facts of power than were Marx and Engels in their utopian mood. They were not influenced by Rousseau but by Hobbes, Locke, and Montesquieu. But one can argue that even they were not realistic enough. "If men were angels," they tell us, "they would have no need of government"—the inference being that conflicts of interest and will are rooted *only* in material things, that without the passions and distractions of the body, the spirit could be pure, without concupiscence or conflict. How odd a notion! For on every known account of Heaven where neither matter nor material interests exist, it turns out that the celestial community has a very complex form of government. The science or theology of angelology exhibits a highly complex hierarchical structure in which the duties, rights, and powers of the angelic hosts are not reciprocal. Having read Milton, it is surprising that the authors of the *Federalist* did not ponder the fate of the fallen angel, Lucifer, who challenged the governance of Paradise. If pride, ambition, envy, and love of power can move angels in Heaven where there are no riches or material scarcities, where there is no marriage or giving in marriage, they can also move men and women in the classless society, however that be defined.

We may therefore conclude that there will always be a need for law in any society, terrestrial or not, where only one man can be number one, whether in political office or in the heart of a woman, and where more than one man dearly wants to be that one. The existence of law is involved in the very existence of man as a *zoon politikon*.

This brings us to the second assumption behind current contemptuous strictures against the necessity for law and order, namely, that law rests purely upon physical force or the threat of force. If the end of law is justice, it is argued, or even if justice is one of its important ends, why does it require physical sanctions? One can no more *compel* a person to recognize or acknowledge to himself what is just than one can compel him to love or feel loyal to others. One can only convince him or persuade him by example. If authority is based on justice and reason, it is sometimes said, we need no state and its hangmen to enforce their injunctions. Justice and reason are all the patents of authority we require.

Here several considerations are in order. It is empirically false to assert that obedience to law is based on force and the fear of force alone. This is false, because laws are obeyed even when they are widely regarded as unjust or foolish. Laws operate largely in virtue of the acquiescence and inertia among those who are affected by them. It is obvious that large scale disobedience to law, almost any law, would make that law ineffective whether it was a tax law or a traffic law or criminal law, since it could not be enforced. Even if there were no active resistance to an unpopular law and those who violated the law passively accepted their punishment, it would be impossible to arrest or imprison multitudes. That is why it is safe to say that most of the time, except in circumstances where mass uprisings have been brutally repressed, the laws of the state are obeyed more out of habit and tradition than out of fear. Even in most countries which are not democratic, it would be an exaggeration to say that the law rests on naked force alone. It would be more accurate to say it rests on the people's sufferance rather than on their genuine explicit consent. The explanation of the sufferance may reveal deep fear of the personal sufferings that would result from attempting to withdraw the sufferance.

It is all the more true that in democratic societies the existence of the legal order and obedience to it among the vast majority of citizens depend on respect for the law rather than on fear of its sanctions. Once that respect is destroyed, and the *presumptive* validity of law as the upshot of the democratic process is challenged or denied, we approach a state of civil war in which every man's hand is raised either in defense or aggression against his neighbor. Hobbes, to the contrary notwithstanding, the state of nature, taken historically, is not the *bellum omnium contra omnes*—the war of all against all—in which the life of man is "nasty, brutish, ugly and short." All primitive societies known to anthropologists are organized societies, not anarchic societies in Hobbes's sense. The Hobbesian war of all against all is most closely approximated when the prevailing system of existing laws has broken down, when the principle of authority has been eroded and its jurisdiction fragmented, and private individuals or groups seek to impose their own will or demands upon the community.

Force as such, although not sufficient to explain the observance of law, is nonetheless indispensable in every society. For not *all* interests are common, and the interests that are common are not always strong enough to override the passions of human beings unequally endowed with powers of intelligence, foresight, discipline, and the capacities for empathetic identification. When Edmund Burke says that "obedience is what makes government and not the names by which it is called," he overlooks the other half of the truth, namely, the element of force, however concealed in the background or inexplicit in utterance, that checks the temptations and impulses to disobedience and cools the fire of errant rages of revolt. The use of force as such cannot be legitimately condemned by anyone except absolute pacifists, and even then at the cost of palpable inconsistencies. Without some force or threat of force, our Bill of Rights would be only pious aspirations, unenforced and unenforceable and, therefore, no danger to "the burly sinners that run the world." The basic questions are: How and for what ends are the law and the force behind it to be used and controlled? To whom are they to be ultimately responsible?

There can be only three generic answers to this last question. Responsibility that sets the ends of law and controls the occasions and direction of force is to be entrusted either 1) to some elite groups, whether of Platonic philosophers or efficiency experts or a compassionate corps of social welfare workers who exercise an open or disguised dictatorship; or 2) to the private judgment or conscience of each individual citizen whose convictions are the final court of authority; or 3) to the delegated representatives of the majority of citizens in the community—where the delegation of authority rests upon the *freely given* consent of the electorate and therefore presupposes the presence of the civil and political rights whose operation makes it possible for a minority peacefully to win over and become a majority.

Our choice then is among three basic political alternatives—some kind of despotism or dictatorship, anarchy, or democracy.

We need not take much time to discuss the alternative of despotism, for we live in an age in which even those who secretly believe in its validity and scheme for its realization profess to be democrats. Nonetheless, the honest arguments for the dictatorship of the wise (or just or good) from Plato to Santayana are quite formidable. They all suffer, however, from the questionable assumption that one must be an expert in order to judge the recommendations of experts, that unless one knows expertly how to make shoes or soup, he cannot tell whether or where the shoes he wears pinch or whether the soup he eats tastes good. When we are dealing with normal or sane human beings who are not children, the same principle that warrants our choosing our cook or our shoes justifies our choosing our rulers, to wit, those who wear the shoes know best where they pinch.

It is the anarchist view which has recently become fashionable among the young and some of the younger teachers of the young. It asserts, in the words of one of its recent champions, that "there is not, and there could not be, a state that has a right to command and whose subjects have a binding obligation to obey."[4] "Each of us," says the anarchist, "must make himself the author of his actions and take responsibility for them by refusing to act save on the basis of reasons he can see for himself to be good."[5] The fact that a democracy is a form of self-government in which the citizens are both rulers and ruled, law-givers as well as law-obeyers, does not alter matters. "For neither majority rule nor any other method of making decisions in the absence of unanimity can be shown to preserve the autonomy of the individual citizen,"[6] that is, his right and duty to follow his own judgment.

A similar view is expressed in a recent book on *The Problem of Crime* by Quinney which carries the crusade for politicalization, so to speak, from education and the university into the field of law, crime, and the administration of justice. "In the end," he writes, "it is the individual's conscience that guides his actions."[7]

On the basis of a reference to the intellectual heritage of the American Revolution and a quotation from Staughton Lynd, Quinney implies that each person has the moral right to violate any law he regards as particularly oppressive. No reference is made to the

---

4. Robert Paul Wolff, "On Violence," *Journal of Philosophy* 66 (1969): 607.
5. Ibid.
6. Ibid.
7. Richard Quinney, *The Problem of Crime* (New York: Dodd, Mead and Co., 1970), p. 185.

relevance of the democratic or nondemocratic character of the political system which enacts this law.

Following this view the individual not only has a moral right to violate any law he regards as unjust that represents an illegitimate *government*, but also of a mistaken government *policy*.

In other words, even when the government is considered legitimate, if any policy of that legitimate government seems wrong, there is as much justification in violating the law that embodies the incorrect policy as in repudiating a wholly illegitimate government. This puts on the same moral and political level the law of the tyrant and the laws of a self-governing community when the individual finds himself at odds or disagreeing with either one or both.

Is there no difference between a law proclaimed by a tyranny or despotism, in whose making we have no voice or vote, direct or indirect, and a law in whose making we *have* played some part within a process that permits appeal from, repeal of, and therefore redress of grievances? In the end, to be sure, the individual's consent or conscience is decisive; but doesn't "in the end" mean different things in the two kinds of situation or context? Is there no difference in the prima facie validity of a law that comes from the iron hand of King George III and one that comes from a democratic representative assembly with an official and respected legal opposition? If we recognize no difference, if all laws, no matter what their source, derive their sole authority from the individual's conscience, how do we differentiate this position from the view *that a person is subject to a law in any society only so long as he chooses to be?* What does conscience mean here precisely? Can one have an authoritative conscience without being conscientious? Can one be conscientious without acknowledging that conscience too must be checked, that it must submit to rational controls, to evidence, and to argument? If with respect to law, we are prepared to give our blessings to our fellow citizens merely with the pious injunction: "Let your conscience be your guide!"—why should we expect consequences different—except in largeness of scale—from those that would ensue if we posted signs on our highways reading "Let your reflexes be your guide!"

Nonetheless, today the reconstruction of social life on a massive scale is being advocated all along the line in the name of conscience and in behalf of a freedom which, behind the glitter of the rhetoric, is interpreted as a freedom to act as one pleases. In *The Problem of Crime* it is noted:

Without an explicit ideology, the new men of conscience have through intelligence and experience found the necessity of building a new society—a society that allows for the expression of human sensitivities and capabilities. We are attempting to create new forms of community, new family patterns, new kinds of livelihood, new artistic forms, and new personal identities. Since the law represents and embodies the ethos of the old institutions, an attack on these laws *(through their violation)* is a logical outcome of the social and personal changes that are currently taking place. Whether we intend them to be or not, our actions are indeed political. And the actions of the state—in the invoking of the laws to preserve its existence—are political as well. We are likely to experience a confrontation of old laws and new consciousness for some time to come. An increasing proportion of *crime* in American society will be a reflection of this political confrontation.[8]

The significant feature of this passage is not the recognition of the necessity of social change and the desirability of growth in social institutions before they become fossilized, but the acceptance of the *manner* by which these changes are to be welcomed. Laws are not to be changed by legislative reforms and other mechanisms of due process but by *violation*, not by political behavior but by *criminal* political behavior. A political confrontation in the legislative assemblies of the nation is one thing; a political confrontation through deliberate mass violation of law in the streets and public squares is something quite different. It is the beginning of civil war or a preface to social chaos that eventuates in civil war.

Whatever apparent plausibility such a view possesses rests on the untenable assumption that the only alternative view to it is juridical absolutism, that no matter how evil a law is it should always be obeyed. It ignores the difference between a law which is a dictate of an arbitrary will and one that emerges from the reasoned give and take of argument and evidence in which the individual is free to persuade and convince others. It ignores situations in which there are irresolvable conflicts of human interest that cannot be harmoniously settled and in which the adoption of certain rules of due process is more important to the community, since it enables us to avoid bloodshed and violence, than any particular decision reached by due process. It overlooks the impossibility of guiding social action by principles of justice without reference to some utilitarian considerations, that is, to the *consequences* of applying principles rather than only to the *consistency* of principles. Even if the individual is resolved to obey only laws that are just and to disobey all others, is justice always enough? May there not be other relevant moral considerations to be taken into account, as, for example, human suffering? This is obvious if the principle of justice is defined in terms of

8. Ibid., p. 186 [emphasis added].

equality of treatment since *formally* such an approach cannot distinguish between treating and mistreating human beings equally. Nor is it possible to reach determinate conclusions on the basis of universalizing any principle, since with some ingenuity *all* principles can be universalized without formal inconsistency. Consistency is at best a necessary and not a sufficient condition of justice.

The anarchist position overlooks the practical consequence that would result if each citizen recognized only the authority of his own conscience or his own reading of moral law as a guide to legal obedience. The authority of the positive law may be derived from reflection on the sufferings that would result if the presumptive validity of law was disregarded and every law became a matter of debate and dispute not only before it was adopted but even after it was adopted. The anarchist's own freedoms of action in many respects are made possible by the law which protects him against those who would interfere with him and which in several ways enables him to acquire and exercise certain powers of citizenship and to develop himself as a human being. In profiting from the operation of the legal system but refusing to abide by its results whenever his private conception of justice condemns these results, even when the legal system provides the means by which these results may be legally altered, the anarchist is behaving unfairly. He is acting as a freeloader.

If the anarchist is asserting no more than that the moral authority of a law for him rests at some point on his voluntary approval of it or of the mechanisms or processes by which it comes into being, then his position is no more than a stupendous tautology. For the very meaning of a moral principle is such that it must recommend itself to a rational agent. But if he is asserting that he is under no obligation whatsoever to obey any *specific* law which he deems foolish or unjust, and which indeed may be such, then he is giving expression to an absurdity. That the obligation is not absolute, that it may ultimately be overridden by another obligation does not gainsay the fact that the first obligation has prima facie validity—any more than that we sometimes have to break a promise originally made in good faith nullifies its initial binding quality.

The demand that unanimity be at least a necessary condition morally for legitimate law or authority opens up a perspective of unlimited and chronic social disorder. Further, in any intelligent moral economy, as we have suggested, justice is only one value among others. If this be overlooked in the pursuit of a chimerical absolute justice, then other legitimate values may be ruthlessly and needlessly sacrificed. One cannot assess the obligation to obey a law without at the same time assessing the consequences of *not* obeying it. Many ethical, and especially political, choices must be choices of the lesser evil in relation to which the origin and source of authority of the law may be irrelevant and certainly not decisive. There is no escaping the ethics of consequences.

I have been assuming that despotism, anarchism, and democracy are the three political parameters of social organization. But it is instructive to observe the tendency among some who subscribe to anarchism as an ideal in which freedom is to find expression under no control except completely autonomous reason and good will to attach this ideal to despotic means of achieving it. The anarchist who has not lost his sense of reality completely is aware that men and women as he knows them are not yet fit to live in a society where their own rational wills are sufficient guides. They must be made fit. Their motives or springs of action must be liberated from cramping institutional restraints, socialized, harmonized, and humanized. This can only be accomplished by proper institutional change. To rely on existing possibilities and processes of political persuasion is hopeless because the will to change, as well as the capacity to grasp the truth and moral superiority of a society of perfect freedom, has allegedly been corrupted by the synthetically contrived needs to which existing selves have become addicted. Men and women accordingly, on this view are so enslaved by their present wants that they define felicity not in terms of the ideal society worthy of man but in terms of the gratification of more wants of the present variety—wants created as much by their society as by their biology. Molded by their present society, how can they voluntarily accept the superior moral validity of an ideal which condemns that society?

The vicious circle, say the apostles of absolute freedom, must be broken! It can only be broken by a revolution led by those who know what the basic human needs of men and women *should* be, who know not only what these needs are but what they require *better* than those who have them or should have them. This leadership—in the nature of the case an elite—pledges itself at the auspicious time and under auspicious circumstances, to engineer a political, economic, social, cultural, in short a total revolution, peacefully if possible, violently if necessary.

Once in political control the leaders face immense social and educational tasks. They must rebuild the economy and the institutional structure of society. They must see that the proper social values are inculcated and that there is no backsliding to the spiritual morass of the past. They must be cruel to be kind, discipline the dissenters and antisocial elements firmly and effectively. To do so, obviously, they must have *positive* laws—to make provision for the new future society in which laws will not be necessary, and, of course, *negative* laws forbidding certain kinds of action, especially of speech, press, and education—so that the masses will not again be corrupted. If tempted, they will know what to avoid doing in order to escape punishment and liquidation.

This conjunction of anarchism and despotism is found among certain kinds of Leninists. It is sometimes called the theory of "repressive tolerance." Whatever guise it takes, it is a mixture of arrogance and ignorance. It is arrogant in denying the right of freedom of choice to those who are considered autonomous, rational persons, and in denying them the right to be wrong, a right without which there can be no genuine growth. It is arrogant in assuming that some self-selected elite can better determine what the best interests of other citizens are than those citizens themselves. It is ignorant of the historical truth that no dictatorial elite has ever voluntarily abandoned the power it has usurped ostensibly for the good of others. It is ignorant of the psychological and moral truth that our ends are determined not by our rhetoric about future freedoms but by the means used to achieve those ends. The Leninist view that a minority dictatorship based on ruthless use of force, force without stint or measure, will usher in a classless society so pacific that there will be no need of any state, gradually and inescapably is transformed into the Stalinist view that the stronger the state becomes, the greater is the certainty of its *ultimate* disappearance—which is not only dialectical nonsense but plain nonsense.

These observations, rejecting the alternatives of anarchy and despotism, strengthen the case for resting the authority of law on the democratic process and procedures by which laws are made, amended, and repealed and which provide for the possibility of airing and remedying the grievances of individuals and groups. Whatever other reason exists for recognizing the *presumptive* validity of a law, it is strengthened when the law is the outcome or upshot of a genuinely democratic community.

This means that when authority is entrusted to the democratic process, it must be accompanied by the surrender of the power of private force to the democratic state which enjoys on various levels the monopoly of force. It requires that the use of force by some members of the democratic community against others to resolve their conflicts of interest be eschewed. It justifies the expectation that the democratic state will seek to make the exercise of force peripheral in social life, to use force, so to speak, only in defense of the due process designed to prevent force from deciding issues. It means that the officers and agents of the democratic state must be subject to the same rules of law as other citizens. It means that in-sofar as one accepts the democratic system, private judgment may justify within certain limits civil disobedience, but not uncivil dis-obedience or the use of violence. To a principled democrat there are limits to civil disobedience, too. These limits are reached when-ever civil disobedience becomes so widespread or contagious that it threatens the stability of the democratic process itself. A citizen or anyone else may invoke a moral right to revolution in a genuine democracy but he cannot legitimately or consistently do so in behalf of the principles of democracy. And when we speak of an *abstract* moral right to revolution, under any system, let us remember that it is on the same footing as an *abstract* moral right to suppress revolu-tion, that one man's mandate from Heaven may seem to another man's horrified vision, the judgment of Hell.

In the light of this analysis I wish to turn to the contemporary scene to show that some influential attitudes and beliefs concerning the function of dissent in a democratic society, and their relation to the use of force and violence, are so confused that they lend a cover of legitimacy to actions destructive of the democratic process.

I shall take as the foil to my argument one of the most bizarre writings ever penned by a member of the highest body of the United States judiciary, *Points of Rebellion* by Justice William Douglas.

Its first serious confusion is between the nature and place of dis-sent in a democratic society, and the nature and place of violence. On our analysis, freedom of *dissent* is integral to any democratic society based on freely given *consent*. But violence is not a legiti-mate form of dissent in a democratic society, because, among other evils, it is coercive of consent.

Justice Douglas is not altogether clear about whether or not there exists significant freedom to dissent in the United States today. In one breath he tells us that "a black silence of fear possesses the na-tion"[9] and that "we have fostered a climate of conformity."[10] In an-other he comments that we have "a current regime of dissent," so much so that "dissent looms ominously" over the country after "a decade of protests that is in many ways unique."[11] The actual facts, if measured by the frequency of its occasions and the intensity of its expression, reveal that dissent has never been so free, so unrestrained and uninhibited, so widespread in the history of the nation as it is today.

9. William O. Douglas, *Points of Rebellion* (New York: Random House, 1970), p. 6.
10. Ibid., p. 12.
11. Ibid., pp. 8, 9.

Dissent in a democracy is one thing but violence is quite another, and Justice Douglas fails to distinguish them properly. Dissent that does not take the form of illegal action or incitement to such action cannot "loom ominously" over us. Only violence or the threat of violence can. Although Justice Douglas presumably is speaking from a democratic point of view, he seems to be identifying legitimate dissent with violence or regarding violence as a species of legitimate dissent. This compounds the confusion. Speaking of the use of violence in the United States, he tells us: "The historic instances of violence have been episodic and have never become a constant feature of American life. Today that pattern has changed. Some demonstrations go on for months: and the protests at colleges have spread like prairie grass fire." [12]

If this means anything, it explicitly asserts that today violence is no longer episodic but systematic. It implicitly acknowledges that the demonstrations and protests are instances of violence and embrace the assaults, vandalism, fire bombing, and other types of confrontation spreading "like prairie fire" from one campus to another.

Then, as if to mystify us further, Justice Douglas goes on to say that these "modern day dissenters and protesters are functioning as the loyal opposition functions in England." [13] Surely there must be some error here. The loyal opposition in England—whether it be Tory to Labor or Labor to Tory—does not resort to violence of any kind. If anything, the loyal opposition is a stickler for the niceties of tradition. Surely Justice Douglas is aware that the violent dissenters "calling for revolutionary changes in our institutions" emphatically declare that they do *not* consider themselves a loyal opposition within the existing system but wish to bring it down about our heads.

This raises a fundamental question to which Justice Douglas gives an uncertain answer: Can a person or group of persons who profess allegiance to the democratic system and wish to function as a loyal opposition within it systematically or even recurrently resort to violence to impose their will on the majority, if and when they believe that the majority is too slow or torpid or stupidly mistaken? Not only has he become doubtful about the Holmesian doctrine of "the clear and present danger" as limiting dissent if it incites unlawful action, but he has explicitly endorsed an opinion in which the following sentence appears: "I believe that The First Amendment forbids Congress to punish people for talking about public affairs, whether or not such discussion incites to action, legal or

12. Ibid., p. 57.
13. Ibid.

illegal."[14] A racist demagogue denouncing school desegregation, whose words incite to mob action, is certainly talking about public affairs. Factions of the Black Panthers and Students for a Democratic Society that not only advocate but incite and passionately urge the use of violence always do so in the course of talking about public affairs. Morally, if an action is wrong, the incitement of the action is also wrong. In law, if an action is criminal, the incitement of it is also illegal although punishable to a lesser degree. In a democracy, political due process cannot prevail if dissent takes the form of direct action whenever a minority fails to persuade the majority. The "exceptional case"—where violence is used to bring about what subsequently is regarded as good—still signifies the breakdown of democratic authority. Every violation of due process, every resort to violence appears as an "exceptional case" to those who perpetrate it. Even then we must not forget that as Carlyle once put it, "violence done is always sure to be injustice done, for violence does even justice unjustly."[15]

There is a naïveté from which some of our Justices are not free in ignoring the fact that in a democracy every case of successful defiance of law by resort to violence tends to make successive cases of defiance more likely. "In a democracy," Justice Frankfurter once wrote, "the appeal from an unenlightened majority must be made to an enlightened majority." Justice Douglas feels, however, that the appeal from an unenlightened majority may justifiably be to rebellion. Whether such counsel is wise, given the Anglo-American political tradition, is very doubtful. What is not doubtful at all is that it cannot be justified by any principle of democracy.

Just as surprising as Justice Douglas's ambiguities about dissent and violence and their place in democratic society is his conception of American society. It approaches the view sometimes characterized as "vulgar Marxism" to distinguish it from more sophisticated varieties of Marxism. According to this view the economic class differences among men are so basic that democracy can function only as an institutional device by which one group retains its power of control and exploitation over other groups. It is sometimes true that the differences among men, economic and noneconomic, are so deep, or are conceived to be such, that they cannot be negotiated. Under some circumstances it is impossible to find some shared value or interest—whether of peace or survival—on the basis of which human beings can live in comity if not in community or

14. Yates v. United States, 354 U.S. 298, 340 (1957).
15. Thomas Carlyle, *The Works of Thomas Carlyle*, vol. 10, *Past and Present* (London: Chapman and Hall, 1899), p. 21.

fraternity. In that case political rule must rest on myth, fraud, or force.

One cannot generalize for all countries, but the historical evidence, especially in the post–World War II period in Western Europe and America, shows it is possible for different economic classes to live, despite their conflicts, in relative peace with each other. This is achieved by virtue of the fact that the political process has jurisdiction over all issues—whether of wealth, status, power—that divide men. Economics does not merely determine politics but politics determines economics as well. A bold tax policy, for example, can redistribute wealth in a generation. Marx was right when he said that man's consciousness is determined by his social existence, but he failed to recognize that man's political consciousness can redetermine his social existence. Because he overlooked this, Marx's predictions went wrong.

This in effect is denied by Justice Douglas in his slap dash characterizations. He conceives of the United States Establishment, as C. Wright Mills did, as one intetgrated power-elite, monolithic in structure, ruthlessly exploitative of men, driven only by quest for ever renewed profit, arrayed against the downtrodden and poor who are denied access to the political levers by which social change can be achieved. The fact that Justice Douglas and his colleagues are a powerful part of the Establishment, that the organized labor movement plays a substantial part in reorienting the economy, that the standards of living and civil liberties have risen very perceptibly— although they still have far to go to be satisfactory—reveals the shallowness and empirical inadequacy of this model of American power. To ask one out of a myriad of questions: What made the right to collective bargaining part of the law of the land; what changed the character of the pre-Roosevelt Court; what induced the federal government to recognize the principle of social responsibility for the minimum welfare subsistence of its citizens, thus permitting escalation to more adequate levels—if not the democratic political process?

Here is how Justice Douglas sees the picture in the United States today: "On the one side are powerful lobbies such as the military-industrial complex, the agro-business lobby, and the highway lobby. These have powerful spokesmen." Opposed to them are "the poor, the unemployed and the disemployed—and they are not well organized."

But what has happened to the rest of us—the at least 70 or 80 percent who do not appear in this confrontation? Justice Douglas does not tell us, but he does comment on the opposition between the Establishment and the poor. "The use of violence as an instrument of persuasion is therefore inviting and seems to the discontented to be the only effective protest."[16]

However, the use of violence, especially in the white community, comes not from the poor, the hungry, and the unemployed but from the affluent middle classes in the North, and from lower middle classes in all sections, especially the South, resisting measures aimed at desegregation. The violence which we have experienced is not so much inspired by hunger, unemployment, and similar physical needs as it is by ideology rooted more in psychological needs to find scapegoats and vent their frustrations on them, than in objective conditions. For when these objective conditions were far worse than they are today, the violence was far less. If it were true that the poor are confronted by the all-powerful panoply of military-industrial power, how can "the use of violence as an instrument of persuasion [appear] inviting" rather than as an invitation to disaster? Justice Douglas is a bad analyst of the plight of the poor and a worse counselor. The poor, the hungry, the unemployed in coalition with other groups in the population can do much more to improve their lot, as they have shown in England and in some of our own states, by political action, by agitation, peaceful organization and demonstration, and by effective use of the ballot than by resorting to violence whose only certain effect is to feed the backlash against all reforms.

The most mischievous and irresponsible of Justice Douglas's views is his use of what I have elsewhere called the "Boston tea-party syndrome," which in some quarters is being used as a "patriotic" justification for violence against democratic society. One rubs one's eyes in astonishment when he reads: "We must realize that today's Establishment is the new George III. Whether it will continue to adhere to his tactics, we do not know. If it does, the redress, honored in tradition, is also revolution."[17]

What were the tactics of George III, against which the American colonists revolted? It was his refusal to give them adequate representation, his refusal to approve laws for the public good adopted by existing legislative bodies, his refusal to respect an independent judiciary, his refusal to submit tax laws and other requisitions to the consent of the people, in short, his refusal to permit the establishment of political mechanisms by which grievances could be peacefully redressed. But once the methods of registering and implementing freely given consent have been introduced, there is no longer the same moral basis for revolution that exists against tyrannies that deny political freedom. The American colonists were not self-gov-

16. Douglas, *Points of Rebellion*, p. 78.
17. Ibid., p. 95.

erning when they made their revolution. And when they did establish self-government they placed all sorts of restrictions on the franchise. Today when the conditions of the American franchise are wider and freer than they have ever been in the past, when dissent is more institutionalized and protected than ever before, when despite its many shortcomings and imperfections, the level of human welfare is higher than ever in the past, and recognized for the first time as the moral responsibility of the government, Justice Douglas makes the preposterous comparison between our democratic political system and the brutal tyranny of George III. Actually, the only branch of the American government whose powers in certain respects are comparable to the despotism of the British crown is the judicial despotism, to use Jefferson's phrase, of the Supreme Court in its nonrepresentative and nonresponsible power (that is, responsible only to itself) to nullify congressional legislation, something that our British cousins, who recognize the supremacy of Parliament as the highest elected body in the commonwealth, would not tolerate for a moment.

Apparently it makes no relevant difference in the eyes of Justice Douglas that, with all our failings, which are many, we are still a representative democracy, more so *today* than when only white men with property voted, or when only white men voted, or even when only men voted. The situation, according to him, is no different from what it was when George III, to quote from the Declaration of Independence, fomented "domestic insurrection" and launched "on works of death, desolation and tyranny, already begun with circumstances of cruelty and perfidy scarcely paralleled in the most barbarous ages."

Presumably the situation confronting dissenters today in the United States is comparable to that which confronted the American colonists when subjected to the despotism of George III. Otherwise Justice Douglas could hardly write, "Where grievances pile high and most of the elected spokesmen represent the Establishment, violence may be the only effective response."[18]

Whether violence is the most effective response in such circumstances is questionable. What is not questionable is that response by violence violates both the letter and spirit of democracy. If the elected spokesmen of the people have been properly elected and can be turned out of office, what is the objection to them? That they vote differently from the way Justice Douglas would have them vote? Then let us elect others if he can convince us that his program is better for the Republic. The crucial question is whether we are free

18. Ibid., p. 89.

to elect others. Although there are obstacles to that freedom, we are freer today than we have ever been before. Why, then, the resort to violence? Democracy is impossible if those who lose elections are prepared to recontest them by violence.

What Justice Douglas's *Points of Rebellion* indicates is that he is more concerned about specific programs of social change than he is about the methods and processes of change, that he is willing—as seen clearly through the pattern of his verbal confusions—to sacrifice democratic due process for some specific social desideratum. I submit that whoever places greater emphasis upon the product rather than the process, upon the result rather than upon the methods of achieving them, upon an all-sanctifying end rather than upon the means of achieving it, is opening the doors of anarchy. Anarchy is just as much a perversion of democracy as is tyranny. Both Plato and Aristotle, the great critics of democracy, recognized that where human beings are compelled to choose between anarchy and despotism, they will more readily choose despotism because anarchy is the shifting and precarious rule of a thousand tyrants. Democracy is the only viable alternative that rejects both.

Faith in democracy is on trial today, just as much as, although in a different way than, it was during the Civil War when the existence of the Union was at stake. If every grievance, genuine or fancied, every demand, justified or not, is to be remedied by direct action, or threats of direct action, if it cannot be rectified through the democratic process, then we are moving toward protracted civil conflict from which only the enemies of American democracy can profit. Those who are the victims of direct action, no matter in what righteous cause, will follow suit to redress their own grievances. "The villainy you teach us," they say, "we shall execute. It will go hard but we will better the instruction." These are the sentiments that guarantee escalation of violence.

Justice Douglas, among others, is much more concerned about the force used to contain or restrain violence than about the outbreak of violence itself. The usual ground is that this response neglects causes and treats only symptoms. It overlooks the obvious fact that the search and quest for causes cannot be undertaken unless the symptoms are properly treated. Confronted by mass hunger, what sensible or compassionate person would say, "Let us first deal with causes!" Suppose one of the causes is overpopulation. Shall we defer actions to relieve the immediate pangs of hunger while we seek to convince the population in question to limit its increase?

In the last analysis the future of democracy depends upon preserving the conditions of rational discourse. Actions that disrupt its possibility cannot be tolerated if we really believe in tolerance. Ideas which challenge democracy, on the other hand, no matter how extreme or mistaken should be welcomed as providing opportunity for clarification and mutual enlightenment.

The avenues of democratic reform are still open in this country. Whether we can use them effectively depends on our courage, our intelligence, our willingness to work harder in the face of occasional defeats, and on our political skills in surmounting the obstacles of ignorance, indifference, prejudice and entrenched vested interest. The difficulties are great enough. Let us not increase them by loose thinking and loose talk.

1970

Chapter 3

The Concept and

Realities of Power

In discussing power one must begin with a dis-
claimer. Not all usages of the term *power* will concern me. I shall
not write of natural energy or of the awesomeness of the powers of
nature. I shall write only of *human* power, of human beings as subjects and objects of power, and of nature and natural resources only
insofar as they are used by man to control the behavior of other men
and women. That is what August Blanqui meant when he said,
"Who has iron, has bread." Today he would have said, "Who has oil,
has bread." Potentially oil was always a source of natural energy
but only recently has it become a source of economic and political
power.

In its most generic sense power is the ability to influence the behavior of others in order to further our desires and purposes. This
reference to the production of intended effects means that we cannot literally speak of natural power without anthropomorphizing
nature. Power in my sense must be either human or divine. In any
case whether it is human or divine, power cannot be omnipotent.
Only an existentialist can believe the absurd notion that God can
make two plus two equal five, or unmake the past.

Even so, the concept of power as influence on the behavior of
others is too vast a theme, and we shall have to delimit it. We shall
not therefore discuss the purely personal uses of power—whether in
friendship or love, commerce or sport. No one except a hermit can
forego exercising some power to influence the conduct of others or

avoid being influenced in turn by their conduct. Our concern will be with the power exercised in a *social* context by individuals or groups on other individuals and groups either directly or through events they bring to pass.

There are a few more qualifications we must make in the interest of clarification. Power is often used interchangeably with influence and authority but although they are related it is a source of confusion to overlook the differences. Not *all* influence is a form of power in the sense which gives us concern. If I influence someone by rational argument to behave in a manner of which I approve, even if I am a salesman, am I exercising power *over* him? Hardly. If someone is *voluntarily* taken as a model of deportment or dress, of social behavior, etiquette, or manners, does he or she thereby become a source or wielder of power? Not in an objectionable sense. When we speak of the "authority of power," the term *power* has a somewhat different meaning from what it has in the phrase "the power of authority." The pope has an authority among Catholics that is independent of his secular power although his authority may depend upon the communicants' *belief* in his spiritual power. When Stalin asked Churchill who had proposed that the pope be consulted about the postwar world: "How many battalions has the pope?" he recognized the difference between authority and power, and at the same time revealed his naïveté about the limits of power. Neither God, in whom Stalin did not believe, nor History, in which he did, is always on the side of the strongest battalions.

One undesirable consequence of equating power with influence or authority or persuasion is that almost by semantic fiat it converts everyone into a seeker of power. So, for example, Hans Morgenthau speaks of "the ubiquitous lust for power" as if it were an essential trait of man. So do those who quote the maxim "Those who have power want more of it; those who don't have it want it more." By bringing in the unconscious, one can, of course, hold on to the view that man is by nature a power-questing creature. This makes the assertion as unempirical a notion as the adolescent view that all human actions are egoistic and that no one acts out of disinterested or unselfish motives. But there are a series of phenomena that would make it difficult to hold to the view that "everyone is power hungry"—if that were asserted as an empirical proposition. For example, the widespread attitude of reluctance to serve, when posts of power have to be filled, expressed in the remark, "Let George do it," or the widespread abstention from the political process altogether are sufficient to refute this oversimple view.

What differentiates power, as I shall use the term, from mere influence, authority, and persuasion, is the element of *constraint* or the threat of constraint which is integral to its meaning. That is why as necessary as power is in human relationships, we are somewhat fearful of it, and seek to curb, tame, or limit it. This insight is recognized by Max Weber in his *Theory of Economic and Social Organization* where the presence of power is defined as "the probability that one actor within a social relationship will be in a position to carry out his will despite resistance, regardless of the basis upon which the probability rests."[1] Without implicit reference to the overcoming of actual or potential resistance, the power of a command would hardly differ from that of a wish.

If we return now to a modified formulation of the conception of power as the ability to impose one's will upon others even in the face of resistance, it is clear that this may be done in various ways and by varied means. The most obvious way, and to some extent always in the background when conflicts arise, is by the exercise of physical force or by threat of its exercise. But this is by far not the only way power shows itself. Otherwise the *physically* stronger would always be the most powerful in history and social life. Whatever may be the case among the lower orders of the animal kingdom, it is not so in human affairs. Unless we define the physically stronger merely in terms of the victorious outcome of any struggle, it is not true that the physically stronger is always the most powerful. David was certainly not stronger than Goliath. A hypnotist can make his physically stronger subject do things he would be unable to get him to do outside of the hypnotic trance. By playing on the fears, natural or supernatural, of multitudes, secular or religious leaders may impose restraints and taboos on their cohorts without any physical sanctions whatsoever. The sacred sometimes is stronger than the drive for self-preservation. Men have died of hunger in the sight of food forbidden to them by their religious faith.

History is replete with illustrations that military strength by itself is not always decisive for victory. When the Russian General Kornilov marched against Kerensky in August 1917 at the head of well armed troops, Kerensky could hardly muster a military defense with the only forces available—the war weary, semimutinous garrison of St. Petersburg. But it was not necessary. In one of the most remarkable examples of the power of propaganda, the coalition that rallied around him mobilized a horde of agitators against Kornilov's troops whose ranks, subjected to the techniques of fraternization, dissolved like snow under a hot sun. The defeat of the U.S. military

---

1. Max Weber, *The Theory of Social and Economic Organization*, trans. A. M. Henderson and Talcott Parsons, ed. Talcott Parsons (Glencoe, IL: Free Press, 1947), p. 152.

forces in Vietnam was not due to their military weakness vis-à-vis their opponents, but to the absence of resoluteness of American political leadership and the erosion of popular support induced by a variety of factors that had nothing to do with military strength. Two of the most far-reaching turning points in the history of Western civilization, the defeat of the Persian forces at Marathon and Salamis and, 500 years later, the triumph of Christianity over the Roman Empire and its mighty legions, may be taken as paradigm cases of the insufficiency of physical power to prevail.

There are many other kinds of power in the world that can be employed to determine, if not completely control, the behavior of others. There is the power of money, and other forms of wealth, particularly property, the power of social position, the power of offices, public or private, the power of expert skill, especially when it is in short supply, and the power of ideas—which may or may not be rationalizations of individual or class interests—religious ideas, nationalistic ideas, racial and ethical ideals.

Libraries of literature have been written about these varieties of power, a great deal of it in the vain attempt to reduce them to one fundamental form either material or ideal. Usually those who seek to reduce all types of power to forms of one, mean no more than that the effects of different power relations in society are the same— namely, control by a few persons over the destinies of many others. But this seems to me to be a great oversimplification. The *way* power is exercised and the *means* employed in its exercise make a difference both to those who use power and those against whom it is used. Power won by the speaking of truths (leaving blackmail aside) will be different at least in some respects from power won by propaganda or outright coercion. Lord Acton's dictum that all power corrupts is no more true than that all powerlessness corrupts, but to the extent it is true, the corruption will vary with the mode of its exercise.

The very fact that all exercise of power is limited by other power, or depends for its success on something else besides itself, shows that power is a matter of degree. We need not worry that it cannot be precisely measured. It is an intensive magnitude. It is sufficient in most contexts, without quantifying power, to assign it greater or lesser weight, and to determine when it is growing stronger or weaker, for example, we can say that the power of religious organizations is greater in some periods than in others. No pope can compel a king to crawl to Canossa today. Although power is a matter of degree—so that there is always something that limits it—we cannot lay down any exact limits to its operation. Force or physical power can by the infliction of death or suffering, or the threat of such, enforce compliant behavior. However, regardless of how harshly physical force is exercised or threatened, there are some things it cannot do. You cannot successfully compel or even command someone to love or respect you although you can make them *say* they do. At the same time, naked power gets clothed with a kind of authority by sheer endurance, if it is not too intense or is not embroiled in revolutionary struggle. Time gilds naked power with a patina of legitimacy. The sons of the conqueror become inheritors, and their sons legitimate rulers. If a tyranny lasts long enough the popular mood goes from hostility, to indifference, to acquiescence, and unfortunately sometimes even to acclaim.

Nonetheless recognizing as we must the limitations of naked power, let us not underestimate how effective a ruthless terror can be. Whoever said (Napoleon?) one can do everything with bayonets except sit on them—overlooks the ways in which bayonets can insure peaceful and comfortable slumber for tyrants by making others sit on them. In passing, it may be noted that fear of death or the belief that mere survival is the be-all and end-all of existence can be the unwitting ally of terror. Power, no matter how arbitrary or absolute, has little hold on those who have no fear of death or unpopularity or public disgrace.

The enumeration of different forms of power should not prevent us from recognizing that they usually reinforce each other in most historical circumstances. At any given time, throne and altar, state and church, economic and cultural, and especially educational, institutions usually tend to support a common structure of values. But rifts and differences always develop in time. Those who have power —or their elites or leadership—*may* have a common interest but their conceptions of that common interest often conflict, and may make a difference between war and peace as an expression of national policy. Conflicts among different groups among the ruling classes —the ins and the outs—produce changes in power relations that neither anticipate, like growth in the power of other classes. The struggle between the nobles and kings strengthened the middle classes, and the struggle between the agricultural and manufacturing interests in England contributed to the rise of the Labor party. When the need for allies in a struggle requires coalitions, a concessionary price may have to be paid for an increased temporary strength whose consequences may be weakness in the long run. In such situations a small group may exercise a disproportionate power —one of the drawbacks of proportional representation.

Many writers on the nature of power seek to find its root or first cause in some one psychological or social trait, but this seems to me to be an exercise in futility. There are varying conditions on which different forms of power depend. The successful manifestation of power depends not only on the qualities, physical or mental, of those over whom power is wielded. One cannot plausibly explain the operations of power merely in terms of the amount of physical force available to the power holders. No police force could enforce the law if a sufficiently large number of people chose to disobey. Kingly, presidential, or judicial power is often more effective in virtue of the power of authority than in terms of threatened sanctions. This leads to references to the power of habit, the power of tradition, or the power of imitation in human behavior. The existence of such psychological factors cannot be disputed, but they cannot account for variations in power relations which are historical in nature. They do not explain who has power over whom, when, where, and how. That is why I refer to them as conditions for the exercise of power. The relationship is somewhat like that of literacy to what is called the power of the press. Unless a people is literate and able to purchase newspapers, we cannot properly speak of the power of the press. But the existence of literacy does not generate the power of the press: it makes it possible. Only when the press exhibits in the selection and emphasis of its news—as well as in its editorial policy—a sustained bias, can we use the expression, "the power of the press" intelligibly.

Because of the tendency to use the term *power* for what are conditions and causes of power, I believe it is a mistake to assume that by semantic legislation or fiat we can establish consistency in usage. We must look beyond the words to locate the phenomenon and the problem. For example, we sometimes talk about "the power of the weak" or "the power of the powerless" to get their way in virtue of their weakness to curb the behavior of those who are stronger than they are. But such power is only enjoyed because of the sufferance or tolerance of those who possess the greater power. It can be extinguished in a moment. Like "the power of a woman's tears" to get her way—which novelists used to write about—despite her legal, financial, and social inequality, its success rests on the patronizing indulgence of those who have greater power because of the institutional structure of society. I am not calling into question the psychological reality of the phenomenon, but only the misleading connotations of the expression. The weak have little power in the absence of the sympathy, compassion, or pity of the powerful. It is only where they are in a position to inflict unacceptable harm on those capable of destroying them that they can win concessions.

Granting that there is a plurality of interacting powers that determine human behavior, and that they are irreducible to each other, it still may be true that one kind of power may be more decisive than others. It may be taken as the independent variable whose changes have an overriding effect on all others. It would hardly be an exaggeration to say that today the most pervasive doctrine about the nature of power is the view that economic power is the predominant factor in politics and history. And because of the ambiguities of the term "economic," we must specify that by "economic" here we mean "the mode of economic production." Whether held in sophisticated or vulgarized form, it is undeniable that there has been an amazing recrudescence of the theory of historical materialism not only in the marketplace, but also in academic quarters.

That economic relationships have a profound influence on human behavior can hardly be gainsaid. But that these relationships are necessarily expressed as power *over persons*, in virtue of power over things, and that it is the foundation which explains not only the distribution of wealth, but everything of cultural importance, is extremely difficult to establish in the light of the historical record. For one thing, it cannot do justice to the economic transformations that have resulted from the exercise of political power. Nonetheless it is widely believed—even among many who have no allegiance to Marxist doctrine, indeed, among some who are outspokenly anti-Marxist. Anyone who asserts that the fundamental issue of our age is between capitalism and socialism as economic systems, rather than between democracy and totalitarianism, as political systems, subscribes to some variant of historical materialism. For what they are asserting is that the clue or key to the complex maze of power relationships that prevail in our society or any society, can be derived from the existing mode of economic production and the legal relations of ownership under which it functions. The Marxists maintain that true democracy can be furthered only by socialization of the means of production; their critics of this school—unconscious crypto-Marxists—contend that socialization will destroy democracy and freedom. But they both agree that the economy is all-determining. Their contrary positions cannot be both true—but both may be false. The most fundamental question of our age is not socialism or capitalism (however they are defined), but the freedom to choose between them. And our free choice may be, and for my part, *should be* not socialism *or* capitalism but *more or less* of one and the other.

There are a number of considerations which make the monistic economic view of history, politics, and culture questionable. Some are rather obvious, and were passed over too lightly by Marx himself. In replying to those who stressed the power of ideas or consciousness in history, Marx wrote, "It is not consciousness that determines existence but social existence that determines consciousness." By "social existence," he meant one's class position, the web of economic relations that define the area in which all historical agents act. But it is clear that Marx's own social existence does not explain *his* ideas or consciousness or that of his lieutenants and leading disciples. The retort that Marx is not speaking of the social existence or consciousness of individuals, but only of classes, is beside the point. For after all, classes are made up of individuals and class consciousness would be a mystical and mystifying notion unless it is related at least statistically to the thought and behavior of individuals. In any event if ideas merely reflected antecedent social existence, the historical influence of Marx's revolutionary ideas would be inexplicable.

Further, if this simplistic view of economic power were valid, nationalism in its varied expressions would be the result of the thrust of economic interests, and religion no more than a mask for such interests. I defy anyone to explain modern nationalist movements in the light of this dogma. Economic interests played a minor role in the movement for Indian independence. And if one essayed to interpret Zionism or Irish nationalism, or the budding nationalist movements for independence in terms of economic interest—where independence usually results in a *decline* in the standard of economic life—he would be cutting the cloth of historical reality to fit an ideological dogma.

Nonetheless leaving these difficulties aside, I want to restate the view that economic power is the predominant power in its strongest and most plausible form. (After all, a theory should be considered in its strongest form.)

In this form it locates the source of power in the nature of social property itself and contends that property over things entails power over persons. The question is: How does property do this? Briefly, the analysis runs as follows: Property is not a thing but a legal relation or title, a legal right. A legal right is a claim to goods or services that society through its authorized agencies stands ready to enforce. One may have a *moral* right regardless of whether it is enforced. But if over an extended time a legal right is not enforced or enforcible, then for all practical purposes it is nonexistent.

What is the nature of property as a legal right? How do you know you have it? Some say that property is the right to use or abuse whatever you have title to. This is not so. The law will not enforce your legal right to harvest your crop or run your factory if you are physically or mentally incapable of doing so. In other words, the law recognizes no obligation to help the individual to use or exploit his or her property. On the other hand, the law will not permit *any* kind of use or abuse of one's property. It will not permit you to harvest a crop of marihuana or construct on your property an abattoir or a horse farm or any other establishment forbidden by the zoning laws. Even the freedom of testamentary disposition is restricted.

What then does the legal right to property amount to? To this— the power through law to *exclude* others from the possession or use of what you own. This brings us to the crux of the argument. If you have property in the social means of production—factories, mines, mills, large tracts of arable land—you have the power to exclude others from their use. If their use is necessary for the employment of others, if it is their only or chief means of livelihood, then you have a very real power over the lives of those who must live by their use. The power to deny access to the means of earning a living is power over life. Power over economic *things* gives power over *persons*.

The paradigm case of such power is illustrated in the case of a town in which almost all employment centers in one large factory, and the service industries that cater to it and its employees. If the owners decide to shut it down for any reason at all, the dislocation in the lives of those who must subsist by their labor radiates to all areas of human experience.

It can be and has been argued that this economic power is the basic form of power, that therefore such power must be made responsible, and that the best way of doing this is by sharing economic power by changing the legal ownership of social property from a private to a collective basis.

What shall we make of this argument? We must recognize the truth of the basic insight that the central fact about property is not so much legal title as *control*. But if that be so, then the nature of the control is central, and it is an open question whether the mere fact of title determines control. In our own economy it has been widely recognized since the publication of *The Modern Corporation and Private Property*, by Berle and Means, that in the giant corporations there has been a progressive dissociation between titular ownership and managerial power. The stockholders own the corporation and legally vote for the board of directors who rarely own a majority of the stock. Profits are still the goal but whether they are to be distributed as dividends or paid out as bonuses or to grant demands for increased wages depends largely on decisions of management.

Secondly, if this analysis is sound, then the power of property over persons depends upon law and the character of the state. Whoever controls the law and the state ultimately controls the economy in diverse ways: by direct and indirect taxation, tariffs, subsidies, and currency reform. The struggle for control of the law and state then becomes a *political* tug of war in which all sorts of interest and pressure groups contend. In democratic communities, now one group, now another, or a coalition of groups acquire preponderant influence. It becomes an empirical question which class or group can impose its will. The economic vector is always present but not always decisive. The Prohibition Amendment in the United States with its fateful cultural consequences and which in effect expropriated without compensation a billion-dollar industry in 1917, was the result not of economic interest but of the pressures of the Woman's Christian Temperance Union.

Thirdly, particularly important is the existence of free trade unions as a countervailing force both to the economic power of corporate management and, save for exceptional areas bearing on public safety, to the power of the state itself. So long as any entrepreneur decides to stay in business, the trade unions can exact concessions to limit his power over the lives of those who work for him. That is why the right to strike is central to free trade unionism. Without it, we have a system tantamount to forced labor. The very existence and survival of trade unions, as history shows, depended on protective legislation. In other words the economic power of both capital and labor stems substantially from political power.

Finally, the same conclusion can be derived from an analysis of the economic system in which the title to ownership of the social means of production is vested in the collectivity. It so happens that today in every country of the world in which a collectivist economy is found, the power to exclude workers from access to the means of production and life is a monopoly of a minority political party which in the name of the proletariat exercises a ruthless, absolute dictatorship *over* the proletariat. If we define property functionally, we can say that, in effect, the leaders of these totalitarian organizations control the economic plant of their countries with much greater power than either the owners or managers control the corporations of so-called capitalist societies. They do not have to contend with free trade unions, strikes, interventions by an independent judiciary, and the myriads of regulations that limit their activities.

Oddly enough the central point I am making, to wit, that control over access to work and living conditions is of greater significance than titles of ownership, was acknowledged by none other than Leon Trotsky many years ago in his devastating indictment of the Soviet economy. He failed to recognize that his analysis shattered the basic assumption of his own historical materialist faith. Trotsky writes:

If a ship is declared collective property, but the passengers continue to be divided into first, second and third class, it is clear that, to the third class passengers, differences in the conditions of life will have infinitely more importance than juridical changes in proprietorship. The first class passengers, on the other hand, will propound together with their coffee and cigars, the thought that collective ownership is everything and a comfortable cabin nothing at all.[2]

I draw two important conclusions from this analysis: First, that although they are interrelated in many ways, to the extent that we can distinguish between economics and politics, the mode of political decision—that is, whether democracy or totalitarianism prevails—is of far greater weight in determining the actual power relations in a society than the mode of economic production; and second, with respect to democracy, the existence of political democracy *by itself* is incomplete in that it does not guarantee, although it makes possible, economic, ethnic and cultural democracy but—and this is the nub of the argument—*without* political democracy, economic, ethnic, cultural, or any other meaningful kind of democracy is impossible.

Once we acknowledge the centrality of the mode of political decision, we must recognize the variations in the locus and strength of the power determinants in different political systems. To do this we must overcome what seems to me to be the profound error of Mosca, Pareto, Michels, and their many disciples. They argue that because in every society the actual laws and the exercise of power are derived not from the thoughts, passions, and will of the many but from the decisions of an elite few in legislative, judicial, and executive roles, that therefore democracy is a myth, majority rule an empty shibboleth, and all political change consists in a succession of power elites.

This overlooks the great dissimilarities—dissimilarities that may spell the difference between life and death—between, on the one hand, political systems which enable a freely expressed public opinion to alter public policy and peacefully get rid of existing elites, and, on the other, systems in which public opinion has no institutional voice or effect, and ruling elites can be replaced only by force and violence. The position I am criticizing is comparable to arguing that because no one possesses infallibility or absolute truth that therefore there are no degrees of truth, no principled difference between inexactness or error and a barefaced lie.

To be sure, literally no majority can rule. No democracy is possible, not even the direct democracy of ancient Athens or the New England town meeting, without some delegation of power. And delegated power may be usurped or abused. Consequently, we must concentrate our attention on the ways in which political power is exercised in democratic societies, the ways in which it must be

2. Leon Trotsky, *The Revolution Betrayed*, trans. Max Eastman (Garden City, NY: Doubleday, Doran and Co., 1937), p. 239.

made more responsible, and also the ways in which under certain conditions it must be curbed or tamed without making it vulnerable to anarchy from within and totalitarian aggression from without.

It is an important truth—but far from the whole truth—to say that political power in a democracy rests on public opinion which is a compound of majority sentiments or ideals, regardless of whether they are true or false. At the end of his life John Maynard Keynes, the great economist, maintained that the strongest factor in public affairs was the dominant ideas, inherited from the past, usually those discredited by contemporary scientific inquiry. In nondemocratic societies these are the ideas of the dominant elites. In democracies there are plural centers of opinion, greater interplay and interaction, more input from more sources, and at the very least a legally recognized opposition to the positions expressed by the official holders of power.

Nonetheless, unless one subscribes to some form of magical idealism, the power of concepts or ideas to affect human conduct cannot be understood without taking note of the channels and media through which they are communicated. Not all ideas get a hearing, and some not much of a hearing. *Whose* ideas predominate, and how? Here we must note the growing power of those who control the sources of information, the selective criteria of what constitutes news, and the way in which reporting the news makes the news, not to mention the distortions and bias of advocacy journalism. There are many problems here which should be explored in depth.

It has been widely alleged that those who control the public media —television, radio, and the press—are the true lords of public opinion in that they exercise the greatest single influence on public opinion, and not only an influence but a one-sided influence. Many illustrations have been cited of this pervasive influence. One of the most recent and impressive is a two-volume study entitled *Big Story* by Peter Braestrop—sponsored by Freedom House. It is a study of the treatment of the famous 1968 Tet Offensive of the Viet Cong by the American press, television, and radio. The actual facts show that this was a disastrous military defeat for the Viet Cong. However, it was systematically played up by the public media as a smashing and humiliating defeat of the South Vietnamese and American forces. This distortion of the true situation, it is alleged, produced a turning point in the public support of American involvement in Vietnam, enabled the Viet Cong to snatch a political victory out of the jaws of a military defeat, and ultimately contributed to President Johnson's decision not to run again.

Even if true, it would require more than this and other cases to validate the thesis that public opinion in the United States is at the mercy of those who control the public media. But it points up the problem. Regardless of what a sober empirical analysis of the facts discloses, we take it for granted that the spirit, if not the letter, of democratic self-government is undermined if public opinion, which ultimately should control the direction of public policy, is manipulated. Of course, we do not want the government to control the public media. But neither do we want the public media to control the government or unduly influence it by systematic campaigns against selected targets, by threats of leaks with bureaucratic connivance for acts of omission or commission that were ignored or played down when committed by a friendly administration.

In a democracy the power of government ultimately rests upon the freely given consent of the governed. Where there is no possibility of effective dissent, there is no democracy, no matter what it calls itself, "new," "higher," "directed," "organic," or "people's" democracy. Power in a democracy by the very nature of the way in which freely given consent is established must be limited. For it must be possible for a minority peacefully to become a majority. No person or group can be permitted to become so powerful as to foreclose that possibility. That is why majority rule in a genuine democracy must respect the basic human rights of minorities.

From this it follows that the best hope of avoiding the abuse of power is to share it. Sharing of power is rendered difficult by the size of our democracy which generates a feeling of individual helplessness, a sense of not being in control of the domestic events affecting one's life, of not counting, of being subject to the power of others— whether government bureaucrats, pressure groups, multinational corporations, trade unions, or other vaguely identified groups referred to as "they" or "them" in opposition to "us." I am not referring to the impatience with legislative delays—the price we pay for brakes on rash or ill-considered actions by the people's representatives in a federal system of divided powers. In time the errors of political action yield to better political judgment. I am referring to actions outside the legislative process which are sensed by a majority of citizens as arbitrary, unwise, or unfair. They range from trivial matters like denying freedom of choice to individuals about what to eat, drink, or wear when information is made available about the likely or unlikely consequences of their consumption, to very important matters affecting their life careers.

An example of the latter is the use of the quota system, preferential hiring, and reverse discrimination in employment. Time and time again every segment of the population regardless of race, ethnicity, and sex has expressed its opposition to such practices. In May 1977 the Gallup poll reported that 85 percent of Americans polled opposed preferential treatment by race or sex for jobs or college places: 64 percent of non-whites polled, that is, members of groups whom today's preferential treatment is supposed to benefit also opposed such preference. Women, who are also favored by many quota practices, opposed them by 83 percent. As the pollsters pointed out, there has seldom been such overwhelming agreement among Americans on a controversial issue. Yet the bureaucrats in the Department of Health, Education, and Welfare and other government agencies are imposing this practice without any legislative warrant, and in defiance of the Civil Rights Act of 1964 which forbids preferential hiring or quotas of any kind. (I am not discussing the validity of this practice which violates the merit system or civil service principle, but citing it as the kind of action that produces the malaise with our democratic system, and the belief that things are out of control.)

Strictly speaking we cannot literally share most forms of power that affect us. What is meant by the phrase "sharing power" is that we want power to be responsible, that it not act arbitrarily in determining our lives, preventing the personal and group initiatives and growth that are not harmful to others.

There are various ways of sharing or diffusing power. The first is by decentralizing organizations. Whatever a local association or group can do at no greater cost than a larger one should be transferred to its jurisdiction. Decentralization, however, is not a panacea. There are some things that must be centralized like the monetary system, immigration policy, national defense. The development of our own federal system shows that the protection of the civil rights of all citizens requires the intervention of federal laws. Nonetheless the current outcry against the growth of big government, reflected in the tremendous increase in the public bureaucracy, which "expanded three times faster than private employment in the last 20 years," and a regulatory mania that goes beyond honest labeling are symptomatic of an increase in arbitrary power that needlessly interferes with the styles of personal life.

Secondly, in addition to reawakening a sense of the strategic importance of local government, stress must be placed upon the varieties of citizen participation that it makes possible. The idea is as old as Thomas Jefferson and its philosophy was elaborated most fully by John Dewey in his theories of shared experience. But it is not enough to cry up participation—its forms must be institutionalized. The forms of participation should reflect equality of concern in a common project, informed awareness, and delegation of power, although not necessarily equality of power. As with decentralization, so with participation. It is not a panacea. There are some problems like that of nuclear control that cannot be settled by mass participation. Such participation is more likely to result in confrontation with delegated authority than in resolution of problems. There is participation and participation. In a democracy it cannot take the form of mob action. It is one thing for citizens to cooperate with law enforcement agencies. It is quite another to organize vigilante groups to enforce the law. It is one thing to hold mass meetings, draw up petitions and addresses to legislatures with respect, say, to the construction of nuclear energy plants. It is quite another form of participation to attempt to take possession of nuclear sites and plants in defiance of law. Usually it is a nonrepresentative minority that engages in actions of this sort, in the course of which it violates the rights of the majority which is willing to accept the arbitrament of the democratic process.

It is not only in politics that we must seek to increase participatory activities. It must also be done in the most difficult and yet the most significant area of human experience—one's vocation and career. For the ordinary person who does not live on an inherited income—the points at which one feels the impact of power is at his or her place of work. Whether or not one finds fulfillment in one's work is next to satisfactory personal relations in love and family, the chief determinants of personal happiness. The trade union or professional association may stand between the worker and the arbitrary actions and petty tyrannies of management. Government through various forms of insurance may remove the nightmare fear of unemployment. But the problem of satisfaction and significance at work—so that earning one's living is not a burden in living one's life, but a meaningful and fulfilling experience—cannot be solved merely by higher trade union settlements or hope of early retirement. No one knows how to meet the challenges in an industrial society geared to assembly lines. The most fruitful prospect lies in the proposals and practices that would provide incentives for retraining and promotion, and that seek to draw workers into participation with management in considering problems related not only to health and plant safety but to the industrial operation itself.

West Germany has blazed an original path with its policy of codetermination in which representatives of the workers sit on governing or managing boards. But this does not meet the needs of the rank and file. It may be that as work becomes more mechanized hours can be reduced to make for more leisure. But unless there is a *creative use* of leisure, killing time, as the tell-tale expression suggests, can be just as boring as monotonous work. Whether at work or leisure, both education and industry must provide an opportunity for individuals to develop a center around which to organize a pattern of experience that expresses their free reflective choice. The more citizens there are who have succeeded in fulfilling themselves in their callings, the greater the likelihood that the excesses of power will be resisted.

One final word. In considering the realities of power today, we must never forget that the democracies of the world represent the smaller segment of the world's population, and that they have existed for an even smaller segment of recorded history than non-democratic forms of society and government. In his second inaugural address Lincoln observed that democracy with its principles of majority rule and respect for minority rights was the only alternative to despotism, on the one hand, and anarchism, on the other. And as we should know from history—anarchism is the rule of a thousand despots.

The perpetual task of democracy is to see to it that in sharing power through the democratic process, it does not weaken its power to defend the democratic process against external and internal foes. At the same time we must not treat opponents within the democratic process as if they were the enemies of that process. We live in a dangerous world—more hazardous than the world of Hobbes who justified the power of government in order to avoid a life which was nasty, brutish, ugly and short. Hobbes's great fear was of sudden death—not from natural causes—but at the hands of his fellow man. We live in an age much more dangerous than that of Hobbes because among other reasons it is one in which as a consequence of scientific technology the sudden death of cultures is possible. This means that the use of power cannot intelligently be forsworn by those who love freedom—and that its exercise must always be justified in the light of the preservation of a free society.

1977

Chapter 4
Intelligence, Morality, and Foreign Policy

In the conduct of foreign affairs, as in personal matters, there are situations in which silence or secrecy demonstrates a form of morality. There are also times when secrecy alone is not enough: The defense of a free society or the maintenance of peace in the world may require the uncovering of complex information about the committed adversaries of freedom. If, in that process, abuses develop in the intelligence systems of a free nation, then appropriate methods must be devised for safely counteracting the morally illegitimate activities. We must unquestionably, however, maintain *intelligent* intelligence operations.

There are at least three fundamental questions whose answers have a direct bearing on the conduct and outcome of American foreign policy. The first is whether the normal political process can cope effectively with the problems and perennial crises of foreign policy, or whether this is a domain in which ultimate decisions must be entrusted to a dedicated corps of trained specialists responsible to the executive power. The second is whether principles of morality can and should operate in guiding the conduct of foreign policy, and to what extent the national interest should be subordinated to such principles when their role is acknowledged. The third is what moral choices are open to a democratic nation like our own in a world in which it is threatened by aggressive totalitarian powers and ideologies.

From de Tocqueville to Walter Lippmann democracies have been faulted because of their inability to conduct intelligent foreign policies. The argument is quite familiar. Where domestic policies are concerned their fruits can be roughly but properly determined by consequences perceived not too long after they have been adopted. If unsatisfactory, they can be corrected or agitation against them developed. But the consequences of a foreign policy are rarely immediate. Critical judgment usually follows only after the experience of bitter fruits of disaster. On the other hand, where the urgencies of a crisis situation require immediate response the democratic process is too slow and unwieldy. It is therefore concluded that because of the delicacy, complexity, and sometimes the necessary secrecy of foreign policy, negotiations and actions cannot be subjected to public discussion. The strategies to meet acts of foreign aggression must be initiated before their outcome confronts the nation and limits its choice of alternatives of response. There is great danger to the national interest—today even to national survival—in deferring to the vagaries of public opinion that tend to swing pendularly from one extreme to another. De Tocqueville's words are often cited to drive these points home. "Foreign politics demand scarcely any of those qualities which a democracy possesses; and they require, on the contrary, the perfect use of almost all those faculties in which it is deficient. . . . A democracy is unable to regulate the details of an important undertaking, to persevere in a design, and to work out its execution in the presence of serious obstacles. It cannot combine its measures with secrecy, and it will not await their consequences with patience."

De Tocqueville's indictment can be substantiated from the historical record. When memories of past wars are faint, public opinion can too easily be aroused in support of armed conflict. This was apparent in 1914. And once hostilities begin, the slogans of total victory or unconditional surrender become extremely popular. Proposals for a negotiated peace are denounced as treasonable. On the other hand, after a costly war popular opinion is apt to become fearful and defeatist and to resist policies which, had they been adopted in time, might have prevented the very outcome that was feared most. The popular opposition to the rearmament of Britain in the thirties is a case in point. Another is the failure to act vigorously— urged only by two public figures, Pilsudski and Trotsky—against Hitler's reentry into the Rhineland in defiance of the Treaty of Versailles. And although it is often ignored, the capitulation to Hitler at Munich was approved with wild popular enthusiasm as insuring peace in our time.

Other considerations make much of the instability and ignorance of popular opinion. Those who stress them tend to argue that the only alternative to the paralysis of the national will in foreign policy in a nation like our own is not to share the power but to entrust it to the executive branch. In an address delivered in New York in 1963, Senator Fulbright voiced sentiments in this vein which contrast sharply with some of his later pronouncements. "Public opinion must be educated and led if it is to bolster a wise and effective foreign policy. This is preeminently a task for Presidential leadership because the Presidential office is the only one under our constitutional system that constitutes a forum for moral and political leadership on a national scale. Accordingly I think that we must contemplate the further enhancement of Presidential authority in foreign affairs."

Granted all this and more, there are overwhelming considerations that make it dubious to entrust the direction of foreign policy (always excluding specific emergency actions whose continuation must be subject to later congressional ratification) to the exclusive purview of the executive power. First, in a democratic community which assumes that those who are affected by basic decisions should have some voice in influencing them, foreign policy must be a matter of high public concern. Especially today in the era of nuclear technology, foreign policy may center on decisions that spell national freedom or enslavement, or the life and death of tens of millions. Foreign policy is everybody's business.

Second, where U.S. foreign policy has been determined by the executive branch independently of public opinion, the consequences have not been very happy for the preservation of freedom and the safeguarding of peace. Woodrow Wilson, elected in 1916 to keep the country out of World War I, a year later took the United States into war and in all likelihood prevented a negotiated peace. Even if the Central Powers had emerged from the conflict relatively stronger than the Allied Powers, Lenin and his faction would probably not have come to power in Russia. (Kerensky has admitted that the continuation of the war was a decisive factor in their triumph.) Without Lenin, the socialist and labor movements of Italy and Germany would not have been disastrously split and we might have been spared Mussolini and Hitler, not to speak of Stalin and Mao. In any event, no matter who had won, in the absence of American intervention it would be hard to imagine a world worse than the Nazi and Gulag Archipelagoes.

Roosevelt during the Second World War regarded the Soviet Union as a genuine ally rather than as a cobelligerent, allaying deep popular distrust of the Kremlin's postwar intentions. Truman expressed Roosevelt's policy in the remark addressed to Senator Wheeler's committee which waited on him, after his accession to the presidency, to caution against the extension of Soviet rule in Eastern Europe. "Gentlemen, it is not Soviet Communism I fear but rather British Imperialism"—and this on the eve of the grant of independence to India and the disintegration of the British Empire.

Third, in the long run the success of any foreign policy, even when initiated by the executive in a crisis, as was the case in Korea (a needless war largely precipitated by the withdrawal of American troops and the declaration that Korea was outside the bounds of our national interest), depends upon the understanding and support of the people. The disaster in Vietnam to a large extent flowed from the absence of popular understanding of what justified our continued presence there after the initial error of involvement had been made. There are good pragmatic grounds therefore for sharing with the citizenry the determination of foreign policy.

This brings to the fore the second question—one that can be posed in the form of a further criticism of a democratic approach to foreign policy. It is often argued that popular influence on foreign policy is undesirable because it tends to be naïve and moralistic. It assumes that what is good or bad, right or wrong, honorable or dishonorable, in private ordinary life is no less so in the life of nations at peace or at war. But many experts in foreign policy assure us that standards of morality in private and public life are profoundly different. Who does not recall the words of statesmen warning against a too simple identification of personal and public morality? Cavour, the Italian statesman, not the worst of the great unifiers, uttered a sentiment that all of them would have approved. "If we did for ourselves what we did for our country, what scoundrels we would be."

Our former Secretary of State Dean Acheson, in an address to those contemplating a career in foreign service, observed, "Generally speaking, morality often imposes upon those who exercise the powers of government standards of conduct quite different from what might seem right to them as private citizens."

Although this is a plausible and widely held view, it seems to me to rest on a confusion between moral standards or basic moral values which, if valid, are invariant for all situations in which human beings must act, and the specific situations in which the decision must be made. No moral principle by itself determines what action should be taken because, when we are in an agony of doubt about what we should do, more than one moral principle applies. This is as true in the area of personal relations as in public policy. Because we should tell the truth, it does not follow that we should tell the truth to someone intent upon killing or maiming or robbing others, if not telling the truth will tend to prevent such action. There are always other values involved. Even in less extreme situations we may rightly prefer to be kind rather than needlessly truthful if the truth speaking will result in great cruelty and no benefit to anyone else.

It is wrong to steal but we cannot morally condemn the man who steals to provide food for his starving family if no other means exist to alleviate their condition. Every situation of moral choice is one in which the choice is not between good and bad, right or wrong, but between good and good, right and right, the good and the right. One good may be overridden by a greater good; one obligation by a more pressing one. Ordinary human life would be impossible if we did not recognize and act on these considerations. It is wrong to kill a human being but *if the only way* to prevent him from blowing up a plane or city was by killing him it would be right to do so. To be sure the weight of experience is behind the moral injunctions and ideals expressed in the testaments and commandments of the great religions and ethical systems of the past. But they cannot all be categorical in all situations because they sometimes conflict. Reflection is required in order to determine which is to be subordinate to which. The only moral absolute is, to use a phrase of John Erskine's, the moral obligation to be intelligent in the choice we make of that course of conduct among possible alternatives whose consequences will strengthen the structure of the reflective values that define our philosophy of life.

This does not justify some current degenerate forms of existentialism according to which individuals are free to decide for themselves what is right or wrong without any appeal to moral principles or ideals but merely on the basis of what they desire. They seem to assume that because principles or ideals do not possess an absolutely categorical character that therefore they have no validity whatsoever. They thereby overlook the fact that when a legitimate exception is made to a moral rule, this does not destroy the validity and binding character of that rule within certain limits and conditions. They fail to recognize the overriding obligation of another rule that holds when the conditions are different. The better is the enemy of the good, and the bad is preferable to what is worse—when these are the only alternatives.

The situation is quite familiar in the area of civil and political rights. We all know that the right to know may conflict with the right to privacy, the freedom to publish may destroy a person's right to a fair trial, the freedom to speak (falsely to shout "Fire!" in a crowded theatre) with the right to life. Even the right to worship according to one's conscience may be abridged if it involves human sacrifice or polygamy. In this country it is the Supreme Court which determines the order of priority these freedoms have and under what conditions. In England, it is Parliament. None of these rights can be considered as absolute in the sense that they can never be overridden in any circumstance.

It is when we approach the field of foreign policy that the greatest confusion abounds. A foreign policy must further the interests and safety of the nation. But any nation worthy of the support of moral men and women must be committed to certain moral ideals—freedom, self-determination, peace, and human welfare. But no more in this case than in the case of personal morality does that mean that we can deduce what our policy should be in specific foreign policy situations. If we espouse "the right to self-determination" as we should, that will not mean that in any and every circumstance of international affairs, we should support it, regardless of other moral values involved, any more than that we should always tell the truth about everything to everyone, or give alms in any and every circumstance. Self-determination is one value among others and we must evaluate a claim for it in a specific case in the light of its consequences on these other values. Not every province of every country that raises the cry warrants our support any more than the demand for self-determination of the southern states warranted moral support when they sought to dissolve the Union. If a country or region of a country demands self-determination in order to impose slavery on others or to unleash an aggressive war, there is good reason not to support it. No group that raises the banner of self-determination really believes that the principle should be universalized. Indian intellectuals under British rule were eloquent about self-determination but they regarded the slogan as treasonable when raised by the inhabitants of Goa and Kashmir. The same was true for the Greek Cypriots in relation to the Turkish enclaves after independence was won by Cyprus.

There are those who are impatient with considerations about moral principles where national interest is involved. They take as their guide Lord Palmerston's pronouncement: "We have no eternal allies and we have no eternal enemies. Our interests are eternal and perpetual, and those interests it is our duty to follow." In the light of American relations with Russia and China in the past sixty years one can certainly agree with this but read a different implication out of it. Why should the national interest exclude moral ideals? Despite the ambiguities and complexities of the concept of national interest, it presupposes at the very least national survival. Even on the plane of personal morality, survival—except under extraordinary conditions—is integral to the good life. In order to be blessed, says Spinoza, one must at least be. The real question is how narrowly the national interest is to be conceived. We are not talking about national survival under any circumstances but of our survival as a free and open society. To some moral and patriotic Frenchmen the acceptance of Churchill's proposal to Vichy to accept union with Great Britain, even if this meant that France as a separate nation would exist no more, was preferable to the continued existence of France under fascist rule.

Once the survival of our free society with all its imperfections and limitations is regarded as desirable, to what measures are we therewith committed in its defense? Certainly not to any measures regardless of their consequences to our security and the character of the society we seek to defend. The untenability of the doctrine that the end of national security justifies the use of any means to insure it is, first, that often the means employed are *not* the most intelligent means of securing that end; and, second, that the consequences of using some means may adversely and unacceptably affect the constellation of other ends—our institutionalized rights, freedoms, and services—whose security we are defending. Nonetheless there are occasions when the ends and values whose presence defines a free and open society conflict, and we must choose between them. There are occasions when freedom of the press does severely prejudice a person's right to a fair trial. There are occasions when speech is used to incite a lynch mob to deprive a person of life or limb. At any definite time the conflict of freedoms is resolved or should be resolved by the action whose consequences are more likely than those of any other action to further the total structure of freedoms in the community. Normally the suspension of freedom of the press for a few days with respect to certain features of a case, with unlimited freedom to comment subsequently, is considered by reflective judgment to be less undesirable than the miscarriage of justice that may result if such freedom remains unabridged. Some of those who protest in the interests of a free press that there is an absolute right to know in such cases do not extend it to the right to know the sources that the press relies on in its investigatory reports.

The great danger, of course, in invoking the sanctions of national security to curb any of the normal traditional freedoms of the marketplace of ideas is that the national security may not be involved at all, that it may be used as a pretext for arbitrary and illegal personal or factional interest. Measures that under proper safeguards may sometimes be both morally and legally legitimate in times of clear and present danger to the primary security of the nation, may be abused and misemployed against fellow citizens with whom we differ about policies. This was illustrated in the Watergate episode in which opponents *within* the democratic process were treated as if they were *enemies* of the democratic process.

This makes focal the third question: What moral choices are open to a democratic society faced by an armed and powerful enemy whose declared objective is the destruction of free institutions like our own? If our society with all its imperfections—and with its multiple mechanisms for improvement—is worth surviving, it is worth defending. How can it legitimately defend itself?

At this point it is necessary to distinguish between two types of totalitarian powers and ideologies. Although as democrats we are morally committed to condemning both, both are not of the same direct and pressing concern to a culture that seeks to preserve its freedom. The first type has very unpleasant consequences for citizens who live within its borders but such nations do not threaten the peace of the world—for example, Franco's Spain and Tito's Yugoslavia. We need no present defense against them. The other type is aggressive and expansionist. It seeks overtly and sometimes covertly to undermine the strength and security of free countries and their allies. Today that characterizes the policy of the Soviet Union and in lesser measure, Communist China. The nature of the struggle to defend and preserve the free world requires at the very least some measures of secrecy. For example, any agreement on multilateral limitation on nuclear weapons is not worth the paper it is written on unless there exists some method of checking on the performance of the principals. If the United States has discovered a method of checking compliance by the Soviet Union, making such knowledge public would invite the Kremlin to devise methods of escaping detection of violations and encourage it to stockpile nuclear weapons to a point where its predominance would make it relatively invulnerable to any response the United States could make if the Kremlin launched a nuclear Pearl Harbor. Secrecy on these and related matters is an axiom of political morality, one is tempted to write, of political sanity.

Our secrecy is not enough. We require in the interests of our defense—and of the peace of the world—intelligence information concerning the Kremlin's success in penetrating our secrecy and its progress in devising methods by which it can undermine our defense. What is true for military measures, *mutatis mutandis*, is true for some political measures, too.

What this entails is that "intelligence measures" be intelligent.

The revelations concerning certain unsavory and foolish CIA operations is not an argument for the abolition of the agency but for its improvement. As well argue that we can remedy defective vision by poking the eyes out of our head, as that the best way of correcting the shortcomings of past intelligence practices is to abolish its functions; or, what is tantamount to the same thing, make the details of its operations known to a large congressional committee whose staffs are in a position to leak secrets to the press. Great Britain and every other democratic nation in the world has an Official Secrets Act or something equivalent. While such an act has never been necessary in America, our system does anticipate that officials and journalists alike will demonstrate a high sense of responsibility. Each must be aware of the inevitable and necessary tension between governmental secrecy and the need of the public to know; yet each must recognize, in the absence of an absolute demarcation of their respective territories, that *some* secrecy is essential to the survival of freedom, and each has the duty to discover where the invisible line rests in each situation.

There have undoubtedly been abuses in CIA activities, particularly in the failure to abide by the restrictions on the field of its surveillance. But these could have been exposed and corrected without destroying the effectiveness of intelligence operations abroad. In other words there is an intelligent way of revealing the inadequacies of intelligence services and an unintelligent way which profits no one but the KGB and other enemies of the relatively free nations of the world.

There seems to be a wilful blindness among some commentators about the necessary role of intelligence services in the defense of a free and open society in an era in which the sudden death of a culture is possible. The blindness is sometimes reinforced by a smug moral posturing which confuses principles with tactical measures. The same considerations—the health and integrity of the democratic process—that condemn the giving of a bribe to a domestic official *may* justify the offer of a bribe to an official of a foreign country for information—not procurable in time by any other way—that may be crucial to the national safety.

Those who on a priori grounds condemn an action without regard for its consequences in preserving the structure of democratic freedoms are guilty at the very least of blatant hypocrisy. This does not give carte blanche to any fool to undertake any project because it seems to him advantageous at the moment. Here as elsewhere there is no substitute for intelligence—for intelligence ultimately responsible to the authorized representatives, legislative or judicial, of the democratic community. It is sometimes necessary to burn a house, or to permit it to burn, in order to save a village. This does not bestow a license for arson. We must recognize the evil we do even when it is the lesser evil. But if it is truly the lesser evil then those who condemn it or would have us do nothing at all are morally responsible for the greater evil that may ensue.

1976

Part Two:
Freedom and Rights

Chapter 5
Reflections on
Human Rights

Social and political theory is often a preface to practice. But often theory lags far behind. The exigencies and opportunities of experience provoke responses which seem appropriate and desirable long before we can justify them. This seems particularly true about movements for human rights. Despite the widespread and growing consciousness of the importance of human rights, and the multiplicity of movements and causes in behalf of one or the other of such rights, there is a paucity of theoretical literature on the subject in comparison with the literature on other philosophical themes. The existing literature betrays a tentativeness and perplexity, and sometimes an outright skepticism, about the nature, reality, and so-called foundations of human rights.

Nonetheless, demands for the recognition of human rights proceed apace. Like the cry for justice in whatever idiom, they flow from feelings of deprivation and resentment which feed the judgment that things can be, and should be, better than they are. Their promulgation is not likely to be affected by difficulties in meta-ethical analysis. Nor does their realization depend upon such difficulties rather than upon the relative power of those who support, and those who oppose these demands—something quite apparent in the agitation for the recognition of new welfare and housing rights in American communities.

To some extent, however, confusions in some interpretations of the meaning of human rights in political and legal discussions have an effect on the recognition of the grounds on which human rights are accepted or rejected. Some writers, interpreting claims to human rights literally as claims to inalienable rights, reject the whole notion as unintelligible. Thus, Santayana, in referring to the rights enumerated in the American Declaration of Independence, characterizes them as "a salad of illusions," and Bentham before him, as "nonsense on stilts." But once rights are cut free from the metaphysics of Blackstone or the religion of Deism—or of any other kind of metaphysics or theology—it can be shown that statements of and about them make perfectly good sense even in terms of Bentham's utilitarianism or Santayana's eudaemonism, albeit not free from some difficulties. At any rate with respect to the cluster of rights which are presupposed by a democratic form of political rule, Bentham's acceptance and Santayana's rejection of them flow not from differences concerning their alleged ontological foundations but from different estimates of their fruits in experience.

The most momentous consequence of skepticism concerning the intelligibility or validity of any theory of human rights is the tendency it encourages to regard them merely as ideological masks of sheer power relations.

A number of grounds have been offered to justify the denial that there are human rights or that we can know of them. I wish briefly to consider them before discussing my conception of human rights.

I. It is sometimes argued that "human rights" do not exist because there are no such things as moral rights altogether. And what this means is that we cannot ever supply a valid or objective foundation for any moral judgment. This wholesale moral skepticism takes two forms. Sometimes it asserts that the expression "right," to the extent that it is intelligible, is wholly reducible to might or power—the familiar Thrasymachian position. Sometimes it is argued that there are various systems of morality, all historically contingent, and that with respect to contrary or contradictory judgments about common practices either both judgments are valid or none is. Nietzsche's philosophy is sometimes cited in support of both varieties of skepticism (the first may be considered a special case of the second).

It seems clear to me that these metaethical questions are really irrelevant to some questions that arise concerning the substantive nature of the rights which should be enumerated in a declaration of human rights. For at any definite time there are more classes of actions that are considered right than can be listed in any declaration. *Differences* concerning what should be listed as "rights" can be intelligently discussed without calling the whole of morality into question. The "right" thing to do in a situation does not automatically give rise to a class of rights. "It is right to speak the truth," "It is right to fulfill one's promises," "It is right to repay a debt," and so forth. But although these may be presupposed by any set of human rights, they are not listed among them. When differences about specific rights do arise, for example, on the right to inheritance, or the control of property, or the privilege against self-incrimination, the determination can be, and is, made independently of metaethical considerations. The situation would be the same were one to deny that we could have adequate grounds for distinguishing between proposed laws to effect certain purposes on the ground that no common definition of law has as yet been reached by jurists.

If the viability of the belief in human rights did depend upon the rejection of the position of Thrasymachus and his modern descendants, then that position seems to me to be refuted by two considerations. The first is the linguistic fact that in none of the major languages of the world are "right" and "strong," "wrong" and "weak" used interchangeably, and that those who claim to do so are never consistent in their usage. The second and more important consideration is this: Even if someone were to be found who sincerely and consistently claimed that he could not distinguish between the concepts of might and right, and that the authority of right was ultimately rooted in the authority of might, a situation could be devised in which his own experience would reveal that there was something askew, something that could not be explained in the equation of might and right. This evidence seems to me just as decisive as that which leads to the acknowledgment by a color-blind person who has failed to distinguish between red and green objects that something is lacking in *his* powers of color discrimination—an acknowledgment induced not by the coercion of numbers but by the deliverances of his own experience.

I can describe the situation only in barest outline. It requires a distinction which could hardly be challenged without abandoning the distinction between sane and insane, between blind *force* that has no direction, and therefore can rend the person who employs it, and *might* whose direction is self-conserving. Let Thrasymachus be the almighty conqueror strong enough to do anything he pleases. To profit by his conquest and to make his rule more secure he lays down the harshest rules imaginable of curfew or what not, rules which enable the population to know what it must do to avoid destruction. A man is brought before him charged with violating the curfew. He denies it. Thrasymachus has the power to kill him whether he broke the rule or not, the power to change the rule or to abolish it altogether. But under the rule Thrasymachus has himself laid down, he knows that the question can intelligibly be asked, whether *he* chooses to ask it or not: Guilty or not guilty? This is not a question of who is stronger or weaker. But whoever asks it or realizes that it can be asked, knows that might and right cannot be identified because questions of guilt or innocence are *in nuce* questions of justice or injustice.[1]

As for the wider or more radical form of skepticism, the position seems to me to rest upon a confusion between objectivity and universality. If it is possible to discover some shared interests among members of a community, one can find good and sufficient reasons in the light of those interests for choosing to perform some action, whose consequences have been carefully compared with the consequences of alternative actions, rather than others. If we encounter creatures on earth or from Mars or Nietzschean supermen with whom we can share no common interest, whether of peace or survival, then we could not have a *common* morality. Nonetheless this does not entail that we cannot have an objectively grounded morality. If human morality is relevant to human interests, needs, and desires, its objectivity is not affected by the existence of other creatures with irreducibly different interests, needs, and desires. There may be questions of how or whether and to what degree these differences are irreducible. These will define the limits of what is common. They will not affect the fact of their objectivity. That certain foods are nourishing to men is objectively true even though they are not nourishing to wolves or tigers. Questions about the objectivity of human morality and its universality are distinct.

Before making inquiry into these questions it is as easy to be pessimistic—and to see in every other man a wolf—as to be too optimistic and not envisage the possibility that we may have to fight to defend our way of life. But no matter what the theoretical foundations of morality are taken to be, secular or religious, formalistic or teleological, no morality can be set up as normative without assuming that with respect to some basic interests that they are shared or shareable. It is only because human beings build gods in their own moral image that they can reasonably hope that the divine commandments can serve as a guideline in human experience.

The very language of those who argue from the theoretical *possibility* of a multiplicity of systems of morality to the denial of the objectivity of human rights within any one of these systems, often betrays confusion on this point. I have heard philosophers declare

---

1. Jonas Cohen, *Theorie der Dialektik: Formenlehre der Philosophie* (Leipzig, 1923), pp. 52 ff.

that they ardently wished to see the UN Universal Declaration of Human Rights "implemented and respected" by all nations at the same time as they asserted it was quite evident to them that we do not know that there are any such rights and that we have no ground for believing that they "ought to be both acknowledged and respected." Actually, for every one of the rights listed a variety of good reasons could easily be offered why it should be acknowledged and respected even though we cannot show that it should be acknowledged and respected for every manner of man and interest *conceivable*.

2. It is sometimes argued that there are no human rights in any system of morals unless these rights are construed as absolute, unconditional, or inalienable. This view is implied in the position taken by some liberal minded jurists with respect to the rights listed in the American Bill of Rights (especially the First Amendment), a few of which appear in the UN Universal Declaration of Human Rights. It is a position that makes no sense in its own terms except on the assumption that there is only one absolute right or, if there is more than one, that we can be provided with convincing reason to believe that all human rights are compatible with each other and that in no foreseeable or credible circumstances will they ever conflict. But this is implausible on its face. It is easy to show that the rights found in every bill of rights often conflict in specific situations. Freedom of speech may not only prejudice a man's right to a fair trial but in the mouth of a demagogue haranguing a lynch mob, imperil a man's right to life.

The illuminating distinctions between prima facie and absolute obligations and rights drawn by Ross and Ewing seem to me to constitute an adequate analysis of the problems we face. All human rights have a prima facie validity in situations in which they are relevant, but they are not absolutely or categorically binding on conduct in any specific case although they must always be considered. We are unable to say which rights are categorically binding not only because we cannot anticipate with what other rights they may conflict but because the consequences of abiding by or violating different prima facie rights and obligations are so complex and of such unequal and inconstant weight that no fixed hierarchy or rank can be established in advance to guide us in all situations. Reflection is required in all grave moral decisions. John Dewey defines the moral experience out of which a genuine quest arises for what is our moral duty to do here and now, as one in which good conflicts with good, or right with right, or good with right. This makes every right, every value, every principle, every rule which we bring to bear upon a moral problem, of presumptive validity until reflective inquiry into the specific situation settles on what is morally best, or at least better, here and now.

Intellectually the procedure is comparable to a decision that must be made in selecting the best or the least objectionable out of any collection in which all members vary in their qualities of shape, color, grace, light, and so forth, and in which no member excels all the others in most respects. But when we must decide between conflicting human policies, with their varied goods and rights, the choice is much more difficult because we cannot sum them up arithmetically or so clearly foresee the consequences of acting upon them.

There are some who believe that there must be, if not absolute rights, then absolute wrongs or absolute obligations of what not to do. Psychologically a powerful case can be made for this position and there are certain things that we may be asked to do in the interests of justice which would make life unendurable. Nonetheless the ironies and tragic cruelties of history create situations in which the choice is between lesser evils, and in which no matter what we do, we cannot avoid guilt. Here our categorical duty is to prevent situations from arising in which such choices must be made; but when they are thrust upon us we cannot say that all alternatives are equally bad. The holy man who refuses to kill the beast or the wicked man who has run amok and is about to kill hundreds of innocents, if killing him is the *only* way of preventing the outrageous evil, is in effect an accomplice in their murders. His holiness cannot wash him morally clean.

The only alternative to this approach, with which I am familiar, which seeks to avoid the fanaticism of absolutism, is to hold that the categorical assertion of inalienable rights presupposes that there are certain exceptions built into the universal judgment, that rules of conduct despite their linguistic form are not intended to convey what is communicated if they are interpreted literally. This has obvious difficulties. No one can foresee all the exceptions. Once it is admitted that all propositions about human rights are open-ended, it becomes semantically impossible to state them in universal form without appearing inconsistent or hypocritical. To attempt to derive the meaning and universal validity of moral utterances (of which statements about human rights are a particular class) from the conditions of linguistic significance under which they are learned so that we know when to disregard the obligation that flows from the statement, "He has a right to be told the truth," seems to me to be hopeless. The conditions of linguistic significance are not universal; and even where they are the same, they cannot by themselves enable us to understand the situations in which a man has a right to be told the truth and when not.[2]

3. Another source of skepticism concerning "human rights" arises because of the differences in the lists of rights as they appear in various declarations of human rights. This objection testifies to a profound misconception of the purpose or point of listing such rights. Such lists are inescapably historical and functional. Any attempt to enumerate human rights without specific reference to a historical situation, or without such reference being presupposed, would give us a schedule of moral rights and duties of such variety and generality that they would be without bite, mere rhetorical pieties, reconcilable with any set of practices. Bills of rights are always historically determined in the sense that their particular provisions depend upon the experience of specific deprivations or oppression or upon the felt need for some service or facility hitherto lacking or not previously acknowledged as a public responsibility. That is why out of an indeterminately large number of rights that are potentially eligible for inclusion, comparatively few are selected.

The fact that rights are always historically determined is apparent in two phenomena. As conditions change, the very meaning of the rights listed is often extended or reinterpreted to cover new situations. Justifications for actions deemed reasonable to meet present-day conditions are read out of, or into, the old formulations. The history of the interpretations of the First Amendment to the United States Constitution is sufficient evidence. Even more striking, new human rights are found presumably carried in words that no one dreamed in previous centuries had such comprehensive connotations. Volumes have recently been published about "the right to privacy" as a fundamental human right enshrined in the American Constitution. Justice Douglas, for example, explicitly maintains that the First Amendment freedoms are derivative from the "right to privacy" which is nowhere mentioned in the text, despite its allegedly ultimate character, or in any of the discussions that accompanied its adoption.[3] It is notorious and yet unavoidable, because of the absence of explicit definition, that new and conflicting meanings have been read into key expressions like "due process of law," "cruel and unusual punishment," "self-incrimination," and so forth.

Secondly, when new declarations or bills of rights are promul-

2. A. I. Melden, "The Concept of Universal Human Rights," in *Science, Language and Human Rights* (Philadelphia: University of Pennsylvania Press, 1952), pp. 167 ff.
3. Griswold v. Connecticut, 381 U.S. 479 (1965).

gated, new rights are often conspicuously added without the subterfuge of exegesis. For example, the right to rest, the right to work, the right to social insurance of various kinds, the right to a nationality, the right to leave one's country, were as a rule not found in earlier formulations because of the absence of the social and economic conditions, and sometimes political conditions, that make them relevant. Certain conditions, of course, are always relevant, especially threats or dangers of arbitrary and despotic government action. This accounts for the presence of some basic human rights in all declarations, for example, the right to life, liberty, freedom of religious worship, speech, press, and assembly. Historical changes may make a profound difference to the meaning of a bill of rights because of the shift of emphasis from one subset of rights to another. In the United States today the right to property, which was the most fiercely defended right in the course of the last century and indeed up to 1936, no longer has the same urgency that it possessed in the days of Locke and even Jefferson, for a variety of reasons, most notably because of the bearing of new forms of social property, as distinct from personal property, on the exercise of the human rights of those who do not possess property.

Finally, whether a right becomes a "human right" does not depend upon whether it gets on a list or declaration. Any moral right can emerge as a focal human right in the course of social and political life. Where human rights are recognized and enforced this is evidence that they have legal force. But their validity does not depend upon their recognition or enforcement. It is or should be obvious that the whole point of asserting, or more accurately, *proposing,* human rights is to win acknowledgment of their validity wherever they are not exercised.

This brings us to the thorny and tangled question of the definition of human rights. Before we can define them we must identify them. There are certain expressions in use, "human rights," or their synonyms, and there are certain practices associated with them that can be described in ways that enable us to determine whether or not they obtain in the community. What definition will best do justice to the following true statements about them?

1. Human rights are a "species" of rights. They are not synonymous therefore with rights per se. The genus of which "human rights" are a species is "moral rights" even when the "human rights" are recognized as legal rights too.

2. When we speak of human rights, if the adjective "human" has any force, they cannot be the same as the rights of animals or the rights of angels, if any, or the rights of corporations or states as such.

3. Although theoretically any moral right can become a human

right, at any given time and place not everything which is a moral right or is morally right is considered a human right. This would be more manifest perhaps if we drew up a declaration of human wrongs. Many things are wrong but only a few would figure in a significant and relevant way on a formal declaration of human wrongs. Declarations of human rights have always been issued in the context of demands for the redress of *grievances*. Most actions which we consider right in a specific context would not be entitled to inclusion among "the rights of man" or "human rights." It is morally right to go out of my way to procure gasoline for a motorist stranded in the desert, but it is not something that can legitimately be included in a declaration of human rights except under theoretically conceivable circumstances of a kind that explain, for example, why the right not to have soldiers quartered in one's home in times of peace was included in the American Bill of Rights (Third Amendment).

4. When human rights are invoked they are cited as *warrants* or good reasons for action or forbearance from actions.

5. Human rights are regarded as general rights as distinguished from special rights that are derived from special relationships to others whether of contract, status, or consanguinity. This is brought home by the question which Felix Cohen addressed to his fellow philosophers shortly after the Second World War. "What rights, if any, can a man [justifiably] claim of me not because he is my brother or my neighbor or my colleague or co-religionist or fellow citizen but just because he is human?" There are certain difficulties with the way in which this question is formulated. Depending upon whether we take the term "human" as a strictly biological characterization or whether we regard it as normative our answers may differ. Anyone who does not answer "none" to the question and enumerates one or more rights may be taken to subscribe to a belief in human rights.

6. Human rights are always regarded as in some sense "basic," "fundamental," or "important."

If this is a sufficient identification of the expression "human rights," and the practices related to their use, how shall we define them? We are seeking a definition that will do justice to the widest variety of usages of the expression "human rights." A considerable number of definitions have been offered on which brief comments are in order.

There is a class of definitions which asserts that human rights are "powers and securities" possessed by individuals. This is inadequate because we speak of the human rights of the powerless and insecure. Another class of definitions makes central the so-called "negative" freedoms from interference by others, and especially by the state. This is inadequate because we speak intelligibly of the human rights of individuals to an education, medical care, work, and not merely of the right to be left alone. There is also a class of definitions which defines human rights as claims made by an individual which society stands ready to enforce. This fails to distinguish between moral rights and legal rights. Human rights are moral rights whether or not they are enforced, whether or not they are the law of the land. It is or should be obvious that some claims are enforced by law that are not considered human rights and many human rights are not legally enforced but should be.

Recently another class of definitions has been put forth by H. J. McCloskey and others, according to which human rights, like other rights, are defined as "entitlements."[4] Of all the single terms that one may substitute in English for "rights" without linguistic awkwardness "entitlement" is the least objectionable. But what illumination is added by the substitution? If one says, "I have a right to *x*," and one is asked for clarification and replies, "I mean I am entitled to *x*," why is this any more satisfactory than if one says, "I am entitled to *x*," and, upon being challenged, replies, "I mean I have a right to *x*"? Like the word "title," the expressions "entitlement" or "entitled to" seem to suggest what is bestowed or conventional, what follows from a rule, and therefore something that may lapse or be canceled, whereas we tend to think of human rights as not so readily cancelable as titles or modifiable as rules. "Entitled" suggests more of a legal term than of a moral term. The very nuance and ambiguities of the terms confirm this. Normally, if we say to someone, "You have no right to the rights you enjoy," it is clear that the first use is of a moral term and the second of a legal one and that we are expressing a moral judgment. If we say, however, "You are not really entitled to your titles," this suggests a legal defect in one's title, a legal judgment.

One of the most interesting definitions of human rights has recently been offered by B. Mayo. "A human right is a claim, on behalf of all men, to corporate action (or perhaps inaction) on the part of whatever institution is in a position to satisfy the claim."[5] Presumably, if no institution exists in a position to satisfy the claim there is an implied moral obligation on all who are in a position to do so, to bring it about.

There are certain difficulties with this definition. A minor one is

4. H. J. McCloskey, "Rights," *Philosophical Quarterly* 15 (April 1965): 115 ff.
5. B. Mayo, *Aristotelian Society Supplementary* 34 (1965): 231.

that there is no limit placed on the scope of the claim. Theoretically it could cover everything or anything at any particular time, whereas all human rights that have hitherto been articulated or sought for have been limited to claims of paramount importance. Secondly, it does not distinguish between rights that *are* claimed and rights that *could be* claimed—a distinction not identical with one that contrasts "claiming" and "being disposed to claim." As I understand this definition, if a person makes no claim for a right or no one else claims it for him or is disposed to do so, it makes no sense to speak of his having a right. On this view presumably, a hundred years ago a man who had resigned himself to his fate, being lynched by a crowd for killing another, had no right to a fair trial until or unless someone spoke up for him or made the claim on his behalf. So if we now say that the man had a human right to a fair trial, whether or not the law enforced it, the right comes into being, so to speak, as well as the violation of the right, with the present claim. A right that was not "possessed" could not have been violated. In defending this view, Mayo argues: "Certainly, an umbrella exists independently of my claiming it [but] it is hard to see that my right (of ownership) exists quite independently of my claims to it. Could an umbrella be *mine* if I never claimed it as mine or ever had the least tendency to do so?"[6]

The answer to this question is, "Of course! I could own the umbrella not only if I never claimed it as mine but even if I claimed it was not mine." To which Mayo retorts that, "The only class of rights which can plausibly be detached from claims seems to be: rights (including ownership) which the *possessor does not know that he has.*" Suppose, however, as man knows that he has rights; can we separate them from his claims to them? Spinoza had both a legal and moral right to his bequest and he knew he had it, but in the end he did not claim what was his by right. In such cases, Mayo holds the rights "are claimed *on his behalf* by someone else."[7] What if they are not? Must Spinoza's rights depend upon the fact that he or someone else in his behalf actually claims them? Is it not necessary to say that the right *could* be claimed? Going further, is it not necessary to say that the existence of the rights does not depend upon whether someone *in fact* claims or *could* claim them, but rather upon whether someone could *justifiably* claim them?

Mayo denies this. There is something odd about a definition of human rights that leads to this denial. It stems from Mayo's belief that a reference to right is embedded in the very meaning of "claim."

6. Ibid., p. 232.
7. Ibid.

He asserts flatly that "all claims are rights" and dismisses the objection that only *justified* or *justifiable* claims are rights on the ground that these qualifications are otiose, that is, futile or functionless and therefore unnecessary. This seems to me to be a piece of arbitrary semantic legislation. "A *demand*," he asserts, "can be (totally) unjustified and unjustifiable" but not a *claim.* Yet every time a host of claims are made to an estate to which there are no known heirs or to large sums of found money, most claims are dismissed as totally unjustified and unjustifiable, and some as fraudulent. Mayo seems to hold that no one uses the word "claim" unless he sincerely believes that his claim is justified or justifiable. This is empirically false. He asserts that the sentence, "I claim x but there is no reason at all why you should give me x," is self-contradictory. I can conceive of situations in which such a sentence would be true. In other situations it might be false. If there is a special sense in which it is self-contradictory, then the sentence in question is no more contradictory than one in which we substitute *demand* for *claim.* "I demand x but there is no reason at all why you should give me x." Actually, in ordinary life situations, no normal man ever makes a claim or demand or even a request without being able to back it up with a reason. The only question is whether the reason is a good one or a morally relevant one. Even in extreme situations where language takes on aberrant uses "demands" are as supportable as "claims." The demands of bank robbers are often supported by reasons (including threats) which may be no weaker than the "reasons" that back up claims.

I conclude therefore that a right is a justifiable claim and offer the following definition of a human right as more adequate to the widest use of the expression "human right" in contemporary discussion:

A human right is a morally justifiable claim made in behalf of all men to the enjoyment and exercise of those basic freedoms, goods, and services which are considered necessary to achieve the human estate. On this definition human rights do not correspond to anything an individual literally possesses as an attribute, whether physical or mental. Morally justifiable claims are *proposals* to treat human beings in certain ways. Human rights are not names of anything. They specify procedures—courses of action—to be followed by agencies of the government and community with respect to a series of liberties, goods, and services.

Before discussing the problem of justification of rights, several features of the definition should be noted. It is clear that the definition is normative or prescriptive in that it interprets human rights as moral rights. It is normative or prescriptive in another sense since the proposal to treat human beings in a certain way reflects a conception of what the human estate *should* be, an idea or ideal of what is worthy of man. It is highly misleading, a category mistake in Ryle's words, to say that man "possesses" his rights in the way he possesses the traits that identify him as a biological creature distinct from other creatures. It is often said that a man possesses his human rights in virtue of his inherent dignity. "Inherent dignity" is ascribed to man presumably in contrast to his acquired dignity. But it is far from clear that all men have "inherent dignity," or how it is to be identified among those who have it, and why it should be the justifying source of human right rather than human sensibility or intelligence. If it makes any sense to speak of human dignity in connection with human rights, it is not as a designation of a trait comparable to grace and style of gait, such as Aristotle's great souled man might have had, but as a method of treating human beings. It is more natural and less obscure to speak of the right of a human being to be *treated* with dignity whether he possesses it or not.

One of the advantages of putting the question, "What rights, if any, can a man claim of me just because he is human?" is that it leaves open the significant possibility that there are *no* rights a man can claim of me merely or just because he is a man. In other words, whatever the answer, it need not be construed as analytic. This can only be denied by overlooking the systematic ambiguity in the terms "man," "human," and cognate expressions. In some contexts, where "man" and "human" mean different things, it makes perfectly good sense to say "The man is not human." So long as any use of the term "man," or a derivative, refers only to membership in a biological species, I for one cannot see why that membership *alone* gives anyone a right he can justifiably claim of me. If I recognize a duty not to impose unnecessary suffering upon him in any of my relationships with him, it is not because he is a member of the species *Homo sapiens* but because he is a creature capable of suffering. This would be true of my relationships towards any animal or other sentient creatures capable of suffering. However, if the term "human" or any of its synonyms or derivatives refer to a member of a moral community, that is, if these are normative terms, the nature and degree of right would depend on the kind of moral community that existed between him and me.

If the derivation of human rights depends upon a normative conception of man's estate it presupposes that we are committed to the view that one set of proposals for treating human beings is better grounded than others. What are these grounds? My answer, most simply put, is that they are of the same order as those invoked in the justification of any ethical judgment. That is to say, the anticipated *consequences* of treating human beings in accordance with the proposals put forward are, upon sustained and careful reflection, believed to fulfill the requirements of moral ideals accepted as valid within the problematic situation which is the context of the inquiry. This justification of human rights rests upon the *consequences* of our purported behavior and not on any presuppositions about the nature of man or antecedently accepted facts about him. This view seems both paradoxical and obviously circular, but I shall try to resolve the paradox and show that it is not viciously circular.

First a few words about an alternative view that argues that there are some theological or physical or psychological facts about a human being (for example, he is created by God, he is a kin of all men, he is endowed with capacity for choice and intelligence, he shares a common fate with others) that presumably are sufficient to justify that he be treated *as* a human being, that is, with the human rights we regard as intrinsic to our conception of a human being. But no one has been able to show why, from the acceptance of antecedent facts about human beings, they should be treated in some determinate way rather than another, although it does exclude some modes of treatment. At most whatever man is or is discovered to be, this must be compatible with the way he should be treated. Whether the characteristics of his existence are compatible with a proposed mode of treating him is something that depends upon experience, not direct or immediate inspection. It is obvious that whatever the nature of human nature is taken to be, it is compatible with at least several proposals of how to act. *Merely* on the basis of man's biological traits alone, one can, with as much or little warrant, derive "the right to kill" as well as "the right not to kill," "the right to eat," and "the right not to be eaten." Grant that all men are children of God or have immortal souls. These premises, although they would exclude some possibilities, would not determine in the least whether men should organize their society democratically or on the hierarchical model of Heaven itself.

The danger of looking for the justification of human rights—especially of equality of treatment which is integral to all proclamations of human rights—in antecedently given facts of equality is that it leads to an overstatement or inflation of the facts of natural equality. One of the great intellectual scandals of the times has been the emergence of political biology; and this is to be deplored whether it takes a reactionary or liberal form. The liberal form of political biology in the interests of a policy of racial equality postulates that the native capacities of intelligence of all branches of the biological human family are equal. This is a proposition which in some formulations is so vague as to permit no determinate answer; and where it is clear it requires suspended judgment until more trustworthy evidence may be had. But my main point here is that the proposal to treat human beings equally in certain respects does not rest upon any assertion of biological equality, but is advanced as a moral policy justified by its consequences. Even if it were established, which is far from being the case, that certain psychological and intellectual differences among the families of men were inherent and not all culturally acquired, this would not necessarily have any bearing on the validity of a policy of equality of concern for the members of all groups to develop themselves to their best capacities. Individual parents may have children whose IQs vary from the range of the mediocre to that of the genius, but would this fact justify denying the requisite food, clothing, shelter, and educational opportunity necessary for each child to develop his full stature as a person? The relevance of real or alleged facts of equality or inequality becomes apparent only when the consequences of certain policies and their alternatives are examined or envisaged.

It is undeniable that equality of treatment is in some sense central to the conception of justice but it seems to me to be a source of great and continuous error to ground this proposal of equality primarily on the equal possession of some antecedent property. This is apparent from the fact that no one really accepts, despite his profession, a completely formal conception of justice as consisting in equality of treatment. For in that case, as I have had occasion to point out elsewhere, we could not distinguish between "Everyone ought to be treated equally" and "Everyone ought to be *mistreated* equally." The just policy cannot regard the presence or absence of human happiness or welfare as irrelevant. And what will produce the acceptable balance of happiness and justice sometimes may depend upon our disregarding the facts of equality.

Actually in the concrete historical situations in which equality of treatment is demanded, the very starting point or presupposition of the demand is not a fact of equality but of inequality or difference. Whether we are urging that members of different races be treated equally, or that communicants of different religious faiths have equal rights of worship, or that men and women receive the same pay for the same work, our recommendations make sense because we are recognizing the fact of prima facie difference rather than of sameness or similarity.

The dialectical expansion of the concept of human rights seems based on a commitment to the *equality of difference* in some relevant respect. The quest for the common rights of man is a demand for the recognition of the right to be different or to remain different without forfeiting the right to equal and humane treatment in relevant respects. This is especially true with respect to natural differences for which human beings have been penalized, so to speak, by nature. With respect to social differences like religion or class, the right to be different and the extent of these differences depend upon the consequences of policies based upon them for certain shared or common values of overriding concern to the community as a whole.

From this point of view we must also consider the attempt to derive human rights from some metaphysics of desire as misconceived. Human rights are claims, and claims are rooted in interests and desires. We have already rejected the view that every claim is a right, but it reappears again in the attempt to find the warrant for a right in some antecedent feature of human existence. It is a position taken by William James and reaffirmed by some contemporary authors. It argues from the mere existence of a claim to an obligation toward it, from the mere fact of a demand to its justification. I would hold that the possibility of a claim or demand constitutes a necessary but not a sufficient condition of its validity, that it is only when we have seen and reflected on the consequences of gratifying the claims or demands in the moral community in which claims and demands are made that we can judge their validity. James, on the other hand, writes: "Take any demand however slight, which any creature, however weak, may make. Ought it not, for its own sake, to be satisfied? If not, prove why not? The only possible kind of proof you can adduce would be the exhibition of another creature who would make a demand that ran the other way. The only possible reason there can be why any phenomenon ought to exist is that such a phenomenon is actually desired."[8]

This view is obviously circular and also leads to conclusions which James would be among the first to reject. Its circularity is obvious when we are confronted with a desire or demand which not merely "ran the other way" but demanded the suppression of the desires of others. If the mere fact that another's demands run counter or different to our own deprives it of validity then *both* demands are invalid. Not everything desired ought to exist since one may desire what is false or foolish or fraught with the death of all desires. Even what is mutually desired may be mutually undesirable if it is unreflectively desired. The very conflicts among our actual desires make it impossible to give them legislative authority. For it is the conflicts among one's own desires, and the conflicts between one's desires and those of others, that provide the occasion for the quest of the desirable. The *de facto* strength alone of desires cannot give them *de jure* status. Only when this quest initiates a reflective

8. William James, *Essays on Faith and Morals*, ed. R. B. Perry (New York: World Publishing Co., Meridian Books, 1962), p. 195.

inquiry and not merely a battle can desire acquire the patents of validity.

Further, if the ontology of desire were the source of the validity of desire why should it be restricted to demands or desires? Why not embrace needs, hopes, wishes, purposes, requests, or commands? Can we not with the same show of tolerance and reasonableness ask not only of demands but of any power in the human psyche: "Ought it not, for its own sake, to be gratified? If not, why not?"

We must now face the problem of the justification of human rights more directly and grapple with the question, "Is the view that human rights are reasonable proposals, defensible in virtue of the consequences of acting on them, any less circular or question-begging than other justifications?"

There are three generic ways in which human rights have been or can be justified (assuming that nothing can be justified by postulation)—by logic, by immediate intuition, or by empirical inquiry.

1. Logic obviously cannot carry us very far in justifying human rights. Contrary claims to "human rights" can be universalized and shown to be equally self-consistent. There are some specific rights in the American Bill of Rights like those involving church-state relations and the privilege against self-incrimination whose prima facie validity would be hard to establish. Any human right can be denied without logical contradiction. Only too often they have been denied in theory and violated in practice. If a human right follows logically from some premise about man, nature, or God, it is these premises that must be justified. And when the attempt is made to do so, invariably a value judgment is surreptitiously introduced into them.

2. Neither the rights listed as human rights nor any premises from which they are presumably derived appear to be self-evident. If they are self-evident, they can only appear so to specially qualified investigators since so many millions of human beings have been unaware of them or have denied them—a fact which is not incompatible with their being valid but is incompatible with their being "self-evidently" valid. There is nothing self-evident even about so basic a right as the right to life, particularly when the loss or destruction of one life is a necessary condition of the survival of another. There are many worthy causes which argue that the right to die is coeval with the right to live, and neither one is self-evident. No rhetoric can conceal from us the fact that men and women do not have an equal right to life in any community in which men are conscripted for active military service in war but women are not.

There is the famous, if apocryphal, episode of the soldier who, in response to Napoleon's rebuke for having abandoned his post under fire, blurted out, "A man must live, Sire!" To which Napoleon is supposed to have retorted, "I do not see the necessity of it." Napoleon's reply, however callous, is literally valid if there is no logical or any other kind of necessity for life. But the soldier certainly had a good reason, if not a conclusive one, for leaving his post if he faced probable death holding it. Some might be tempted to argue that the right to life is not even a prima facie right in the same sense as the right to be repaid for a debt or to the fulfillment of a promise. No one promised the soldier his life. He had not paid for it. And if a volunteer, he has committed himself to taking certain risks. Nonetheless even recognizing that no absolute claim can be made for it, the right to life seems much stronger than the right to be repaid or to have a promise kept. It outweighs the other rights because of the intensity and multiplicity of the evil consequences of violating it.

3. Does not this appeal to consequences founder because of its obvious circularity? I do not believe so, if we do not try to solve all problems at once or regard all problems as facets of one problem. The conventional wisdom on the question of justification of rights is that rights can be ultimately derived from some fundamental ethical principle or insight which is intuitively valid. The most promising, even if inadequate, approach along these lines is a qualified negative utilitarianism in which we justify the specific proposals or decisions we recommend on the ground that we thereby reduce and equalize human suffering in the world. In one form or another the twin principles of welfare and justice appear as ultimate.

It seems to me that there is an element of vagueness, irrelevant abstractness, indeed of unreality, about this whole approach. Very few persuasive cases can be made out on the basis of so-called *ultimate* principles, whether of happiness or justice or inherent dignity, for any specific decision to propose the recognition and adoption of a human right. Who can foresee all the consequences of an action or balance the disparate experiences of pain and pleasure in their various dimensions and qualities? Is it not true that there are moral qualities in experience that are not simply reducible to forms of happiness or welfare and justice—for example, sincerity, kindness, truthfulness, nobility, friendliness—so that we must conclude either that there are many irreducible ultimate values, or, since they are in conflict when a moral situation is experienced, that there are no ultimate values?

It is a commonplace fact of our moral experience that we sometimes choose a just course of action rather than one that maximizes welfare. And it is also true that on some occasions we rationally prefer to forego the just solution if we can thereby raise appreciably the level of welfare for all, even at the cost of privileges for some. It is just as significant that we sometimes judge a kind act (which is not a mode of dispensing welfare) as more praiseworthy than a just act, and a noble or self-sacrificial act as more praiseworthy than one which increases the average or total welfare.

The truth seems to be that the demand for the recognition of a specific human right is justified not only by some envisaged consequences for weal or woe in adopting it or not adopting it, but also by implicit reference to other values accepted as valid or beyond question *at that point*. The demand for women's rights to suffrage, or for the right to a job, or for the right to insurance against want if a job is not forthcoming, or the right to medical insurance all presuppose changes in the structure of family life and in the industrial character of society, but their justification does not rest on such considerations alone. In every problematic situation in which these demands conflict with others, what is presupposed is not only the social-historical material context but the validity of certain ethical values, some of them *already* possessing the authority of human rights, whether it be the right to security, the right to fair procedure, the right not merely to life but to a decent life. Some of these rights may have a complex character like the right not to be punished by ex post facto laws.

To be sure, any one of these values, commitments, rights, which we bring—together with an analysis of the factual situation—into the process of justification can be challenged just as any statement about the factual presuppositions and consequences of introducing or not introducing the proposed new right may be challenged. But note: we do not challenge in one gush *all* the values we bring to the consideration of the specific proposal, else no moral questions would ever be settled; they would all become confrontations of ultimate values, and where we are moved genuinely to challenge some specific value-commitment taken for granted in resolving a problem, we meet it in the same way by reference to *both* fact and other assumed values.

Does this not raise the ghost of an infinite regress? No more so than does any process of scientific explanation. If I coherently explain the cause of a disease I do so only because I have made certain other causal assumptions that, although not in dispute in my inquiry, are theoretically challengeable. I do not have to explain the cause of the cause until I reach a first cause to accept a causal explanation as valid. Nor do I have to reach an ultimate value about which there is universal agreement in order to justify a given proposal to treat human beings in a certain way. So long as the consequences of the proposal are in accord with, or serve to realize the shared values on which, for the problem at hand, there is no dispute, better than the consequences of other proposals, I need inquire no further. The question whether the values declared ultimate in specific situations of moral conflict are really ultimate rather than penultimate is always open. The further question whether if we are committed to many different values, any one of which may be justified in terms of others, the apparent circularity is objectionable, I leave unexplored except to point to C. I. Lewis's reminder that a dictionary, however ideal its definitions, is still useful even if all of its words are defined in terms of other words in the dictionary. Nor am I overlooking the difference between the subject matters of scientific and ethical inquiry, but I am contending that just as we do not put everything we know into dispute in the process of scientific inquiry and confirmation, so we do not put all our values in dispute in the process of ethical validation. We no more have to solve all scientific problems to solve any than we have to resolve all moral conflicts to resolve any.

Actually in the process of reflective inquiry by which we seek to resolve moral conflicts we reach out to find the shared interests and values from which to survey our differences. If the ultimate inarbitrable values from which all our other values allegedly hang (as if from some cosmic hook) guided our deliberations, we could not explain so plausibly those agreements on proximate and intermediate goals on which ordered life in a community depends. To be sure, there are some who claim to invoke ultimate values as decisive, not merely as theoretical postulates dictated by dialectical necessity, but in concrete historical situations—that is, with respect to the use of nuclear weapons or the choice of being red or dead. In every case that has come to light the discussion reveals either that some reason is offered in support of the alleged ultimate value, or more commonly, that the value(s) held and the way they are held depend upon some implicit assumptions of fact about the causes and/or consequences of believing and acting on them. Anyone in a genuine problematic context who espouses a value in complete independence of the factual presupposition of the causes of the conflict situation, or of the consequences of believing and acting on the value, in contrast with courses of conduct guided by alternative values, has offered us a paradigm case of an unreasonable, indeed, a fanatical belief.

The history of human reflection on the nature of values indicates that we are surer of the validity of at least *some* of our moral judgments than we are of the theories or principles we offer in ultimate justification of them. At any definite time there seems to be a set of moral judgments whose acceptance appears necessary for the conduct of civilized life and which function as "intuitive" checks upon proposals. We sometimes reject a theoretical position like that of unrestricted utilitarianism because it leads to conclusions that we find morally unacceptable. But these "intuitive" or "counterintuitive" checks are not absolute, or eternal, or so certain as to be beyond possibility of rational doubt. We do not accept every pronouncement of our moral consciousness as valid without considering the wider context of moral judgments and principles in which it is embedded. We seek to make consistent, as integral to the process of justification, our moral judgments on different practical occasions. Here, too, there is an analogy with the process of verification. The truth of a judgment of fact depends upon observation, and we are more certain of our perceptions than we are of any theory which is tested by them. Nonetheless, any particular judgment of perception or of observation, no matter how certain we may feel about it, may have to be withdrawn if some assumption which guides our observation is challenged, or if some subsequent observation is incompatible with the truth of our previous perception.

On this view of the justification of human rights, they are *proposals* to recognize as binding, on all and sundry who are relevantly situated to defend and/or enforce them, a set of rules which within the historical and cultural context in which they are enunciated are more reasonable than any others. Rights are not derived from the state of affairs we start from. They are not derived from the reason of things or the reason in God, Nature, or Man. They are justified by the consequences of rules of action. Nor can it be said that these consequences are such that they strictly *entail* any proposals or choices, but only that they render some more reasonable or less arbitrary than others. This pragmatic justification needs no metaphysical or theological proposition for logical underpinning any more than moral judgments in ordinary experience require such support. Whatever the incompatible over-beliefs or dogmas that human beings bring to the consideration of moral problems, in the end, if they go on living together instead of fighting each other, they have in effect indicated a working agreement as to what is, comparatively, better among the possible alternatives. That agreement is a necessary condition for the solution of the problem, even if it is not always sufficient.

There are some who have defended the belief in human rights as useful *fictions* justified by happy results. This seems to me just as inadequate as the view which asserts that statements about rights are as descriptive as statements about things and relations, and literally true. It is a belief that reifies valid proposals; that assumes that the attribution of rights could be literally true or false, in the sense in which the "mirage" of an oasis could turn out to be a real oasis; and that commits a category mistake under the guise of intellectual sophistication. It fails to explain why some rather than other rights are useful, thus losing an opportunity to stress the nonfictional reasons for the proposals in question. In addition, it is psychologically self-defeating to characterize beliefs in rights as beliefs in fictions, if it is expected that human beings will run great risks in defense of human rights. Men are not passionately concerned to defend anything publicly identified as "fiction" that shades into "myth" and then into "pious fraud" which, like plain lies, may also be useful. This is not to deny that men have fought and died for unanalyzable abstractions, for lost causes, for gods that have not existed, for the honor of kings and countries that have had no honor, for unrealizable ideals. What I am contending is that to describe the objects of these struggles as "fictions" misconceives and misdescribes human behavior. For in all of these cases it is possible to find a good if not morally adequate reason for their action. Most men may be fools: they are not systematically deluded.

This brings us to a cluster of related questions. How significant is the distinction between negative and positive rights or freedoms? Does it correspond to the distinction between civil and political rights on the one hand, and social and economic rights on the other? Is it confusing to include both sets of rights in the UN Universal Declaration of Human Rights? Are Maurice Cranston and other critics justified in charging that a fundamental incoherence was introduced by Roosevelt in the Atlantic Charter when he spoke of the four freedoms—a confusion perpetuated in the UN Universal Declaration of Human Rights and carried to absurdity in some of the provisions in Articles 21 to 30?

There are distinctions between the so-called positive and negative freedoms or rights. But these do not require that we draw hard and fast lines of separation between them. If we recognize the historical character of human rights, we should be prepared to expand the list or schedule of rights regarded as not only relevant to, but of paramount importance in our conception of the kind of life deemed fit for man. Nonetheless, although the so-called negative and positive rights are interrelated, there is a sense in which we are justified in considering the traditional civil and political rights or freedoms as the most strategic. I believe that this is what the critics of the UN Universal Declaration of Human Rights really have in mind when they object to the inclusion of other rights.

The so-called negative freedoms are ordinarily defined in terms of absence of restraints on human conduct. The right or freedom to speak is present whenever a person is free *from* the interference of others in speaking his mind. Positive freedom is ordinarily defined in terms of powers or guaranteed opportunity to achieve certain desired goals. This freedom "to" or "for" implies that the desire or willingness to do something, its voluntary character so to speak, is not enough, even in the absence of interference by others. There may be other obstacles to overcome. All rights or freedoms can be defined in negative terms if the interferences are not broken down into different types of interference—personal, natural, or social. All rights or freedoms can be defined in positive terms if the power to do what one desires is interpreted as the power to overcome all human obstacles or interferences or the power to prevent others from preventing our action. My point is that what is of the greatest issue here is not whether the analysis of rights is to be made in negative or positive terms, but the substantial question of the relative validity of the specific right at issue, and the difference between the different kinds of conditions preventing its fulfillment.[9]

Freedom from restraint may be freedom from constraint—from direct human interference—or from other preventing conditions. Preventing conditions may be of two kinds: natural and beyond the control of men; and social, for which institutions, and indirectly men, are responsible. To enjoy "the freedom to sail" I must be free from the interference of those who would prevent me from sailing, who would steal or damage my boat. My "freedom to sail," however, may also be frustrated by a storm or other natural conditions no one can do anything about. But, and this is the source of the grievance, even when I am not referring to vandals or pirates, my freedom to sail may be frustrated by the failure of the economy to manufacture boats, or the refusal of those who do to sell them to me at a price I can afford, despite the fact that my livelihood may depend upon the use of a boat. Only the historic context tells us whether the demand for "the right to sail" is a demand for the freedom of the seas or a demand for the acquisition of the means to sail.

The historic context shows that "freedom of belief," especially freedom of religious belief, is almost invariably a demand that there be no interference with religious belief, private or public; no punishment, persecution or, discrimination. On the other hand, where the cry of "freedom to eat" is heard, this is never intended as a plea for prevention of interference with our dietary freedom, but as a demand for positive, reconstructive measures for more food. Yet this positive freedom or right *to* or *for* more food, where its availability depends to some degree on social action, can also be described in negative terms as "freedom *from* hunger."

The rights enumerated in the UN Universal Declaration of Human Rights make up a mixed bag. Articles 6 through 11 are designed

---

9. Cf. the illuminating essay by Gerald C. MacCollum, Jr., "Negative and Positive Freedom," *Philosophical Review* 26 (July 1967): 312 ff.

to protect the individual's right to fair judicial process. This cannot be done *merely* by preventing other members of the community from interfering with the proper norms of due process. On the contrary, the implementation of these articles requires positive actions on an extensive scale by the institutions of the state—measures which would be comparable to those undertaken by the state in *behalf* of some social and economic rights. Think, for example, of what is required to protect a defendant's right to a fair trial. Surely a fair trial cannot be guaranteed merely by negative action, by stopping the use of illegal coercion against a defendant, as in dispersing a lynch mob. It may necessitate the performance of many positive, complex tasks—among them the careful selection of jurors to diminish the likelihood of discrimination, change of venue, the provision of competent counsel, and contribution to the costs of the defense. If the enumeration of human rights were to restrict itself to a statement only of freedoms which should never be invaded, of actions that should never be performed, of liberties that are inviolable and therefore "supremely sacred," it is difficult to understand how we can implement "the right to a fair trial" since this requires not leaving a man alone or refraining from violations of his personal property, but doing, positively, a great deal more than that.

Article 16, however, requires much less in the way of positive action on the part of the state—perhaps only the minimal, positive action of registration. This article gives men and women a right to marry and found a family. This obviously does not mean that the state or community will undertake to provide a wife or husband for those who wish to marry, but only that if they do find someone willing to marry them there will be no coercion permitted to prevent it and no legal hindrance of a discriminatory sort. In other words, what limits this right, as in the prevention of child marriages, is the assertion or defense of another human right. In communities where custom requires, as a necessary condition of marriage, that the bride have a dowry, the spirit of the other articles of the declaration would make it incumbent upon the states in question to provide for those economically disadvantaged.

Article 19 prescribes the right to complete freedom of expression. Here, too, this does not mean that the community is under an obligation to provide any individual with the means necessary for the public expression of his views, but rather, once an individual possesses the means, it will prevent hostile actions designed to interfere with the expression. Under certain circumstances social control to forestall a monopoly of newsprint may be necessary in the interests of freedom of expression. On a priori grounds one might conclude that those who own the press have a greater freedom of expression and therefore greater political influence than those who have limited means. But actually this has not proved true. So long as there is no coercion against expression of opinion in *other* media, and no monopoly, there is no direct relation between political influence and press ownership. Roosevelt and Truman were violently opposed by most of the press.

There are other provisions of the Declaration which focus upon the responsibility of the community to bring into existence constructive and positive programs of action. Article 23 recognizes the "right to work." This obviously means more than if the individual finds a position, he will be protected against others who wish to take it away from him. Indeed, it will not protect him against others if they wish to deprive him of the position by peaceful competition or bargaining. It means that whatever the result of the competition, the community recognizes the obligation to create social conditions in which the individual can find a position or, failing that, in which he can receive unemployment insurance.

The responsibility of the community for even more comprehensive social action is implied in Article 26, on the right to an education. The right to an education was among the rights of citizens recognized as early as 1789. In its first intention it does not even remotely suggest that it is directed against those who would prevent children from attending school. Nor does it provide for an alternative comparable to unemployment insurance for those for whom it cannot arrange to find work. This article calls upon the community to accept the duty of compelling schooling of some sort for all, at least on the elementary level. Its positive enforcement is complex and widespread and cannot be interpreted as freedom *from* preventive human constraints but only as freedom from the preventing condition of ignorance.

The classification of rights as negative or positive is hardly illuminating. When negative rights are identified with the civil and political, and positive rights with the social and economic, and a plea is made to exclude the latter from the list of genuine human rights, confusion results—because, as we have seen, all rights can be defined as either negative or positive; many are interrelated; and whatever sensible hierarchy exists in the economy of values is independent of such classification.

The nub of the argument against including the so-called social and political rights in the UN Universal Declaration of Human Rights is put by Maurice Cranston as follows: "A human right by *definition is a universal moral right*, something which all men, everywhere, at all times ought to have, and something of which no one may be deprived without a grave affront to justice, something which is owing to every human being simply because he is human."[10] Consequently, Cranston argues that to refer to such rights as those provided in Articles 23 and 24, which even go so far as to mention the right to "provide holidays with pay," is simply nonsense. Cranston does not agree with Bentham that all talk about human rights is nonsense. It is only talk about social and economic rights that he dubs nonsense —despite the fact that he acknowledges that under some circumstances they may be "morally compelling." The reasons he gives for this critical judgment are that such alleged rights are neither practicable, nor categorical, nor of paramount importance.

Let us grant that no community is obliged to do what is impossible. But to say that something is impracticable is not to say the same sort of thing as that it is impossible. Practicability is surely a matter of degree. The objective historical situation that determines whether a right is realizable varies from country to country. In a country which is very poor, very illiterate, and internally chaotic, how "practicable" is "freedom of the press" or "a fair trial"? Certainly, not fully. Even so, so long as a beginning can be made, its recognition is justifiable. Not all the civil and political rights that Cranston endorses are fully practicable in many of the new countries, but this does not testify against the desirability of emphasizing them, nor does it justify the abrogation of primitive beginnings of democratic participation in government, called for in Article 21, on the ground that the country is not fully prepared for them. In how many countries of Asia and Africa is it practicable to enforce the right to an education, or the civil right to marriage (Article 15), which specifies that it be entered into *only* with the free and full consent of the intending spouses, who are to enjoy *equal rights* at marriage, during marriage, and upon its dissolution?

Further, it is clear that some social and economic rights are more practicable, even if not completely practicable, than some civil and political rights. I cheerfully acknowledge that the reference to the right to "periodic holidays with pay" (Article 24) is a supererogative demand. It is much too specific. It need not have been listed. Whenever and wherever a case can be made for it, it can be brought under the broader provisions of other articles (specifically Article 23, Sections 1 and 3). But if we look at Article 24, which concludes with the mirth-producing reference to "periodic holidays with pay," we find that it begins: "Everyone has a right to rest and leisure includ-

10. Maurice Cranston, *What Are Human Rights?* (New York: Basic Books, 1962), p. 36.

ing reasonable limitations of working hours." It could have ended there without the addition of the phrase "and periodic holidays with pay," which, when it is feasible, can be construed as an application of the right to rest and leisure and a reasonable limitation of working hours. The right to rest and leisure seems to me as universal, practicable, and relevant as any civil and political right. Labor *without* rest or leisure can kill. It is incompatible with the right to life. It is significant that the importance of this humane provision was recognized as long ago as the promulgation of the Decalogue and was invested with the authority of divine sanction.

If, by "categorical," is meant that human rights cannot ever be legitimately breached for any reason, this makes them "absolute" and "inalienable," and we have seen that no right has that character, not even the right to life which appears on all bills and declarations of rights. If it is admitted that social and economic rights are moral rights, then they have the same categorical character as all moral rights including civil and political rights. To be sure they sometimes conflict with each other but so do the latter.

There remains then, the difference in their degree of urgency or paramountcy. What makes a right of paramount importance? If this is measured by the amount of suffering or the extent of injustice consequent upon the absence or denial of a right, I doubt whether it can be legitimately asserted that in all situations the violation of any civil and political right is productive of more evil than the violation of any social and economic right. Everyone can think of certain historical crises in which the pinch of hunger or hurt of social humiliation has led to a too easy sacrifice of civil and political liberties for the promise of security and welfare. And in times of great need, danger, or famine, the rights of due process are suspended.

If civil and political rights are, as I believe, of paramount importance, it is not for the reasons given by Cranston. Most simply put, the civil and political rights in any statement of rights are of paramount importance to all others in that without them all other rights could be easily ignored, abused, corrupted, and ultimately lost. Without them the very right to eat—the bread-card of welfare—becomes a weapon of tyranny. Where they are present, the evils of monopoly of any kind may be curbed. And where they flourish, they make possible the discovery of other and new rights, and the recognition of these new rights by the moral conscience of the community. Civil and political rights are primary to all others in the same way as political democracy is basic to all other forms of democracy.

One of the unhappiest legacies of the vulgar-Marxist tradition, partly inspired by ambiguities in Marx's own writings, has been the tendency to infer from the fact that civil and political rights are not sufficient *by themselves* to guarantee human rights of a social and economic nature that they were therefore purely abstract and formal, irrelevant to historical progress, and functioning primarily as ideological masks to extend class privilege. The point of view is typified in a statement like this, explaining why "the classical framework of civil and political rights" was deemed inadequate: "The man who stole bread was sure of a fair trial and was free to speak out against the law that condemned him before he was hanged."[11]

When such things were possible, did the man who was *denied* a fair trial and the right to speak out against the law, escape hanging? The freedom to speak out was not the less important because it failed at once to put an end to such outrages. For the historical record shows that it was in virtue of the continued speaking out that the punishment of death for the theft of bread was first abolished, and then, more gradually, bread was supplied to all who needed it, making it unnecessary to steal it. On the other hand, where these scorned "bourgeois" freedoms of speech and press do not exist, it becomes quite easy for the rulers to promise bread to all but never deliver it, and to hang without trial or by means of rigged trials, innocent men who have violated no laws, not even laws against theft.

The history of the last two centuries has shown that respect for civil liberties has not in itself been sufficient to achieve a guaranteed livelihood or decent minimum level of welfare for all without profound changes in the economic order and in the traditional conception of the role of the government. But the same history has shown with even greater vividness that where civil and political liberties have not been respected, the so-called social and economic rights have not been guaranteed to all, that they have always been in a state of precarious dependence upon the whim of a despot or a small political minority. Bread and circuses are notoriously uncertain if those whose decisions determine their distribution are not responsible to those they govern. The assertion that social and economic rights exist in such circumstances is far more of a "sham" and "pretense" than the assertion that civil and political rights can still function effectively in societies where social and economic rights are yet to be introduced. Only in a very Pickwickian sense can one say it is possible to enjoy social security without political freedom since

11. J. E. S. Fawcett, *Political Theory and The Rights of Man*, ed. D. D. Raphael (Bloomington: Indiana University Press, 1967), p. 133.

such security cannot be guaranteed by powers that consider themselves above the law and can withdraw it on the merest suspicion that the citizens—really subjects—are not totally reliable.

The upshot of conceptual analysis reinforces the lessons that can be drawn from history. Unless civil rights and liberties are regarded as of *strategic* importance and become, so to speak, the ribbed frame of the ship of state and its political order, the social and economic rights that define the social order lack the proper safeguard against erosion, or still worse, perversion into support for tyranny. It is not necessary to conceive of civil rights and liberties as absolute; but it is necessary on historical, psychological, and ultimately moral grounds to give them priority of concern in building the social order to meet the needs of the whole man or ideal man or new man—however he be morally conceived. If this is not done, civil rights are easily sacrificed as too costly or inconvenient in the slow and painful progress toward the desirable social order. But once they are sacrificed the shining goals of the new order become more remote. For there is no way now safely to evaluate the goals by criticism of the means used to achieve them, no freedom to expose the folly and even the madness of those who are implementing the goals, no mechanisms of press, radio, or public debate by which the truth may be communicated.

One leading member of the European Commission of Human Rights which limits the jurisdiction of its inquiries only to reported violations of civil and political rights of the classical tradition is critical of the distinction which Cranston and others seek to uphold between these rights and social and economic rights. For he believes that such distinctions have an adverse effect upon their implementation. In the perspective of the unending task of making society more reasonable and humane, such a distinction "is a fixation of human rights in terms of a particular phase in the development of social ideas."[12]

A distinction, however, is not a separation. It is not necessary to confine a declaration of rights to civil and political ones alone. Others may be added. Moreover, an emphasis is not a fixation. Precisely because the development of new social rights is so important, the civil and political rights must be recognized as strategic or central or preferred. And Mr. Fawcett implicitly acknowledges this when he discusses the key question of the implementation of human rights. For unless the rights proclaimed in any declaration can be at some point implemented, they are a cruel mockery of human hope and aspiration. In discussing the most effective method of implementing

12. Ibid.

human rights, Fawcett says: "Fundamental to *all* effective methods of implementation of human rights is independent and objective fact-finding, and its ally, publicity; indeed, *publicity is perhaps the most decisive element of all.*"[13]

This admission sustains my point. If it is true that independent and objective fact-finding and publicity are the most effective methods of implementing rights, then surely the best guarantee that the conclusions reached will be broadcast in available media of communication is the operating presence of civil and political liberties. All the more evident is this when the findings are critical of those in power and challenge entrenched privilege. I believe it is fair to conclude, therefore, that these rights or liberties are, to use Mr. Fawcett's expression, "the most decisive" feature in any declaration of human rights.

An obvious question which arises in this connection is: What is the point of the enunciation of a bill of rights whose most decisive provisions are violated by the signatory governments? Is it not gross hypocrisy for countries which declare their belief in the freedom of the press to jail those who try to exercise this freedom; or which, by total monopoly of the press, paper, and printer's ink, reinforced by prior censorship, deny to anyone not approved by the government an opportunity to voice an opinion?

The obvious answer is provided by the influence of such declarations in the history of nations whose institutional practices violated both the letter and spirit of the rights inscribed in their constitutions. Their presence has an educational influence that in time undercuts the cynicism and Machiavellianism which inspired their adoption as a political maneuver. The disparity between the solemn words and the ignoble deeds raises questions, creates puzzles, awakens doubts in any reasonable mind. It has to be explained. And once an explanation is given, it invites belief or disbelief.

Nonetheless we must not make too great a claim for the effect of *mere* words. They tip the historical spears with which men do battle. But their force and penetration depends upon the length of the shaft—the social interests behind them. The Stalin Constitution with all its "guarantees" of civil rights was proclaimed at the very height of one of the bloodiest terrors in human history. There is no evidence that any group invoked these constitutional guarantees from 1936, when it was promulgated, to the death of Stalin. Even in the United States the educational influence of the Bill of Rights declarations, both in federal and state constitutions, has been slow, accelerating with the pace of events.

13. Ibid., pp. 132–33 [italics mine].

Nonetheless it remains true that if and when opposition movements develop against dictatorial practices or regimes in countries that formally profess allegiance to bills of rights, they can make tremendous headway by appealing to these official declarations. It becomes increasingly difficult to charge the champions of human rights with importing a foreign ideology when they use as their rallying cry the very formula which the representatives of legitimacy have used as rationalizations of their power.[14]

1968

---

14. I am indebted to Richard Brandt for criticisms of a draft of this chapter. He is not responsible, of course, for any of its views or formulations.

Chapter 6

The Social Democratic Prospect

A friend of many years standing who heard that that I was to give the keynote speech at a convention of Social Democrats wrote me in genuine puzzlement. "I know what a Democrat is and I know what a Socialist is, but what is a Social Democrat, and why is he or she necessary?" This is a fair question and I propose to answer it here.

Let us begin with the term *democracy* with a small *d*. Most briefly put, a democrat is one who believes that governmental rule should rest upon the freely given consent of the governed. In this sense, all political parties, except the Communist and other totalitarian groupings, whatever their differing economic and social programs, are democrats. In this sense, political democracy is necessary for every other kind of democracy, for without it, no other kind is possible or even meaningful. And this is no mere truism but an important assertion when counterposed to the claim that although totalitarian societies lack political democracy, they enjoy economic or ethnic or cultural democracy. For it should be clear that without the strategic freedoms of speech, press, assembly, organization, and the rights of criticism and dissent—which constitute the very nature of political democracy—there can be no economic or ethnic or cultural democracy.

Very well, then, granted that political democracy is always essential to any conception of democracy, what is the difference between the political democrat—whether he is a member of the Republican,

Democratic, Conservative, or Libertarian parties—and the Social Democrat?

The difference, I submit, is this: for the Social Democrat, democracy is not merely a political concept but a moral one. It is democracy as a way of life. What is "democracy as a way of life"? It is a society whose basic institutions are animated by an equality of concern for all human beings, regardless of class, race, sex, religion, and national origin, to develop themselves as *persons* to their fullest growth, to be free to live up to their desirable potentials as human beings. It is possible for human beings to be politically equal as voters but yet so unequal in educational, economic, and social opportunities, that ultimately even the nature of their political equality is affected.

The Social Democrat therefore is interested in extending the area of equal opportunity beyond the political sphere to all other areas of social life. He believes that all social institutions to the extent to which they are modifiable must be judged by their fruits or consequences on the lives of individual persons. It is from this premise of "democracy as a way of life," of equal opportunity for all to develop themselves as persons, taken as a regulative moral ideal, not as an inexorable, "dialectical" law of history, that the social democrat derives the justification for multiple programs of social reform—whether it be social security, health and unemployment insurance, a guaranteed minimum family income, occupational safety, or improved and extended public education.

I shall have more to say about social democracy as a moral ideal later but now to the second half of the question: How is social democracy related to socialism? It all depends, of course, upon how "socialism" is understood. Unfortunately socialism has been identified too often, not with the moral ends of democracy as a way of life, but only with one of the *means* by which some socialists in the past hoped that those moral ends could be furthered, namely, with collectivism or the nationalization of all means of production, distribution, and exchange. Unfortunately, socialists have made a fetish of the means without considering the consequences of those means on professed ends or goals. Unfortunately, socialism has been too often identified with a social system in which there is no vestige of political democracy, and in which the slightest expression of dissent brings penalties that have varied from tortured exile in the camps of the Gulag Archipelago, to confinement in insane asylums. The consequence has been that the workers and peasants have suffered more and enjoyed less freedom in the nationalized economies of the "socialist" countries of the world than in the nonsocialist democratic societies of the West. Unfortunately, socialism has too often been identified with a police state in which the inhabitants are penned in by walls, electrified fences, and minefields, and no one is free to leave. Unfortunately, this historical conjunction of socialism and terror has strengthened a widely held view that the only alternative open to those who love freedom is support of the free enterprise system, that any movement away from capitalism as an economic system involves the abandonment of freedom and democracy.

This complex of historical, theoretical, and psychological misfortunes necessitates that we rethink the basic question of property and human freedom, that we liberate ourselves from the traditional clichés and slogans of socialism, and develop new philosophical foundations for a human democratic society. That, it seems to me, is one of the tasks of contemporary social democracy.

We must begin by clearing the ground of some theoretical confusions. We sometimes hear human rights contrasted with property rights. That is a mistake. A property right *is* a human right. Our very personality and its expression, as William James so cogently showed in his *Principles of Psychology*, depends upon the possession of property in the things we own, our clothes, our tools, our pictures, our books, our homes. Even our human right to speak our minds and publish our thoughts depends upon the possession of some property in means of communication—be it no more than the typewriter and paper. But this kind of property is *personal* property—and one of the standard criticisms of traditional capitalism is that it has resulted in an inequitable distribution of personal property among individuals, on which the development of personality depends. (In comparison with other economic systems of the past, capitalism has been a veritable cornucopia of plenty but the distribution of that plenty in terms of personal property has been haphazard and inequitable, characterized periodically by a surfeit for some and a lack of essential goods and services for many more regardless of merit or desert.)

What is true of *personal* property, however, is not necessarily true of *social* property in the large-scale means of production in an industrial society. If I have any human rights as a person, I have some rights to the food, shelter, clothing, education without which these rights are a nullity. But I cannot reasonably contend that my human rights require not only *personal* property but *social* property in the mills, factories, mines, and fields on which the livelihood of others depends. For property in the social means of production gives not only power over inanimate things but over the persons whose lives and welfare depend on their use. In this sector, property means power over human beings. Let us see why.

After all, how do we know that we have a right to property or ownership of anything? Not by mere possession. For what I can dispossess you of, you in turn can dispossess me of. Not by power of use. I may own a great many things I am unable to use or whose use is restricted by law. Normally one cannot use one's home for a glue factory or a hospital where zoning laws exist. Legally, ownership gives power not to use or abuse but power to *exclude others* from the use of what I own. Ownership of land or factory on which the livelihood of others depends gives me power to exclude them from its use or to control the conditions of its use. Where there are no other resources at hand, like an open frontier, my ownership of land or factory therefore gives me a very real power over the lives of those and their families whose income depends on their employment.

From the point of view of democracy as a way of life, since power over the instruments of production means power over the human beings who must live by them, this power, like all power, must be socially *responsible.* It cannot be unlimited. Otherwise, all sorts of inequities would develop. With the development of free trade unions and certain kinds of protective labor legislation in democratic capitalist countries of the West, there has been an impressive movement toward sharing this power. Social Democrats wish to make this shared power more responsible.

On the other hand, where in so-called socialist countries the instruments of social production have been collectivized or nationalized, without the presence of political democracy, the workers on farms or in factories have even less control over their lives than in the most ruthless days of uncontrolled Western capitalism. They can be barred from work and permanently blacklisted or herded to distant places at the command of a small minority which exercises a monopoly of interlocking military, judicial, and economic powers. The agents of this minority decree with the awful authority of a ubiquitous secret police what the conditions and rewards of work shall be. If we define property *functionally,* in terms of access to and control of property, it is hardly an exaggeration to say that, in the absence of forms of democratic participation and free trade unions with a legally recognized right to strike, the collectivized economy of present-day socialist states is the property of the closed political corporation that goes by the name of the Communist party. Where there is no right to strike, we have a system of forced labor. Where there is no independent judiciary, there is no defense against trumped up charges and frame-ups. Where there is no legally recognized political opposition which enables a minority peacefully to become a majority, the regime, despite its semantic disguises, rests on terror. The resoluteness of organized Communist terror is evidenced by the fact that in contrast to other totalitarian and authoritarian regimes no Communist regime that has seized power since Lenin's day has ever been overthrown. (The only exceptions were minor areas in Central Europe.)

In this connection we must say a word or two about the contentions of conservative thinkers like Friedrich von Hayek and Milton Friedman who contend that any attempt to regulate free enterprise is sure to bring with it the erosion of political and cultural freedom, and the inevitable triumph of an industrial serfdom. Such a position, it seems to me, can only be held in defiance of the verifiable historical facts.

First, in every country in the world, without exception, in which economic collectivism now exists, the destruction of political democratic institutions *preceded* the introduction of the collectivist economy. It was only after the Constituent Assembly, the last democratic institution that existed in Russia, was forcibly dissolved, and the minority Communist party dictatorship set up in the Soviet Union, that the collectivist economy was established. It was only after the Red Army destroyed all prospects of democratic political life in the satellite nations, that they followed suit. And if the Nazi and Fascist command economies be regarded as a species of collectivism, it is just as obvious that they *followed* on the violent death of democracy.

Secondly, the largely state-controlled economies of Sweden, Norway, Denmark, Holland, and England, whatever their difficulties, exist in countries in which there has been no abatement of traditional liberties.

Most important of all, in our own country, the intervention of the state into the economy, by direct and indirect subsidies, through tariffs and regulatory agencies, has resulted in the emergence of a substantial public sector. The free enterprise economic system of Adam Smith no more exists today in the U.S.A. than the socialism of Karl Marx in the U.S.S.R. Notice, however, that if the Hayek-Friedman analysis were valid, the rise of the public sector should have been accompanied by a progressive restriction on our political and cultural freedoms. Yet the precise opposite has occurred. With respect to every area of political and civil rights in this country, with respect to the variety, vehemence, and scope of articulate dissent, our freedom is greater today than it has ever been, especially in the halcyon days of unregulated capitalism. To be sure, there have been bureaucratic excesses that are foolish, and sometimes vicious, as in some of the guidelines of the Department of Health, Education, and Welfare (HEW) prescribing numerical goals and quotas in employment, but the remedies for them are available to an aroused citizenry.

As social democrats we frankly recognize that there is a totalitarian potential in any economy which is completely centralized and nationalized. For if political democracy is ever lost, such an economy can become the most powerful engine of repression in human history. In economics as in politics, power must limit power even at the cost of some efficiency. Therefore every move toward government intervention must be carefully weighed for its consequences on the basic freedoms of society. We prefer to leave to private initiative the gratification of social needs if that does not impose onerous costs, burdens, and deceptions on the community. But if these social needs cannot be properly met by private initiative, then the community must accept responsibility for them in the same way that it should provide police and health protection for individuals regardless of their capacity to pay. This responsibility must extend to the employment of those able and willing to work but who for no fault of their own lack the opportunity. When an earthquake levels a city or a plague sweeps a community, we recognize our obligation to alleviate the conditions of the victims. When mass unemployment strikes a society with the effect of a natural disaster, why should our obligation be any less?

We social democrats, therefore, yield to none in putting freedom first. We find that sometimes those who also say that they put freedom first really mean they put the freedom to make profit first. There is room for a fair return on investment and entrepreneurial talent but where issues arise that involve the safety and security of democratic institutions and the basic welfare of the working population, considerations of efficiency and financial responsibility, although always relevant, must be counterbalanced by our concern for human beings. We must regiment *things* sometimes in order *not* to regiment *people*.

In no sphere of life is this so apparent as in international affairs. In our age of military nuclear technology, in which the sudden death of cultures is possible—something unique in human history—foreign policy has an overriding importance. In the present juncture of events it is no exaggeration to say that the outcome of existing international tensions, within the lifetime of most of my readers will determine the political future of the Western World in the next century. As the international situation has grown potentially more dangerous, peace has rested on "the precarious balance of terror" between the two great superpowers—the U.S.A. and the U.S.S.R. That balance can be easily upset if one side acquires a disproportionate superiority over the other, or if one side loses its credibility in the eyes of its adversary as a potential combatant, either because it is unable to defend itself or, because of loss of faith in its way of life or failure of nerve, it is unwilling to do so.

The foreign policy of a democracy, as well as its domestic policy, reflects many elements and interests. But it cannot have any coherence unless it also reflects its common ideals too. Foreign policy ought never to become a football of domestic politics, and especially not in an election year.

My point of departure is that the prospects of a world government able to compose international tensions in a just fashion is extremely remote. The United Nations today, far from creating a unified public world opinion that would support efforts to resolve conflicts among nations, if possible peacefully and if not, equitably, has itself become a cockpit in which these tensions are often exacerbated. Witness its infamous resolution condemning Israel, which is in perpetual danger of extermination from its enemies, as a threat to world peace, and the equating of Zionism with racialism.

There are many social conflicts in the world today that flow from national and racial differences, conflicts over frontiers and access to raw materials, but they are all eclipsed in the danger they pose to world peace by the fundamental opposition between Communist totalitarianism and the relatively free nations of the world, whose chief bulwark and support is the United States. By Communist totalitarianism in this context I mean primarily the Soviet Union. Mainland China ultimately may become a great or even greater threat to the United States and the Free World than the Soviet Union is today. If and when the current Sino-Soviet rift is healed, a rift that has been a moderating influence on both, the prospects for world peace will correspondingly decline.

It is generally recognized that democracies have great difficulty in developing an effective and consistent foreign policy because the very demand for openness threatens the delicacy, complexity, and the secrecy sometimes required to negotiate stubborn differences. The covenants of a free people should be open but they cannot be openly arrived at in the glare of publicity. To negotiate successfully when passions and fears are rife is not always possible when the negotiations themselves are public.

Granted all these difficulties, and others too, it still remains true that in a democracy no foreign policy can succeed if its basic direction does not have popular support. Most Americans, however, currently would be hard put to tell whether we really have a basic foreign policy, and if so, what it is.

The Soviet Union, on the other hand, the chief adversary of the Free World, has a definite foreign policy and one which its rulers do not have to account for to its peoples. That policy is geared to its fundamental objective—an objective spelled out by a whole library of official documents, and reflected in its history. It has sought sometimes by threats and propaganda and sometimes by overt use of force to impose its political, social, and economic system on adjoining countries. It conceives this objective to be necessary not only for its *national defense* but for its *ideological defense* because of the possible subversive influence on its own institutions of the existence of free and open societies elsewhere. That is why it builds its walls and iron curtains, physical and mental, not so much to prevent alien elements from coming in but to prevent its own peoples from running out or becoming infected with dissident ideas. This objective is the source of its unremitting ideological warfare against the Free World. From the very outset of its existence, the Soviet Union has been waging this war through the Communist International, the Comminform, foreign national parties, and its growing powers of communication control. It frankly proclaims that whether it is called "coexistence" or "detente," this ideological warfare will continue and intensify.

The defense against this ideological warfare, and against the accompanying phenomena of episodic aggression after the Second World War, was called the Cold War. Despite its defects and defeats, the Cold War had at least this to be said for it—it prevented a *hot* world war. The great question for the future is whether and how we can prevent a "hot" war and a possible holocaust. If Cold War succeeds in doing that, its cost will be a small price to pay.

After all, what are the only alternatives to waging an intelligent Cold War of defense against totalitarian expansion and its Gulag Archipelago culture? If history can provide an answer, it is either a policy of appeasement which, bit by gradual bit, from one retreat in moments of crisis to another, leads to capitulation and ultimate surrender or it is a policy of appeasement which by encouraging bolder and bolder acts of aggression by the enemy, finally precipitates the war that nobody professes to want. Hitler, you will recall, claimed— and the English historian A. J. P. Taylor seems to support him—that he was lured into the Second World War. After the capitulation to him at Munich, he invaded Poland, assuming that if the West did not resist when he invaded Czechoslovakia—"that distant country somewhere in Europe" as Chamberlain characterized it—it would not resist when he invaded Poland, a country far more distant.

Actual war is *not* inevitable. Even the Communists who believe that their ultimate worldwide triumph is inevitable, no longer believe, as they once did, that their victory will inevitably come about through war. Khrushchev has revised both Lenin and Stalin who firmly believed and proclaimed that the inevitable victory of communism would inevitably be won by war. Here the unexpected advances in technology have undermined one of the deeply rooted dogmas of Bolshevik-Leninist ideology.

Further, Cold War when intelligently waged to forestall "hot" war does not preclude limited agreements and treaties with the adversaries of free societies. But such agreements should be subject to at least three strictly enforced conditions. First, the consequences of any such agreement, especially where nuclear arms limitations and test bans are concerned, should not undermine the position of the free world to defend itself by conventional military means. Secondly—what has sometimes been lacking in implementing past agreements—the conditions must be based on genuine mutuality and reciprocity. Thirdly, before entering on new agreements and treaties, the provisions of the old ones must be faithfully fulfilled.

Anyone aware of the record of our relationships with the Soviet Union will have a vivid recollection of the repeated failures of the Soviet Union to live up to its treaties and agreements. Nonetheless, instead of insisting that the Soviet Union fulfill the terms of the Basic Principles of Agreement on May 29, 1972 between Brezhnev and Nixon, before concluding new agreements, the United States proceeded to sign the ten-point Helsinki Declaration which in effect gave our official recognition and acceptance of Soviet violations of previous agreements with respect to Eastern Europe.

I have previously said, and it is necessary to repeat it, that no foreign policy can succeed in the long run in a democracy unless it enjoys popular support. Especially is this true if the policy involves risks and sacrifices. Popular support is largely a function of popular understanding of the basic issues in dispute between the communist world and our own. What, then, really is the issue for which we some day may be called upon to stake not only our fortunes and our honor but our very lives? I find disheartening the widespread failure to understand it on almost every level of American life.

We sometimes hear that the basic issue is between capitalism and socialism as economic systems. This is actually the constant theme song of Kremlin propaganda despite the absence of either free enterprise or socialism in their classic forms anywhere in the world. This counterposition of capitalism *or* socialism is not only false, for the specific content of economic decisions is not between capitalism and socialism but between more or less of either, it misses the central issue. Human beings do not fight for economic systems. Who would be willing to die for capitalism? Certainly not the capitalists! Who would go to the barricades for a totally nationalized economy? Not even the Webbs. No, the issue is not between capitalism and socialism. *The issue is whether human beings are to be free to choose for themselves the economic system under which they wish to live or whether this is to be imposed upon them forcibly by a small group of self-selected rulers responsible to no one but themselves.*

Or we sometimes hear that the basic issue between the democratic and communist worlds is between religion and irreligion. I have a premonition we may hear more about this in the future. In the past, President Eisenhower, whose charming and vacuous smile matched his knowledge of international affairs, and who confessed himself stumped by General Zhukov's questions as to what ideals inspired the West, repeatedly warned us against the dangers of "atheistic communism" as if a communism that was not atheistic would be any less objectionable. No, the issue is not now, nor has it ever been, between religion and irreligion. It has always been the *freedom to choose* between them, the freedom to worship or not to worship one, many, or no gods; the right of one's conscience to believe or not to believe, or the dogmatic intolerance that makes the state power the arbiter of the faiths of man.

Nor is the issue between formalism or modernism in art or culture, on the one hand, or socialist realism, whatever that is, on the other. Once again the issue is *the right to choose freely one's own values or philosophy,* to experiment with new art forms and lifestyles, or to submit to a state-imposed view. Nor is the issue which system can outproduce the other as in the famous Nixon-Khrushchev debate. The issue is rather whether those who produce society's goods and services have the right at least to some extent to determine, through their free trade unions and other voluntary associations, the conditions and rewards of work, or whether this is to be dictated by bureaucratic decrees backed by the coercive powers of the state.

In short, what is at stake is the most precious principle of liberal civilization whose roots were nurtured in Athens, Jerusalem, and Rome, and which began to bud at the time of the humanist Renaissance, and to flower when the American Declaration of Independence made the principle of freely given consent the hallmark of legitimate political sovereignty. When we say that social democracy puts freedom first, we mean that freedom becomes the touchstone of policy, a principle that cannot be compromised whether for the sale of machinery or oil or wheat or for the benefit of any special economic vested interests that look longingly at the markets of the Soviet Union and China, as their similars once did during the thirties at the markets of Japan and Germany.

When it comes to the principled defense of freedom, and to opposition to all forms of totalitarianism, let it be said that to its eternal credit, the organized labor movement in the United States, in contradiction to all other sectors of American life, especially in industry, the academy, and the churches, has never faltered, or trimmed its sails. Its dedication to the ideals of a free society has been unsullied. Its leaders have never been Munichmen of the spirit.

The sober reality of the present moment is that the credibility of the United States as an active proponent of the principle of freedom first has come into question in important areas of the world. The ineptness and failures of our foreign policy initiatives, indeed of our feeble responses to the contumely, ingratitude, and provocations of nondemocratic powers, have contributed to the growth of neutralism in Western Europe which, if not reversed, can result in the Finlandization of Europe. This failure to develop an active policy in defense of freedom has eclipsed the will of many in our own country to defend it. I conceive it as the historic and continuous function of social democracy in international affairs to stress the centrality of the commitment to freedom first and its political relevance, not only in moments of crisis and confrontation, but in the day-to-day business of international agencies.

We recognize that there are limits to American influence and power and that we must rely on the internal evolution and development of existing totalitarian countries toward freer horizons, not on threats and force of any kind. But just as we permit the waves of totalitarian propaganda to wash over our country, so we must beam the message of freedom, and expressions of our solidarity and support for the Solzhenitsyns and Sakharovs, and the nameless hundreds of other dissenters in Iron Curtain countries. The Soviet regime, its leaders and its controlled press, have never scrupled to discuss American internal affairs even when by their denunciatory exaggerations they have contributed to the gaiety of nations. We should welcome any criticism from any foreign source, however unfriendly, learn from it where it is valid, and respond to it if it is invalid in programs of public education. *We should raise our voice in continued protest against repressions in any country where they occur.* We should not be deterred by the hypocritical outcry that we are interfering in internal affairs that are of no concern to us. Countries that are signatories to the provisions of the Universal Declaration of Human Rights cannot win immunity from criticism of their repressive practices by classifying them as internal affairs. To those who put freedom first, whenever and wherever individuals are deprived of their human rights, it is never a purely internal affair.

I want to conclude with a few remarks about the domestic scene and the role of Social Democrats in it. We are not a political party with our own candidates. We are not alone in our specific programs for more employment, more insurance, more welfare, less discrimination, less bureaucratic inefficiency. Our spiritual task should be to relate these programs and demands to the underlying philosophy of democracy, to express and defend those larger moral ideals that should inform programs for which we wish to develop popular support. These large ideals are not utopian blueprints but perspectives by which to judge the direction and quality of desirable social changes. Without these ideals we cannot formulate any conception of a good society or a better society. The demand for "More!" carries us beyond the *status quo* but "more" is not enough. We must know what is desirable and worth having before wanting more of it. We know that jobs are worth having, and programs of full employment at decent wages, lacking which a comprehensive insurance program should provide relief. But over and above this I believe we must raise our eyes to distant horizons to grasp a vision of society not only abundant and free but in which every person feels he has a significant stake and a sense of worth and esteem regardless of the work one is doing.

It is not unduly optimistic to look forward to a period in which the malaise and evils of poverty, defined as acute deprivation, will be finally overcome. But I am not so optimistic as to assume that this will automatically eliminate what may be paradoxically called "the evils of affluence"—whose effects are observable currently among some of the most alienated sections of youth in our own and other democratic countries. Those who are depraved by drugs or consumed by an insatiable and self-defeating craving for excitement and sensation or caught up in criminal violence for ostensibly high ideals are not children of poverty suffering from acute physical want. What they suffer from most is *lack of meaning* in their lives, a vague discontent with normal life, punctuated by outbursts of rage between listlessness and boredom.

The problem is vast and involves further study and research. But I believe that three fruitful suggestions deserve mention and require concrete implementation. One is to reawaken a sense of the importance of citizen participation in local government and its multiple activities. This kind of participation is an effective antidote to the impression of anonymity and helplessness in a complex world, and a perennial source for the feeling that one counts for something. This participation in local government must not be equated with a mindless drive toward decentralization. The universal enforcement of civil rights requires a strong central government just as a good national transportation system depends upon efficient coordination. But local government in a complex populous society can help to make the sense of citizenship continuous and vital. Another is to develop American variants on the practice of West Germany's co-determination in industry that can counteract to some extent the deadening effect of assembly lines and routinized mechanizations. We cannot, of course, transplant the German practice. The representatives of the consumer, too, must have a voice and a role.

Finally, more important and most difficult is the development of the sense of vocation or calling. Through the appropriate educational nurture, the community must provide the opportunities that give individuals a chance, aside from the felicities of family life, to acquire an abiding sense of significance and meaning in life. I know of no more effective way of developing a center of interest around which human experience can be organized than by finding a career that makes a call upon the creative capacities of the individual.

Look around you and ask: Who are the most integrated persons you know, who seem to have found themselves and, however one defines it, have achieved a satisfactory and happy life? I am confident that they will be persons who are characterized by one or both of two features: 1) They are able to love or be loved in their personal relationships, and 2) they have found a continuing self-fulfillment in their life's work. The first is largely a matter of luck. The second is the responsibility of social and educational institutions broadly conceived. For most people today, even when they are not in want, "earning one's living" and "living one's life" are quite different and opposed experiences. Our task as social democrats—a task not only educational but social and political—is to move society in a direction in which for progressively larger numbers of human beings, "earning one's living" will be at the same time a satisfactory part of "living one's life." We are not utopians and are aware that some tasks may be too boring or degrading to attract those seeking a meaningful career. Mechanization, part-time work, rotating assignments, high compensation may help in getting this work done. Just as some individuals are willing to engage in very hazardous occupations to have time for leisure and amateur pursuits so others may undertake the less attractive tasks that must inescapably be performed. There will of course always be problems. But sufficient unto this day are the problems thereof.

1976

Chapter 7
Capitalism, Socialism, and Freedom

Questions concerning the fate of freedom under socialism and capitalism were widely discussed long before the socialist dream of a community in which all are "free and equal" was transformed into a totalitarian nightmare in the Soviet Union and its satellites. But these questions became especially acute for those among the intellectual classes who had been drawn to socialism not so much because it seemed a feasible means of abolishing poverty as because of its promise to liberate human energies and expand freedom.

The logic of the arguments was explored in depth in my second series of debates with Max Eastman almost thirty-five years ago after he had been converted by Friedrich von Hayek to ardent support of an unregulated free-enterprise system.[1] I was struck at that time by an odd feature of the discussion that has often reappeared in subsequent exchanges on the theme. Staunch critics of Marxism, in their effort to show that socialism necessarily spells the end of political and cultural freedom, seem to rely on the central dogma of orthodox Marxism, namely, the theory of historical materialism. The orthodox Marxists maintain that the mode of economic production determines the dominant character of the culture of capitalist

---

1. The exchange is reproduced in my *Political Power and Personal Freedom* (New York: Macmillan Co., 1959). The first series, in the late 1920s and early 1930s, was about the meaning of Marx.

society, as of all class societies, and that its politics, education, art, philosophy, and religion "reflect" the basic economic structure. The critics of Marxism contend that the mode of economic production would be no less decisive in determining the culture of a socialist society, but that its socialized economy, far from providing the sound basis for a leap from the kingdom of necessity into the kingdom of freedom, would inescapably destroy the political and cultural freedoms that were ushered into the world in the wake of capitalism.

Both views suffer from the simplicities and inadequacies of every historical monism. The economy of a society excludes certain options and always limits alternatives of action, just as the foundation of a building excludes certain types of superstructure. But on the same foundation one can erect either a prison or a luxurious retirement home. And no knowledge of the foundation alone will enable us to predict the precise number of stories that will be built on it, the materials and style of its construction, its interior decorative design, and a multiplicity of other important details.

The influence of economic organization on human ideas, ideals, and behaviors is a matter of degree, and its strength varies from time to time. Whatever may have been the case in the past, in our own era, since the end of World War I, the mode of political decision seems to me to have had at least as much influence on our culture as the mode of economic production. This is not a matter that can be established by conceptual analysis but by empirical, social, and historical inquiry.

Those who contend that any significant intervention of the state in economic affairs either by way of ownership or control ineluctably leads to political tyranny and cultural despotism must meet some obvious difficulties:

1. Capitalism as an economic order has functioned under political systems that have had varied character, either more or less democratic or authoritarian, and even in some countries like Italy, Japan, and Germany that abandoned democratic political forms entirely. If the economic system of capitalism did not uniquely determine the political and cultural institution of the societies in which it functioned, why should we assume that a regulated or socialized economy, regardless of the degree and extent of the regulation or socialization, *must* sooner or later result in totalitarianism?

2. Granted that every completely or predominantly socialized economy today is characterized by a despotism more pervasive and oppressive than any that existed in the past. Nonetheless, the historical record is clear and incontestable: In every such case, political democracy was destroyed *before* the economy was socialized. There is not a single democratic country where the public sector of the

economy has grown substantially over the years, either through socialization or through governmental controls and subsidies (whether it be England, Sweden, Norway, Holland, or the United States), in which the dire predictions concerning the extinction or even the radical restrictions of democratic freedoms have been realized.

3. Compare the economies of the United States and Great Britain and the state of their political and cultural life as they were at the turn of the twentieth century, and as they are today. In the past, their economies, although not completely free because of the tariff system, were certainly far freer from state intervention or control than they are at present. Yet with respect to freedom of expression in politics and all fields of art, freedom of life-styles, openness to heresies within the academy and without, tolerance of dissent, acceptance of unconventional sexual behavior, current practices are so free that in some areas they border on license, as in the violent disruption of public debate. The increasing state control of the economy in democratic countries has not resulted in the progressive diminution of freedoms in political and cultural life.

4. Compare the American economy during and shortly after World Wars I and II. In World War I, business was conducted almost as usual, with very little state control over the economy. During this same period, however, we experienced the worst political terror in American history. During World War II, the government practically took over the control of the American economy with price controls and rationing. Yet the political climate was such that representatives of both the Socialist and Socialist Labor parties—neither of which supported the war—were permitted to address the armed forces. The one great lapse was the cruel and needless internment of the Japanese population in California, engineered by the then-governor, Earl Warren. What made the difference? In part the nature of the enemy we were combating, but even more, an awareness of the excesses of World War I and a desire to avoid them. The only call for the arrest of Norman Thomas, who defended the right to strike in war industries, came from the leaders of the Communist party.

This is not to deny in the least the profound ways in which the economic relations of any society influence its political institutions and behavior, but the latter can, as the emergence of the welfare state itself shows, have a far-reaching reciprocal influence on the development of the economy and the redistribution of wealth within it. It is significant that in none of the welfare states has government control of the economy—regardless of the wisdom and feasibility of the regulatory measures—prevented the electorate from voting the governing political party out of power. Here and there extraparliamentary efforts have been made to throttle the political opposition, but they have been no more frequent than comparable episodes when the economy was unregulated, and they have rarely succeeded when courageously resisted.

In the United States, the bureaucratic usurpation of academic functions by the Department of Health, Education, and Welfare (HEW) through the imposition of a disguised quota system, under penalty of forfeiting all federal subsidies, has sometimes been cited as evidence of the erosion of traditional freedoms in consequence of economic intervention by the state. It is more persuasive evidence of the absence of moral courage on the part of our major universities. Had they made a *concerted* effort to defy the HEW guidelines and taken their case to Congress and the courts, since the defense capacity of the nation depended on them, they could have stopped the bureaucrats of HEW in their tracks. Sometimes it may be economically costly to defy a government decree, even if it is legally mandated by Congress and the courts. But fidelity to the academic mission of the university may require it. Those who cite this unhappy chapter in recent academic history as evidence that encroachment on basic freedoms must necessarily follow on government grants, would interpret even graver capitulations to the power of capital in an unregulated economy not as a violation of basic human rights but as a deplorable weakness of moral fiber. Unpopularity and even genteel poverty may be the costs of defending freedom against bureaucrats in a democratic welfare state, but such defense does not require the courage of a Sakharov or a Bukovsky.

Nonetheless, in the light of historical experience—which only a fanatic or a fool can ignore—we must recast the idea of socialism, whatever the terms used to designate the revision. The emphasis must be placed not so much on the *legal form* of property relations but on the moral ideals of democracy as a way of life, conceived as an equality of concern for all citizens of the community to develop themselves as persons to their full growth. The economy should be considered a means to that end. As far as the quality of human life is concerned, this approach is more radical than mere measures of nationalization in which, in the absence of free trade unions, workers can be exploited more than in the private sector of democratic welfare states.

If we do not place too great a stress on efficiency, I believe that it is still *formally* possible to provide for freedom of choice in occupations and in consumption even in an economy whose major industries have been collectivized. But the totalitarian potential in such a setup makes it too dangerous. The loss of political freedom would transform the economy into a most powerful engine of human repression. Therefore, in the interests of freedom, it is wiser and safer to limit carefully the extent of socialization, relying on some regulated industries, considerable private enterprise, public corporations, cooperatives, increased worker participation in the operation of plants as well as in the directing boards of large corporations, and other means of multiplying centers of economic power.

It is significant that although in some fascist nations political democracy has been restored without civil war, not a single country in which Communists have seized power has been permitted to revert to democracy. The absolute control of the economy by the Communist party has enabled it to reinforce a kind of terror beyond anything previously known in human history, and to use the bread-card and the work-card to enforce conformity.

An additional reason for preserving a private sector is that it can help provide greater incentives to productivity and innovation without which a minimum decent standard of living cannot be sustained —a standard below which human beings should not be permitted to sink in a civilized society, and which could be raised with technological advances. It is significant how little technological and industrial innovation exists in current collectivist societies whose economies from the very outset borrowed, bought, or stole the techniques, know-how, and discoveries of the free Western economies.

If we declare that "we put freedom first," is it more likely to be furthered in the world today by a return to an uncontrolled free-enterprise economy than by the judicious development of the democratic welfare state pruned of its bureaucratic excrescences? By freedom here I do not mean the right to do anything one pleases, which would result in a Hobbesian war of all against all, but the strategic freedoms of speech, press, assembly, independent trade unions and judiciary, and the cluster of rights associated with democracy in its widest sense. Although they are interrelated, there is an order of priority in freedoms to guide us when they conflict. All but anarchists understand that since every freedom logically entails the curtailment of an opposite freedom—if I am to be free to speak, others are not free to prevent me from speaking—the state must exist to enforce the exercise of these civic and political freedoms. Any other functions we entrust to it must be limited by the scrupulous adherence to the strategic freedoms. In a democracy, the state should be considered as a protector of human rights, not its necessary enemy.

Property is a human right but like all human rights not every form or manifestation of it is sacred. It was none other than John Stuart Mill, one of the patron saints of economic liberalism, who observed that, "Society is fully entitled to abrogate or alter any particular right of property which on sufficient consideration it judged to stand in the way of the public good."[2]

Some who say that they put freedom first mean primarily the freedom to buy and sell, which is tantamount to putting profit first. The capitalist *pur sang* is not out of character when he does this. But it is to be hoped that in the defense of the democratic world against the totalitarian assault, the capitalist will be a little less pure, giving political freedom priority. However, when we see the eagerness with which certain groups of financiers, industrialists, and farmers fall all over themselves to expand trade with Communist countries and contrast it with the consistent and principled struggle of the organized American labor movement, the AFL-CIO, against the denial of human rights anywhere in the world, we encounter a different order of priorities. The fact that it was George Meany who gave a public platform to Solzhenitsyn and Bukovsky and not Ford or Carter is of more than symbolic significance in the global struggle for human freedom.

1978

2. John Stuart Mill, *Socialism* (New York: Humboldt Publishing Co., 1891), p. 137.

Chapter 8
The Ethics of Controversy

Democratic society cannot exist without free discussion. One of its basic assumptions is that truth of fact and wisdom of policy can be more readily achieved through the lively interchange of ideas and opinions than by unchallengeable edicts on the part of a self-perpetuating elite—whether of theologians or philosophers or politicians or even scientific experts. Throughout history, controversy and spirited differences have always marked the deliberations of communities of free men. Their pooled judgments, expressed in public decisions, always reflect the criticism of healthy opposition.

But if democratic society cannot exist without free discussion, some kinds of discussion tend to undermine democratic society. Political life, of course, is not a game; yet, it has certain implicit ground rules which must be observed if freely delegated government by majority is not to degenerate into the tyranny of the mob, or the dictatorship of faction.

In a democratic society, what is morally permissible and impermissible in public controversy follows from the commitment to permit all sectional, class and individual interests to express themselves openly and honestly before reaching a consensus of agreement on measures that seek to further the common welfare.

As natural creatures, men have needs and interests whose specific form depends upon the times and society in which they live. Conflicts of interest, conflicts of judgment concerning these interests and the best methods of fulfilling them are inescapable in a world of limited resources and fallible intelligence. The democratic process is the best method so far devised by which these conflicts of interest and judgment may be resolved without repression or violence. Discussion is the lifeblood of the democratic process, and, wherever discussion flourishes, controversy is sure to arise.

Certain methods of controversy, however, poison instead of refresh the lifeblood of democracy. They are characterized by the fact that they do not desire to establish the truth or to approximate it as closely as conditions permit. They seek to discredit persons rather than to consider problems. They ignore or suppress relevant evidence. They aim to create a mood of refusal to listen to views challenging some favored or dominant notions. Instead of exposing, confronting, reconciling, or negotiating the conflicts of interest and opinion, one interest is fanatically identified with the common interest, and one opinion with the loyal opinion.

The cumulative effect of such practices is to generate an atmosphere in which the self-corrective procedures of democracy cannot operate. Fact rarely catches up with rumor. Opponents legitimately at odds with each other within the framework of the democratic system are pictured as enemies of the democratic system itself. The reciprocal esteem which citizens of a democratic community should feel for each other, even in disagreement, is replaced by mutual contempt and hate. Instead of being used as an instrument to explore fresh possibilities in the quest for solutions, intelligence becomes a tool to secure only a narrow partisan advantage. Even the liberal mind, by focusing too intently on achievement of immediate objectives without concern for methods, risks becoming transformed into the crafty mind. Most dispiriting of all, some who recognize and denounce morally objectionable techniques of controversy when practiced by others often use them themselves, thus adding hypocrisy to confusion and forgetting that those who blandly lie in a good cause must continue to lie to avoid being found out.

The abuses of free discussion are legion. Short of criminal libel and incitement to, or advocacy of, violence in a situation of clear and present danger, they should not be the subject of legal restraints. For, just as soon as legal restraints are adopted against the various forms of deliberate untruth, malicious and scurrilous exaggeration, venomous insinuation, and outright fabrication, they become weapons to curb honest error and to hamper the spontaneous expression of free minds. In the last analysis, only self-discipline can prevent the level of public discussion from sinking below the safety-line of democratic health. The restraints entailed by good form in discussion are, therefore, more than a matter of good manners: They are a matter of good public morals.

In a world of universal literacy in which everyone is within earshot of a radio, words have become more potent social forces than ever before. No one can write the history of the Weimar Republic or the Kerensky regime or even of modern France without recognizing the extent to which whispering campaigns, calumniation of public figures, and ill-founded accusations against political opponents undermined civic morale and destroyed mutual confidence.

Totalitarian practices in controversy are at least consistent with totalitarian theory. Both Bolshevik and Fascist doctrine deny that there is, or can be, any such thing as "fair" or "classless" or even "objective" discussion of issues. Truth is identified with partisan interest. This serves as a premise to justify the wildest slander against those whom totalitarians oppose, if only it furthers the interest of the party or race. Hitler exhausted the vocabulary of abuse against the leaders of other political groups. Lenin was amazingly frank in justifying the use of poisoned weapons of controversy even against other working-class groups.

A few years before the Russian Revolution, Lenin was tried in a kind of Court of Honor set up by the Social Democratic party (one of whose factions he headed) for using morally impermissible polemical methods. He was charged with impugning the integrity of party members and thus confusing the Russian workers. Lenin defiantly stood his ground and admitted that the tone of his words and their formulation were

calculated to evoke in the reader hatred, aversion and contempt. . . . Such a formulation is calculated not to convince, but to break up the ranks of an opponent, not to correct the mistakes of an opponent, but to destroy him, to wipe his organization off the face of the earth. This formulation is indeed of such a nature as to evoke the worst thoughts, the worst *suspicions* about the opponents, and indeed, *as contrasted with formulation that convinces and corrects*, it "carries confusion into the ranks of the proletariat."[1]

Only toward members of a *united party* (that is, when they agreed with him or his faction in the Central Committee) did Lenin admit that such methods were morally impermissible. But against all others such methods were mandatory. "Against *such* political enemies I

1. V. I. Lenin, *Selected Works* (New York: International Publishers, 1943), 3:490 [italics mine].

conducted and . . . *shall always conduct* a fight of extermination."[2]

When political feelings run high in democratic communities, many who are firmly opposed to communism and fascism employ techniques of disputation which bear the hallmarks of totalitarian polemics. Anyone who studies the totalitarian press and the proceedings of demonstration trials will find certain recurrent patterns of accusation that show up with alarming frequency in countries this side of the Iron Curtain. One of the most familiar is the systematic confusion between what constitutes evidence of the *consequences* of an action or policy with what constitutes evidence of its *intent*.

No *moral* judgment can be passed upon any individual human action without an appraisal of its intent. Consequences *alone* cannot be a fair test of intentions. A common procedure in Soviet and satellite countries is to charge that the consequences of a policy have been disastrous (the charge is rarely proved), and then to take the alleged disastrous consequences as sufficient proof of the presence of an intention to bring them about. This "justifies" the secret police in torturing the defendant to confess to an intention which has already been objectively established by the consequences. In effect, an accident becomes a crime; ignorance is indistinguishable from treason, and error a form of sabotage. The Bolshevik concept of "objective counterrevolutionary" guilt, inferred not only from the presumed consequences of a man's actions but from his membership in a family or class and other *nonvoluntary* forms of association, led to the liquidation of millions.

Recent political argument in the United States seems to show that, in the heat of controversy, the most elementary distinctions have been overlooked. From the true proposition that policies can be intelligently tested only by their consequences, the false proposition is drawn that the consequences alone are the conclusive test of the intent or motives behind the policies. A bad result is deemed proof of a wicked purpose (particularly if one's political opponents are responsible for the decision), and a good result is proof of good will (particularly if one's political friends initiated it). This summarizes many pages of discussion today.

In nonpolitical contexts, the crudity and cruelty of such simplistic criticism is easily recognized and universally repudiated. It would be tantamount to charging a surgeon whose patient had died under the knife with murder or a general of a defeated army with being in the service of the enemy.

It would be preposterous to equate the systematic employment of

2. Ibid., p. 491 [Lenin's italics].

poisoned instruments of controversy in totalitarian countries with the serious abuses of discussion in free cultures; for, in the former, a single minority party has a total monopoly of the power of denunciation and defamation. But the presence of intellectually dishonest techniques of argument in a free culture, even when they are employed by many parties in the peaceful struggle for political power, is a disquieting phenomenon. It is a betrayal of the spirit of the democratic process even when it abides by its legal forms.

Several books and many articles have been written which persuasively argue that *if* someone had set out to serve the Communist cause, he *would have* advocated certain policies and behaved in certain ways. Evidence is then presented that some individuals *did* advocate these policies and behave in these ways. This is then considered conclusive proof that he did set out to serve the Communist cause. No further inquiry is deemed necessary to determine the independent facts about his memberships, activities, and other data relevant to his intentions or purposes. It is overlooked that, just as the same conclusion can be reached from different premises, so the same policy may be advocated for two entirely different, and sometimes incompatible, sets of motives. A member of the Communist party, for example, may advocate unilateral disarmament for the United States. But so may an absolute pacifist, in the belief that the Kremlin will kiss the other cheek instead of slapping it. The first should not be eligible for government employment, certainly not in a sensitive post; the second, however, may be eligible, and, if ineligible, only on grounds relevant to his competence which have nothing to do with his loyalty.

One of Senator McCarthy's favorite techniques of argument is to insinuate that, since a policy has been followed by the Kremlin, or approved by the Kremlin, anyone else who advocated such a policy is therewith suspect of being a Soviet agent. Unfortunately, some of those who are critical of Senator McCarthy's methods do not hesitate to use some of his techniques of argument against those who disagree with them: Because Senator McCarthy says that the Communist party is a conspiracy, therefore anyone who says that the Communist party is a conspiracy is suspect of McCarthyism. But what makes a thing true is not who says it, but the evidence for it; the evidence that the Communist party is a conspiratorial movement, and not like other American political parties, is by now overwhelming.

The intellectual circles of the country have a responsibility for teaching, and living up to, the highest standards of vigorous controversy. But there are signs even here of infection by the virus of partisanship. One occasionally hears members of the learned professions substitute abuse for logical analysis and, unable to meet argument or evidence for some positions of which they disapprove, inveigh against the presumed "unconscious" of those who uphold them. When the methods of the marketplace—and of the black marketplace—invade the academy, the intellectual life of a country is debased.

The ground rules of controversy in a democracy are simple, and their reaffirmation may sound like truisms. They *are* truisms. But when denied or violated, truisms become very important. That their reaffirmation is necessary is an indication of how low political discussion has sunk. Among these rules are:

1. Nothing and no one is immune from criticism.

2. Everyone involved in a controversy has an intellectual responsibility to inform himself of the available facts.

3. Criticism should be directed first to policies, and against persons only when they are responsible for policies, and against their motives or purposes only when there is some independent evidence of their character.

4. Because certain words are legally permissible, they are not therefore morally permissible.

5. *Before* impugning an opponent's motives, even when they legitimately may be impugned, answer his arguments.

6. Do not treat an opponent of a policy as if he were therefore a personal enemy or an enemy of the country or a concealed enemy of democracy.

7. Since a good cause may be defended by bad arguments, after answering the bad arguments for another's position present positive evidence for your own.

8. Do not hesitate to admit lack of knowledge or to suspend judgment if evidence is not decisive either way.

9. Only in pure logic and mathematics, not in human affairs, can one demonstrate that something is strictly impossible. Because something is logically possible, it is not therefore probable. "It is not impossible" is a preface to an irrelevant statement about human affairs. The question is always one of the balance of probabilities. And the evidence for probabilities must include more than abstract possibilities.

10. The cardinal sin, when we are looking for truth of fact or wisdom of policy, is refusal to discuss, or action which blocks discussion.

These ground rules express *in nuce* the logic and ethics of scientific inquiry. From one point of view, science may be considered as a field of continuing controversy which leaves behind it not burning hatreds, but vast accumulations of knowledge. It is not necessary to deny the vast differences between the *subject-matters* of the natural sciences and the disciplines concerned with human affairs to recognize that, if the spirit of scientific inquiry were brought to bear on most questions of politics, American democracy would be both wiser and more secure.

1954

Chapter 9

Are There Limits to
Freedom of Expression?

From the East to the West coast, from the Great
Lakes to the Gulf, a spirit of unlawfulness lies like a brooding presence over the land. It has seeped into the very fabric of social and
political life and burst into flame in areas where minorities, moving
to break out of the patterns of segregation and discrimination, meet
majorities resisting the pace and method of their movement. Hate-
mongers, black and white, are finding susceptible audiences. All this
is developing in a period in which reliance upon democratic procedures of resolving conflicts has been weakened by open contempt
for law and legal institutions. The spectacle of the late Michael
Quill, with the television eyes of the country upon him, ripping to
pieces a court injunction and cursing the judge who issued it, is a
dramatic symbol of deeply felt attitudes.

Incitement to violence, civil and uncivil disobedience, wild
threats against individuals, group libels, organized chants denouncing the chief magistrates of the nation as "murderers" and "assas-
sins" have come to be regarded in certain quarters, even on some
campuses, as normal methods of political dialogue. At no time in the
twentieth century has expression in America been so uninhibited,
so reckless, so inflammatory.

To those who believe that the First Amendment guarantees absolute freedom of expression to all members of the community, these
unlovely phenomena are merely the price of a free society. But there
are obvious difficulties with this absolutist position. The Constitu-

tion also provides that no one should be deprived of the right to life, liberty, and property without due process of law. What happens when freedom of expression imperils life, threatens a defendant's liberty, leads by malicious falsehood to loss of property, good name, or reputation? Obviously if there is more than one absolute right, and they conflict, as when speech prejudices a man's right to a fair trial or violates his right to privacy, one or both must be abridged. Which right is to yield to which, and when? Granting the strategic importance of freedom of expression in a democratic society, we must still face the problem, growing more acute in recent days, under what circumstances may speech, press, and assembly reasonably be curbed?

Professor Thomas I. Emerson of the Yale University Law School addresses himself to this problem in *Towards a General Theory of the First Amendment* (New York: Random House, 1968). He criticizes with vigor the chief general principles that have been previously advanced to distinguish expression which is constitutionally privileged from expression which is not. He rejects the "bad tendency" test that would limit expression if there are reasonable grounds for believing it would lead to substantial social evil. The "clear and present danger" test of Justices Holmes and Brandeis, once hailed as a libertarian doctrine, is declared too vague and ambiguous to be of any practical use. The *"ad hoc* balancing test" which seeks to strike a judicial balance between interest in freedom of expression and other individual freedoms and social interests is ruled out as untenable, as affording little or no protection to free expression.

Emerson is also somewhat critical of "the absolute test," associated with Justice Black, because some of its formulations suggest that the First Amendment gives unqualified immunity to all expression. On the whole, however, he is very sympathetic to the absolute view; his own theory essays a restatement of the absolute test that would make it less vulnerable to criticism.

Professor Emerson believes that the only adequate theory that can guide us in applying the First Amendment to the troublesome problems is one based on a strict distinction between "expression" and "action." The upshot of his discussion is "if the theory of freedom of expression means anything, therefore, it requires that social control be directed toward the subsequent action." But if the reader takes this to mean that only actions are to be legally punishable while utterances, oral or written, remain immune, he will be mistaken. For Emerson concedes that certain threats, solicitations, insults, libels, obscenities, incitements, and so forth, may justifiably be punished by civil or even criminal sanctions. How is this apparent contradiction to be reconciled? Quite simply! By a process of semantic legislation. Whenever we have good reason to hold that certain expressions or forms of speech should be legally punishable —like a false charge that a judge has taken a bribe, or a leaflet to soldiers in wartime urging them to desert, or threats to a jury to convict a defendant, or a speech inciting a crowd to a lynching bee—we put quotation marks around the term expression and then classify this "expression" as an action. In other words, whenever speech is deemed legally actionable it becomes "speech," a type of action. Conversely, whenever we have good reasons to hold that certain actions, which some citizens regard as evil, like mass picketing or joining a subversive organization, should not be subject to legal restraint, we put quotation marks around the term action and classify "action" as an expression or form of speech.

The term abridgment is the object of the same semantic ploy. An employer is properly forbidden to distribute a statement to his employees, who are being polled on whether they want a union, to the effect that he may have to go out of business if a union is voted in. This is a clear and justifiable abridgment of his speech. Not so according to Emerson. It is not an abridgment but only an "abridgment" because his expression is "an expression," and therefore to be classified as an *action*.

This procedure seems to me to be an outrage both on common usage and common sense. The "clear and present danger" test, for all its difficulties, which are not as great as Emerson contends, is intellectually more forthright in recognizing that it is the use of certain *words* and *expressions* that is being punished because of their tendency to bring about "substantive evils Congress has a right to prevent." It does not pretend with brazen indifference to the ethics of words that when a speech is being punished, it is not speech but something else. It would be less bizarre to repudiate the strict distinction between expression and action, regard all expressions or acts of speech as forms of behavior or action, and employ various moral criteria to determine the degree of freedom these speech-acts should enjoy.

What Professor Emerson is proposing may be more apparent if we apply the same technique of redefinition to "freedom of religion." This is not discussed by him although it comes first in the First Amendment and is as "absolute" as the other provisions. The "free exercise of religion" was considered by the framers as every whit as important as freedom of expression. Nonetheless a man whose religious conscience justifies the practice of plural marriages, or human bloodletting, or refusal to permit administration of lifesaving drugs to his critically ill child may find himself in jail. Since the absolutists do not object to the laws that would send him to jail, they presumably must hold that he is not exercising his religion but only "religion," and that therefore his freedom of religion is not being abridged, but merely "abridged," that he is not a sincere martyr to his faith but a criminal masking his action under "religion"— thus adding insult to injury. The simple truth overlooked by both Justice Black and Professor Emerson is that the framers were too intelligent to be absolutists about freedom of religion, expression, or any other specific freedom.

It is not necessary to resort to desperate expedients of redefinition to honor the strategic or central importance of freedom of expression in a democratic society, and yet recognize that at certain times, places, and occasions, in the interest of preserving the whole cluster of freedoms essential to a functioning democracy, some expressions may have to be curbed. I do not believe that any one criterion or test can be found that will satisfy our reflective moral sense in all situations where some limit on expression is justified.

What Emerson pejoratively calls *"ad hoc* balancing" is not itself a criterion, like the clear and present danger test, but a process of weighing and weighting the relevant considerations, involving various criteria, of which reflective judgment must take note when right conflicts with right, good with good, and right with good. He himself is aware that one resorts to some balancing of rights and interests even in distinguishing between "expression" and expression. Every genuine *problem* of conflict of rights requires some balancing. That is why his objections, as well as those of Frantz and Meiklejohn, seem to me to lack cogency and to be based on misunderstanding. Intelligent balancing does not mean we must reopen all questions in considering all issues of conflict, that nothing is ever presumptively settled, and that the rights and interests balanced against each other are always of equal weight.

The notion that whatever balancing of rights is required, where the limits of freedom of expression are in question, has already been done by the framers of the Constitution is bad history, bad logic, and bad ethics. It is bad history because not only may the ends or values of the Preamble to the Constitution obviously conflict with each other—justice does not always ensure domestic tranquility—but because the rights enumerated to achieve them may conflict, a fact that could hardly have escaped the architects of the Constitution. It is bad logic because the very language of key sections of the Constitution, including the First Amendment, is not sufficiently precise to give determinate answers to many questions. It does not tell us what the limits of free expression are, nor even, as Court opinions show, what constitutes a religious establishment or religious freedom. It is bad ethics because it implies a willingness to be bound by the presumed mandate of persons who, however worthy, could not possibly have anticipated many of the conflicts of rights which arise over freedom of communication in an electronic age. If we eschewed balancing when rights conflict we would have to resort to the complicated and cumbersome process of amendment in the face of each fresh situation.

Ultimately all the arguments against the process of balancing turn out to be variations of the view that it is dangerous and perhaps ultimately disastrous to make exceptions to general rules. Emerson declares that "once the principle of governmental restriction is accepted for any purpose, it becomes difficult to establish a stopping place." Surely, even if this were true, it would be no argument against the use of police power or taxation that are also forms of restriction. But it is truer for some purposes than for others, and the degree of difficulty varies. After all, what is our intelligence for, if not to find appropriate stopping places? We do not have to do everything whole hog.

Freedom of expression is intrinsically and instrumentally so valuable in a good society that there is a presumption in its favor when it conflicts with other rights and interests. But presumptions are always rebuttable. There is no greater paradox here than in the realization that food is of central importance for life, but that sometimes in order to preserve life it is necessary to fast. Emerson is like the man who warns us that the fast may end in starvation. Nonetheless he willingly admits that despite the dangers of governmental regulation, where individuals need protection against *private* organizations, it may be a lesser evil. But he is extremely reluctant to recognize that sometimes it may also be a lesser evil in the area of public expression. In part this flows from a mistaken underestimate of the power of words to injure and incite to mob action, particularly in the present period. In part it seems to me the result of not stressing sufficiently that whenever the right of expression is properly limited, it is in behalf of other human rights, and not out of a fetishism of "law and order" as such. Like other ritualistic liberals, Professor Emerson fails to do justice to the position of realistic liberals like Justice Frankfurter, who do not share his absolutist prepossessions. When a community is threatened with the breakdown of law and order, we are told that "the remedy lies in using other means which will restore a basic consensus rather than in abandoning the system of free expression." But this is a false disjunction, and far from exhaustive. *Until* the consensus is established, what do we do? Specifically, what do we do about speech inciting to riot and violence? Suppose a consensus cannot be easily established? In such situations intelligence requires not "the abandonment of the system of free expression"—which no one proposes—but only its reasonable and temporary limitation. Despotism is not the only alternative to anarchy. Failure to appreciate this is one of the differentia of ritualistic liberalism as over against the realistic liberalism of Holmes, Brandeis, and Frankfurter. *

The invariable response to any legislative proposal or judicial decision that limits freedom of expression, even if there are good and sufficient reasons to believe that it will incite violence, is that such a limitation will have a chilling effect on legitimate expressions of opinion. Reasonable attempts to curb the public distribution of hard core pornography in the streets, it is sometimes argued, will have a chilling effect on the distribution of unpopular political and religious tracts. These are dogmatic a priori asseverations comparable to the objection against fluoridation on the ground that once we introduce even a minimal amount of a noneliminable poison like fluorides in our drinking water, we may end up by injecting massive doses of potassium cyanide into our reservoirs. A far better case can be made in such situations for the chilling effect of our failure to limit utterances that because they incite violence, in Justice Holmes's words, "may have all the effect of force," on other human rights and freedoms.

1966

---

* I have developed this position at length in the chapter "Absolutism and Human Rights" in my *Pragmatism and the Tragic Sense of Life* (New York: Basic Books, 1976).

Chapter 10

The Rights of
the Victims

One of the great paradoxes of our time is that as
the danger of major international wars recedes and the standard of
living rises, the level of domestic violence and crime increases at a
frightening rate. We need not rehearse the statistics that confirm the
observations and experiences of concerned and intelligent citizens
throughout the nation, especially of those who live in or visit our
chief metropolitan centers. We know that the situation is even worse
than the figures indicate because many crimes are not reported.

Accompanying this increase in violence and crimes of violence
has been an impressive, sympathetic concern—some have unfairly
called it a preoccupation—with the human and civil rights of criminals and of those accused of crime. Judicial opinions as well as academic treatises on criminology reveal a growing and thoughtful
sensitivity to the possibility that the procedures by which defendants in criminal cases are booked and tried, and the evidence
against them evaluated, may lead to the miscarriage of justice. Legal
practices that were once accepted without any qualms and doubts at
a time when the Bill of Rights was adopted to safeguard the basic
liberties of the people against possible tyranny of the state, practices
that endured far into the twentieth century, have been discarded in
recent years in consequence of new, ostensibly more enlightened
readings or interpretations of our constitutional rights.

There are those who maintain that the alarming increase in
crimes of violence is a direct consequence of the liberal modifica-

tions of our arrest and indictment procedures, of Supreme Court decisions that allegedly have shackled the law enforcement authorities and resulted in an ever larger number of recidivists or repeaters among criminal defendants. However, such an inference may be a case of *post hoc propter hoc.* Causal questions in human affairs are notoriously difficult to resolve because of the number of variables involved. Striking correlations are not always evidence of the causal connections. For the purposes of our analysis, it is not necessary either to reject or accept the view—asserted by some with great confidence—concerning the influence of court decisions on criminal behavior. We suspend judgment about the *causes* of the increase in crimes of violence. We take our point of departure only from the indisputable fact that the marked and alarming increase in domestic violence has occurred.

What I propose to do is to raise some fundamental questions about the basic ethical and jurisprudential issues involved. Why should we as citizens be concerned with the human and legal rights of persons accused of breaking the law? Why should we seek to liberalize the processes of law enforcement by raising protective hedges around such persons by making their conviction more difficult?

The answers summarize a library of literature. First, over and above any considerations of humanitarianism, we wish to avoid the danger of convicting the accused on the basis of plausible evidence, who in ultimate fact may be innocent. Second, even if we do not make the presumption of innocence, there is a good reason why we should want to defend and extend the rights of those accused of crime. For hard as it may be for us to imagine, someday we ourselves may be in the dock facing criminal charges of one kind or another. The quirks of fate or hazard of fortune or the hidden purpose of providence—call it what you will!—have caught up even the most straitlaced and proper individuals in tragic and violent situations, as bizarre as they were unexpected. And not all of them have been crimes of passion. There is a perennial and humbling wisdom in the Puritan's admonition to his son witnessing a wretch being dragged to the gallows, "There but for the Grace of God go I!" Both Goethe and Tolstoy have acknowledged that there is no crime in the calendar of human folly and bestiality which in some situations they could not conceive themselves committing. And if we pride ourselves on our own immunity from temptation, it may testify not so much to our incorruptibility, as to our lack of imaginative power.

This is the case for the rights of the criminal or the person accused of crime—and a powerful case it is. But before we bring in judgment we must perform an act of imaginative identification much simpler and more natural, and that is with ourselves as victims of crimes of violence. Granted that I am a potential criminal, I am also a potential victim of crime. The statistics of mounting violence show that cases of murder, nonnegligent manslaughter, and forcible rape have skyrocketed. It has been estimated that in large metropolitan centers, the risk of becoming the victim of a serious crime has more than doubled in the last decade. Since many crimes of violence are committed by repeaters, the likelihood of my becoming a victim of crime is much greater than the likelihood of my becoming a criminal. Therefore, the protection of my legitimate rights not to be mugged, assaulted, or murdered looms much larger in my mind than my legitimate rights as a criminal defendant.

Let us be clear about some things that have become obscure in virtue of our legitimate concern with the rights of criminals and those accused of crime. The potential victim has at least just as much a human right not to be violently molested, interfered with, and outraged as the person accused of such crimes has to a fair trial and a skillful defense. As a citizen, most of the rights guaranteed me under the Bill of Rights become nugatory if I am hopelessly crippled by violence, and all of them become extinguished if I am killed. The rights of victims are recognized in some legal jurisdictions which compensate them for disasters in which they become involved through no fault of their own. In England, it has been suggested that the assets of apprehended criminals who have committed capital crimes be distributed to the dependents of their victims. But my point here is that this emerging legal right of the victim is dependent upon the prior recognition of his moral right not to be victimized by the lawbreaker.

No matter how we seek to escape from acknowledging it, there is a direct conflict between the rights of the criminal and of persons accused of crime and the rights of their past and potential victims. In some classes of cases it is clear that the greater the right of the person accused of crime, the less the right of his future victim. For example, the right of a person out on bail for a crime of violence to receive bail when he is charged with committing the same type of violent offense, and to be granted bail even when he is charged with committing the offense a third time—a right which he legitimately claims since he has not yet been found guilty of the first offense— conflicts head on with the rights of his victims who can legitimately claim that they suffered this violence because the person at bar enjoyed his constitutional right to be free on bail. Those who fail to see this do not understand the nature of moral decision. They also fail to see that this conflict of rights is expressed in our very Bill of Rights in which the free exercise of religion conflicts with the principle of separation of state and church, and in which the right to a free press conflicts with the right to a fair trial. They therefore fail to understand the law-making powers of the Supreme Court, some of whose justices in the past deceived themselves with the absurd view that the rights of the Bill of Rights are absolute and cannot be abridged under any circumstances.

Why has this conflict between the rights of the potential criminals and the rights of the potential victims not been previously recognized? Among the reasons undoubtedly has been the fact that in all periods when the rights of criminals and those accused of crime were being recognized the incidence of violent crime was, relative to preceding periods, declining. Where crime was rife, the human rights of those accused of crime were hardly recognized or ruthlessly sacrificed on the altar of law and order. The recognition and appreciation of the human rights of criminals and those accused of crimes go back a long way, as the right of sanctuary in biblical times indicates. When crime became a mass phenomenon, however, these rights were honored more in the breach than in the observance.

Actually, although the protection of the rights in the Bill of Rights has been extended by the Court to state jurisdictions of criminal law, originally they were intended to curb primarily the violation of political rights by the federal government. The judicial legislation that reinterpreted and extended these guarantees to hold for criminal defendants in state courts was in large measure certainly justified because of changes in social needs and the development of more humane attitudes. But today, a humane concern for the increasing number of victims of violent crimes requires a reinterpretation, another emphasis. When we read that preventive detention at the discretion of the judge by denial of bail to repeated offenders charged with extremely violent crimes is denounced by some liberals as a betrayal of elementary justice, as smacking of the concentration camps of Hitler and Stalin; when we read that a person jailed for the death of twelve persons is freed from jail and the case against him dismissed because the prosecution's only evidence against him was a voluntary confession to the police who had failed to inform him of his rights; when we read that a man who murdered one of three hostages he had taken had a record of twenty-five arrests ranging from armed robbery to aggravated assault and battery and that at the time of his arrest was free on bail awaiting grand jury action on charges in five separate cases in a two-month period preceding the murder; when we read that a man whose speeding car had been stopped by a motorcycle policeman, who without a search warrant forced him to open his trunk that contained the corpses of a woman and two children, walks out of court scot-free because the evidence is ruled inadmissible*—we can only conclude that the law is an ass. The true wisdom of the law consists in recognizing the conflict of rights and adjudicating the conflict by a decision that strengthens the whole structure of rights in the community. At a time when crime is rife, if the proof of a grave crime like murder is incontestable on the basis of evidence that may be tainted because the law enforcement officers disregarded the niceties of procedure, then legal action should be taken against these officers by the state or the defendant rather than giving in effect a grant of immunity to a murderer.

How, then, should we resolve the conflict between the rights of the criminally accused and the rights of the potential victims? I submit that at the present juncture of events because our cities have become more dangerous to life and limb than the darkest jungle we must give priority to the rights of potential victims. I am prepared to weaken the guarantees and privileges to which I am entitled as a potential criminal or as a defendant in order to strengthen my rights and safeguards as a potential victim. Purely on the basis of probabilities, I am convinced that I run a greater danger of suffering disaster as a potential victim than as a potential criminal or defendant. It is these probabilities, that shift from one historical period to another, that must be the guide to wise, prudent, and just administration of the law.

Until 1961 evidence obtained in a criminal proceeding in the United States could be used and examined in state courts for their probative bearing on the guilt or innocence of the accused regardless of the circumstances under which it was obtained. The state of affairs was illustrated in a class of cases whose essential features are exemplified in the following incident. A robbery and murder had been committed by masked men who fled in an automobile with the loot, weapons, and other conclusive evidence of their guilt. The car was stopped by a traffic policeman for making a wrong turn. On the strength of a hunch he ordered the occupants out of the car at gunpoint, examined the trunk and floor of the vehicle, and found the incriminating evidence. The fact that the officer had violated the local search and seizure law would not bar the prosecuting authorities from introducing the evidence and bringing the criminals to justice. Since the case of *Mapp v. Ohio* this kind of evidence cannot be used in any criminal jurisdiction of the United States even if it means that the defendants would get off scot-free for the most dastardly of crimes.

---

* According to Judge Joseph Lodge of the Santa Barbara–Goleta Municipal Court the case occurred in the late 1960s in a California jurisdiction.

In 1966 in another five to four decision the U.S. Supreme Court in *Miranda v. Arizona* declared that regardless of the voluntary nature of any confession, it was not admissible as evidence unless the person arrested or in police custody was specifically advised, prior to any questioning, not only that he had a right to remain silent but in addition that he had the right to the presence of an attorney before answering any questions.

The justification of these two decisions is that they would have a deterrent effect on the behavior of law enforcement authorities tempted to take illegal shortcuts to procure evidence. Judging by the number of cases in which serious criminal charges have been made that have been thrown out of court or reversed on appeal on grounds of violation of *Mapp* and/or *Miranda*, there is no persuasive evidence that these decisions have achieved their purpose. What is indisputable is that the rights of the victims of those liberated by the Court's rulings as well as the future victims of any further criminal action by them have been completely disregarded. Not even the pretense of balancing the risks of injustice in such cases was made by the Court.

In England and other enlightened criminal jurisdictions, the violation of procedural requirements by members of the law enforcement agencies is punished not by violating the rights of the innocent victims, past and future, of the criminal action, but by punishment through demotion, fines, or dismissal, of those responsible for not properly exercising their professional tasks. But not in the United States where the Exclusionary Rule forbids the introduction of evidence "tainted" not because it is false or irrelevant or immaterial but because the arresting officer in the heat of the moment disregarded the niceties of the search and seizure regulations. Actually *Miranda* and other rulings that protect criminals and those accused of crime from the lawlessness of the police could remain on the books without resulting in injustices provided that the Exclusionary Rule is abolished.

We wish to reduce the role of violence in human affairs without sacrificing the principles of justice. The extension of the privileges against self-incrimination to absurd lengths by justices who abandoned common sense in a desire to establish a reputation for liberalism has no parallel in any other national legal jurisdiction. To elicit relevant testimony it has required legislation that has enabled some criminal defendants to purchase an undeserved immunity from punishment for very serious crimes. The statistics of violent crimes show that our situation is much too serious to indulge in sentimentalism at the expense of our fellow citizens. When crimes of violence are rare and infrequent we may justifiably lean over backward to protect those accused of serious crime from a possible miscarriage of justice. But it is not justice but only compassion that leads us to say that it is better that nine or ninety-nine guilty men escape punishment for their crime than that one innocent man be convicted. For that is certainly not doing justice either to the nine or ninety-nine guilty or to their potential victims. When crime is as rampant as it is today, those who invoke this dictum to justify strengthening the rights of individuals accused of violent crime at the expense of the rights of the potential victims of violent crimes are not even entitled to the self-righteous claim that they are moved by compassion. Compassion, if it is a virtue, must itself be balanced and equitable. Where, we ask, is their compassion for the myriad victims of violent crime? At what point, we ask, do the victims come into the ethical reckoning?

There are no easy answers. What I am proposing is a reconsideration of some of our basic jurisprudential assumptions in this age of growing violent crime. In times of crises we suspend certain traditional guarantees. We can avoid such crises and the panic response to them by reflective action—measured, firm, and humane. This requires a rethinking of our first principles in the ethics of law and punishment, a more pragmatic consideration of the historical context, and a greater awareness of social needs.

Liberalism in social life may be defined as devotion to human freedom pursued and tested by the arts of intelligence. But not all who call themselves liberal understand either themselves or the doctrines they profess. In other contexts, I have referred to "ritualistic liberals" as those who think they can be liberal without being intelligent. A particularly conspicuous species of the genus of ritualistic liberal is found among those writers on crime and law enforcement for whom the victims of crime are only incidental rather than central to the problem of crime prevention. Such writers in their mournful assessment of tragic encounters between lawbreakers and law officers tend to equate with a fine moral impartiality those who are slain while attempting or committing murder with those who lose their life preventing it. Both kinds of fatality are deplored but, strangely enough, as if there were no moral distinction between them.

A similar absurd equation is being drawn today by those who proclaim that "the *fear* of crime is almost as serious a problem as the crime problem itself"—the implication being that the fear of crime is almost as great a threat to society as crime. Such a judgment is as bizarre as it is irresponsible. Where crime exists, especially violent crime of unusual magnitude, fear of crime is natural and reasonable, and not a form of hysteria or paranoia. Only in the absence of genuine persecution can a person be called a victim of a persecution complex. Only in the absence of widespread crime is the fear of crime a likely sign of hysteria.

In a dangerous world, the human race might not survive unless there were intelligent fear. That is why, for example, intelligent fear of nuclear warfare, of large-scale global pollution, and of the grim effects of the population explosion is justified. Only a sociological mad-hatter would say that the fear of a nuclear holocaust is almost as serious a problem as the threat of one, or the fear of the population explosion as dangerous as the pressure of unrestricted growth.

Let us have done with extremists who would mindlessly substitute either toughness or permissiveness for intelligence in their simplistic response to the mounting crime wave. A fruitful way to begin the quest for intelligent solutions is to reorient our thinking in the current period to the rights of the potential victims of crime, and to the task of reducing their number and suffering. In this way we can best serve the interests both of justice and compassion.

1971

Chapter 11
Reverse Discrimination

The phrase *reverse discrimination* has come into recent English usage in consequence of efforts to eliminate the unjust discrimination against human beings on the basis of race, color, sex, religion, or national origin. The conscience of the American community has caught up with the immoral practices of its past history. The Civil Rights Act of 1964 and the presidential executive orders which it inspired have made the absence of open or hidden discrimination of the kind described a required condition of government contracts. An equal opportunity employer is one who pledges himself to a program of affirmative action in order to insure that the invidious discriminations of the past are not perpetuated in masked or subtle form.

An appropriate affirmative action program requires that an intensive and extensive recruitment search be undertaken in good faith, sometimes supplemented by remedial educational measures, in order to equalize opportunities for employment or study. Such programs presuppose that once the recruitment search is over, once the remedial training is completed, the actual selection of the candidates for the post will be determined by one set of equitable standards applied to all. If the standards or tests are not equitable, if they are not related to or relevant to the actual posts that are to be filled, then the standards or tests must be modified until they are deemed satisfactory. In no case must a double standard be employed which enables one group to benefit at the expense of any other. Customarily this adhesion to one set of standards designed to test merit or to determine who of all contending candidates is the best qualified for the post has been known as the civil service principle. It is the only way by which incompetence, corruption, and invidious discrimination can be eliminated. Preferential hiring on the basis of sex, race, color, religion, or national origin clearly violates the civil service principle and the programs of affirmative action that seek to enlarge the areas of equal opportunity.

Why, then, is the demand made for reverse discrimination under various semantic disguises? If all invidious or unfair discrimination is wrong, how can reverse discrimination be justified? The answer sometimes made is that reverse discrimination is not unfair, for it seeks to undo the injustice of the past and the effects of that injustice in the present, by compensating the victims of past injustice at the expense of those responsible for their plight. Were this the case with respect to any particular individual who has suffered from discriminatory practice there would be no moral objection to compensating him or her for the loss and depriving or punishing those responsible for the past act of discrimination. This would be a simple matter of justice, redressing the grievance of the past, and in no sense an act of discrimination—direct or reverse.

It is an altogether different situation, however, when we discriminate against members of any group today in favor of members of another group, not because the individuals of the first group have been guilty of past or present oppression or discrimination against members of the second group, but because the ancestors of the latter have been victimized in previous times. Yet this is precisely what is being done today when preferential hiring practices on the basis of race or sex are followed or when numerical goals or quotas are used as guidelines instead of criteria of merit or qualification.

All such practices which stem from the distortions or misreading of the Civil Rights Act of 1964 and the presidential executive orders are attempts to undo the injustices of the past against members of minority groups and women by perpetrating injustices against members of nonminority groups and men in the present. Can such practices be defended on moral grounds? Let us consider a few historic cases to get our moral bearings:

It is commonly acknowledged that the Chinese laborers who were employed during the last century in building the transcontinental railroad were abominably treated, underpaid, overworked, wretchedly housed, and subjected to all sorts of humiliating discriminations. Is anyone prepared to argue that their descendants today or other Chinese should therefore be paid more than non-Chinese or given preference over non-Chinese with respect to employment regardless of merit or specific qualifications?

Until the Nineteenth Amendment of the U.S. Constitution was

adopted in 1920, American women, who were citizens of the country and subject to all its laws, were denied the right to vote. Would it be reasonable to contend that women should have been compensated for past discrimination against their maternal forebears by being given an extra vote or two at the expense of their male fellow citizens? Would it have been just to deprive the male descendants of prejudiced white men of the past of their vote in order to even the score?

Take a more relevant case. For many years blacks were shamelessly and unfairly barred from professional sports until Jackie Robinson broke the color bar. Would it not be manifestly absurd to urge therefore today that in compensation for the long history of deprivation of blacks there should be discrimination against whites in professional athletics? Would any sensible or fair person try to determine what the proportion of whites and blacks should be on our basketball or football or baseball teams in relation to racial availability or utilizability? What could be fairer than the quest for the best players for the open positions regardless of the percentage distribution in relation to the general population or the pool of candidates trying out? What would be the relevance of numerical goals or quotas here? Why should it be any different in any situation in which we are looking for the best qualified person to fill a post? If we oppose, as we should, all invidious discrimination, why not drop all color, sex, religious, and national bars in an honest quest for the best qualified—regardless of what the numerical distribution turns out to be. Of course, the quest must be public and not only be fair but must be seen to be fair.

Whenever we judge a person primarily on the basis of membership in a group, except where membership in a group bears on the task to be performed (soprano voices, wet nurses, clergymen of the same denomination), an injustice is done to individuals. This is the point of my final illustration. When I graduated from the City College of New York in the early twenties, many of my classmates who had taken the premedical course applied to American medical schools. Most of them were rejected because at the time a thinly disguised quota system existed limiting the number of Jewish applicants. This was a great blow to those affected. A few went abroad. Some entered the Post Office system and prepared for other vocations. Now consider the position of their grandchildren who apply to medical schools that have admission practices based on numerical goals or quotas designed to counteract the discriminatory practices of the past against women and minorities. These candidates do not request preferential treatment but only that they be evaluated by equitable standards applicable to all. Is it fair to them to select those who are less qualified under professionally relevant standards? Can they or their forebears be taxed with responsibility for the unjust discriminatory practices of the past which victimized them as well as others? And cannot students of Italian, Polish, Slovak, Armenian, Irish, and Ukrainian origin ask the same questions?

There are certain questionable assumptions in the rationale behind the practices of reverse discrimination. The first is that preferential hiring (or promotion) on the basis of race or sex to correct past bias is like school desegregation rulings to correct the admittedly immoral segregation practices of the past. This overlooks the key difference. In correcting the immorality of past segregation we are not discriminating *against* white students. They are not being injured or deprived of anything by the color of their classmates' skin. All students may profit in virtue of desegregation. But the situation with respect to the allocation of jobs is different. If X and Y are competing for a post, my decision to hire X is in the nature of the case a decision not to hire Y. And if my decision is based on X's sex or race, and not on merit, then it is a case of racial or sexual discrimination *against* Y, which is morally wrong. All invidious discrimination *in favor* of anyone is invidious discrimination *against* someone else.

A second assumption is that one can tell by statistical distribution alone whether objectionable discrimination exists that calls for corrective action. This is absurd on its face. Unless there is specific evidence of individual discrimination, at most only a suspicion of discrimination can be drawn warranting further inquiry. Only when we are dealing with random selection where no criteria of merit are involved, as in jury rolls or in registration procedures or voting behavior, are statistical disproportions at variance with population distribution prima facie evidence of bias in the process of selection. My favorite example of nondiscriminatory statistical disproportion is that in the past the overwhelming majority of the captains of the tug boats in New York Harbor were of Swedish origin but this constituted no evidence of the presence of anti-Semitism or prejudice against blacks. The disproportion of black teachers in black college faculties is certainly not evidence of a policy of discrimination against whites.

A third related assumption is a particularly mischievous one. It holds that where there is no overt or covert discrimination, and equal opportunities are offered, the various minorities within the community will be represented in all disciplines, professions, and areas of work in roughly numerical proportionality to their distribution in the total pool of the population or in the community pool or in the pool of the potentially utilizable. There is not a shred of evidence for this assumption. Human beings do not constitute a homogenized mass in which interest, ambitions, historical and social traditions are equally shared. Potentially all groups may be capable of acquiring or developing any cultural interest just as at birth any normal child is equipped with the capacity to speak any language. But in actual practice family, national, regional traditions, and allegiances as well as the accidents of history incline some groups toward some occupational activities rather than others even where there are no legal obstacles to the pursuit of any. For historical reasons, Polish immigrants and their descendants did not go into sheepherding or fishing while Basques and Portuguese did. Whenever anyone maintains, in the absence of discriminatory practices, that minority persons or women are "underrepresented" or "underutilized," the assumption is unconsciously being made that there is a "natural" or "proper" or "correct" norm or level of their representation. Who determines what is the "natural" representation of women among fire fighters, of Irish among policemen and politicians, of Italians among opera singers, of blacks among actors, of Jews among pants pressers, diamond cutters, and mathematical physicists? In time there will undoubtedly be *some* representation from all groups in all fields but only political absolutisms will impose fixed quotas.

A fourth assumption is that with respect to minorities and women, even if all present forms of discrimination against them were completely eliminated, this would still not enable them to compete on an equal basis with others because of the continuing debilitating effects of past generations of discrimination against them. It is sometimes said in emphasizing this point, "If you handicap a runner at the outset by burdening him with heavy weights and let him run half the race, you cannot make it a fair race by removing the weights when the race has been half run. He will still suffer unfairly from the effects of that handicap." This is perfectly true for that individual runner in that race and possibly in other races he engages in. He is certainly entitled to special consideration to overcome his handicap on the same principle that any specific individual who has been discriminated against in the past is entitled to compensatory treatment. But surely this does not entitle a descendant of this person who is running against others in a subsequent race to a privilege or handicap over them. Who knows but that the ancestors of the others were also handicapped in past races?

This entire analogy breaks down because it really assumes the inheritance of acquired characteristics. Women in Elizabethan times were barred from acting in the theatre and from certain industrial pursuits in the nineteenth century. Did this have a continuing debilitating effect upon their capacities in the twentieth century? If past discrimination has a continuing debilitating effect, how can we explain the tens of thousands of cases of members of minorities who have made good in their professions and vocations without benefit of preferential treatment or reverse discrimination?

Another conscience-appeasing justification for the manifestly immoral violations of the principle of equal treatment under just law is the claim that measures adopted to implement reverse discrimination are "merely temporary" or "transitional," until such time as the necessity for it disappears, and race and sex can be disregarded in hiring and promotion practices. This is the position among others of the American Civil Liberties Union. It is obviously question-begging. When will the necessity for reverse discrimination disappear? When all minorities and women are represented in all avenues of work in proportion to their numbers in the population? The American Civil Liberties Union would be outraged at the proposal "to suspend temporarily" a person's right to a fair trial until the crime wave subsides. Why should any morally principled clear-headed opponent of all forms of discrimination temporarily suspend the protection of equal rights under the law?

We know from other situations that nothing is so permanent as the temporary, especially when vested interest develops in its perpetuation. Once numerical goals or quotas are introduced as "temporary expedients" to overcome the alleged discriminations of the past, psychologically any subsequent effort to abandon or even to modify the goals or quotas is likely to be interpreted as a rebirth of invidious discrimination. On the other hand, the mandatory application of goals or quotas in the hiring and promotion of members of minorities and women is certain to generate resentment among members of non-minorities and men who will regard racial and sexual criteria of appointment as arbitrary, motivated by political considerations for which they pay the costs. They will visit this resentment even on those minority persons and women who have obtained advancement purely on the basis of their own merit. The collegiality among workers will be shattered, and existing racial and sexual antagonisms that may abate in time when fair standards of merit are strictly enforced will instead be intensified.

Another dubious assumption is that once careers are truly opened to talents members of minorities and women will never make it on their own without the crutch of reverse discrimination in their favor. This either gratuitously takes for granted that the practices of invidious discrimination of the past will continue, despite the laws against them, or it is an expression of racism and sexism. The absence of members of minorities and women in many areas today is not a consequence of their failure to perform satisfactorily in them but to social attitudes, stereotyped expectations of what roles men and women are fit for, which happily are now changing, but which in the past discouraged them from trying out. There is no cogent reason to doubt that just as members of ethnic immigrant groups who suffered from the prejudiced judgments of native Americans have overcome the obstacles thrown up in their path, so the blacks and Chicanos will in time also succeed. The main reason why today larger numbers of these minorities are not found in the professions and specialized academic pursuits is not invidious discrimination against them but rather the absence of qualified applicants in consequence of educational and economic disadvantages. Here is where vigorous remedial action must be undertaken not only by public agencies but by private organizations along the lines of the Reverend Jesse Jackson's "Push Towards Excellence."

Special educational measures must be adopted to improve the quality of schooling on the elementary and secondary school levels and to encourage career choices oriented toward professional and academic life. It cannot be too strongly emphasized that despite the social disadvantages from which minority groups suffer, and which the community as a whole has the responsibility to mitigate and ultimately remove, the minorities themselves are not merely passive recipients of what befalls them, helpless wards of the state whose future is shaped by what others decide for them. They can do, and often have done, much to reshape the educational opportunities, to rekindle the pride and strengthen the drive to succeed in a world that requires more skills and more knowledge, and more schooling to acquire them, than in the past. Studies of the adjustments of immigrant groups to the hardships and environmental deprivation they initially encountered have shown that the family atmosphere, the presence or absence of strong parental guidance, has been more decisive in determining the willingness to avail oneself of educational opportunities than the legislative action itself that prolonged the age of mandatory schooling.

Our educational system must be geared not only to meet the educational needs of the superior students but of ordinary students and even of those who are not scholastically gifted. A vast range of talents is found among all peoples and races. The focus must be on each individual student, regardless of sex or color, in order to determine what his or her educational needs are. Provision must be made therefore for various types of educational institutions, beyond the elementary and secondary level, for students of varying capacities and interests, and for continuing adult education in both the liberal and vocational arts to accommodate both personal development and social change. There is a uniqueness about every student which the spirit and practice of a democratic education must respect. This respect is perfectly compatible with the application of a single and relevant standard of achievement or reward for all in any given institution, according to which some pass and some fail. We may and should guarantee the basic needs of food, shelter, health and education of all citizens but we cannot guarantee anyone against educational failure. Further, everyone in a democratic welfare society such as ours has a right to employment (or to some kind of unemployment insurance) but no one regardless of merit and experience can claim a right to any specific job.

It is apparent that this analysis is based on the belief that it is the individual person who is the carrier of human rights and not the ethnic, national, sexual, or racial group. Once we disregard this universalistic approach which is blind to color, deaf to religious dogma, indifferent to national origin or sex where merit should count, we practically insure the presence of endemic conflicts in which invidious discriminations are rife. This has been the sad story of the past which we are or should be trying to get away from. Some progress has been made and much more is possible. Reverse discrimination, however, threatens that progress. It increases the existing tensions among different groups and converts our pluralistic society into a more polarized society. The evidence that this is already happening is at hand whenever the admirable, original purposes of affirmative action programs have been misconstrued by arbitrary bureaucratic fiat, and guidelines promulgated that mandate numerical goals or quotas.

Successive polls have shown that the overwhelming majority of the population have endorsed equality of opportunity but at the same time have strongly disapproved of numerical goals, quotas, or preferential hiring. A majority may be wrong but with respect to the theory and practice of reverse discrimination, the logic and ethics of the argument support the condemnation. The reasons that lead us morally to disapprove of discrimination in the past are the same as those that justify disapproval of reverse discrimination in the present and future.

1978

SINCE THE FOREGOING was written, the United States Supreme Court has rendered a decision in the case of *Regents of the University of California v. Bakke.* Allan Bakke was an applicant for admission to the Medical School of the Davis campus of the University of California who was rejected despite the fact that his qualifications were higher than those of students admitted under a program which reserved sixteen places out of a hundred for members of minority groups. There had been no history of discrimination against minority students at Davis. Bakke brought a legal action against the University of California and his suit was upheld by the Supreme Court of the State of California which ordered that Bakke be admitted to the Medical School at Davis and that the university be barred from according any consideration to race in assessing the eligibility of candidates for admission to any of its educational programs. The University of California appealed the case to the United States Supreme Court which granted certiorari. The intensity of the public interest generated by the case may be gauged by the fact that the number of *amicus curiae* briefs filed in connection with it was the greatest in the history of the Court.

A careful reading of the opinions of the Supreme Court's judgment in the Allan Bakke case will bring little comfort to those who believe that in a genuinely democratic society there should be no invidious discrimination on grounds of race, color, religion, sex, or national origin. In effect, despite the relief awarded to Allan Bakke as an individual, the Court has nullified the key provision of the 1964 Civil Rights Act which specified that, "No person in the United States shall, on the ground of race, color, or national origin be excluded from participation in, be denied the benefits of, or be subjected to discrimination under any program or activity receiving Federal financial assistance."

That four justices found the clearly designed quota system of admissions at the University of California's Davis Medical School compatible with this provision as well as with the equal-protection clause of the Fourteenth Amendment is disquieting enough. That four other justices in refusing to assess the constitutional issue also refuse to bar the consideration and use of racial criteria in admissions policy, despite the plain language of the statute and its legislative history, indicates that they are not really opposed to educational institutions doing in other ways what they have disapproved of in the case of Davis. Finally, in Justice Lewis F. Powell, Jr.'s, opinion which announced the judgment of the Court, we have an explicit reversal of the action of the Supreme Court of the State of California that enjoined the university from according any consideration to race in admissions.

No wonder Secretary Joseph Califano, Jr., has hailed the Supreme Court's decision as a complete vindication for the position of the Department of Health, Education, and Welfare, not only with respect to admissions but also with respect to its imposition of numerical goals and time schedules in the hiring practices of universities and other institutions.

The fundamental principle animating the judgment of the Court is expressed in a statement in Justice Harry A. Blackmun's opinion. "In order to get beyond racism, we must first take account of race." This has been echoed in the *New York Times* editorial endorsing the Court's overall judgment. It apparently underlies, among other considerations, Justice Powell's view that the race of a candidate may be considered in the admissions process.

The ambiguity of the statement, "In order to get beyond racism, we must first take account of race," is glaringly obvious. In one sense it is a simple truism—in order to get beyond racism, we must take note of its *existence* or *presence*. No one can dispute this. In order to get beyond any evil—and racism *is* an evil—we must recognize the evil. In order to get beyond anti-Semitism, we must also take note of anti-Semitism. Otherwise, how could we get beyond it?

But in another sense, the statement, "In order to get beyond racism, we must first take account of race," is an absurdity. In this sense it means that in order to get beyond racism, we must practice it, that in order not to discriminate against race, we must discriminate in favor of it. This, as I read it, is actually the position of the Court disguised under the pretext that race is being used as an *educational* criterion. If it is true that, in order to get beyond racism, we must practice a little racism, then it is tantamount to saying that to get beyond lawlessness we must be a little lawless, that to uphold freedom we must begin by violating freedom. It is instructive here to note that the *New York Times*, which approved Justice Blackmun's dictum, severely criticized President Nixon and his confederates for acting on it in their attempt to uphold the law.

Justice Powell's opinion represents a defeat for clear thinking and consistent, principled practice. It confuses the fact that in order to achieve one value or good, we must sacrifice another value or good, with a position that insists that in pursuit of a good or value no other value can be sacrificed. It makes sense to say that, in the interests of security or safety, we must go beyond justice or fairness. But it makes no sense to say that in the interests of justice, we must go beyond justice. It would have been perfectly comprehensible and perhaps legitimate had the Court maintained that we must become racist in order to achieve some highly desirable state interest that could not be attained in any other way. But the Court does not succeed in showing this.

What in effect it did in ruling that race could be used as a criterion for selection is to assert that in order to improve the quality of undergraduate education it was necessary to violate Title VI of the Civil Rights Act of 1964 as well as the constitutional provisions for equal treatment under the laws.

Justice Powell asserts that the First Amendment guarantees the right to academic freedom. The universities must therefore have a right to select students in such a way as to improve the quality of education. Whatever "contributes to a robust exchange of ideas" improves the quality of education. Such an exchange is furthered by "educational diversity," and selection on the basis of race is one means of reaching educational diversity. This mode of selection characterizes the Harvard Plan of admission, in which race is one factor that may therefore be considered legitimately in determining who is to be enrolled. Justice Powell concludes therefore that on the basis of the First Amendment there is a compelling state interest in furthering educational diversity that overrides constitutional and statutory bans against racial discrimination.

The argument is dubious in every particular, but, before taking it apart, it should be noted that this approach would also justify taking religion into account. Indeed, *any* factor could be taken into account as relevant to the creation of greater educational diversity. A few years ago Harvard made the accidental fact of geographical locus a relevant matter for educational consideration, and today racial membership can count, too. "A farm boy from Idaho can bring something to Harvard College that a Bostonian cannot offer. Similarly, a black student can usually bring something that a white person cannot offer." But the same can be said of a redhead, a poker player, a runaway, Siamese twins—anyone imaginable can bring something of value to the educational process.

What does educational diversity mean in this context? And what is the evidence that it contributes to a superior *educational* experience? No one can reasonably contend that diversity among students *as such* is educationally desirable, since that would justify lumping the unqualified and qualified together and students of different tongues who are unable even to communicate with each other.

There is not a particle of evidence that the wider geographical distribution of students admitted to Harvard *after* 1922 has contributed to a richer educational experience than existed before. It is an open secret that the geographical categories were introduced at Harvard primarily to prevent an influx of Jewish students from the Eastern seaboard whose academic qualifications surpassed all others. Those in a position to know contend that when the ethnic composition of students at the City College of New York was 90 percent Jewish, the intellectual life of the academic community was far more stimulating than when the composition radically changed. If diversity of ideas, opinions, and outlook is essential to educational diversity, this is not to be wondered at, since, according to some observers, whenever there are two Jewish students present, we find three opinions expressed. The contention that the geographical criterion was introduced to enrich the educational experience, is a hollow rationalization. It was introduced primarily to keep down the number of Jewish students at Harvard.

The notion that the right to academic freedom, like freedom of speech and press, is entailed by the First Amendment is preposterous, for the simple reason that everyone enjoys the First Amendment rights as a member of the political community. They are part of our democratic birthright. They do not have to be earned, whereas the right to academic freedom must be earned. Academic freedom is the right of the *professionally qualified* teachers or researchers to investigate, publish, and teach the truth as they see it in the field of their competence. The First Amendment guarantees anyone's freedom to speak, not anyone's freedom to teach.

The Court buys, without any critical reflection, the Harvard rationalization of that university's use of competitive consideration of race, ethnic origin, and geographical distribution in admissions. It assumes that any experience is itself an educational experience or contributes to one. But some experiences for all their diversity may be miseducational. To the extent that an experience is genuinely educational, it is the *character* of that experience, not the color or ethnic origin of the person undergoing that experience, which is relevant to the educational process. That a student has been a *victim* of political, economic, or religious persecution may be educationally relevant, and not whether he is an American or black or Jew or Slovak.

If educational diversity on an undergraduate level means varied representation of racial, religious, or national groups, it is hard to see how the same kind of diversity contributes to excellence of educational achievement on the graduate or professional level. Justice Powell reaches into the air for a plausible ground and asserts that, since "physicians serve a heterogeneous population," the more heterogeneous the student body the more likely it is that students will be better trained physicians. This is truly homeopathic education! There is no evidence whatsoever that the improvement in medical education and practice in recent years has anything to do with the ethnic or religious composition of the medical student body. Growth in medical knowledge and skills, as well as professional dedication and concern for patients, are more the results of improvement in teaching than of manipulation in admissions.

Finally, if in contravention of the Civil Rights Act of 1964, race is to be a legitimate criterion for purposes of admission, why should it not in time become a legitimate criterion for purposes of grading and, subsequently, for graduation, too? Many of the considerations adduced against a color-blind policy for admissions, can be brought to bear against a color-blind policy for grading (we have already heard that tests are culturally biased), and against a color-blind policy in graduation (how else remedy the chronic neglect of the health needs of racial ghettos?).

In no field of American life was deplorable racial prejudice so widespread as in organized sport. After Jackie Robinson broke the color bar, merit and merit alone became the criterion for the selection of members of our football, basketball, and baseball teams. Who cares what the racial composition of those teams should be? Who speaks of quotas and numerical goals here, or of the continuing effects of past discrimination? Why should the situation be any different in any other field? The absence of minorities in considerable numbers in our professional schools today is not due to any lack of inherent capacity, but to educational deprivation on elementary and secondary levels, a deprivation largely reflecting economic conditions. Through remedial education programs and economic aid these historical handicaps can be overcome. Affirmative action programs in the original sense envisaged by the presidential executive orders implementing the Civil Rights Act of 1964 do not call for preferential hiring or selection. They can be administered with the understanding that a single equitable criterion of merit will be applied to all.

More important than the constitutionality of any provision is its wisdom or lack of it. The meaning of the Constitution is what a shifting majority of justices declares it to be. But what is wise or foolish is independent of the opinions of the Court. And it is demonstrably foolish to hold that, in order to get beyond racism, we must begin by practicing it.

1978

Part Three:
Heroes and Anti-Heroes

Chapter 12

The Hero in History:

Myth, Power, or Moral Ideal?

The role of personality in history is a theme of perennial interest. It concerns not only scholars but every man and every woman who reflects on the fate of their culture and their place in it. Is our social destiny shaped by forces beyond our power to mold them closer to our heart's desire? Or can we master the future by collective effort under the outstanding leadership of heroic men and women? To these questions easy answers are often made. On the one hand are those who invoke a kind of social astrology. They plot the future of humanity not by reference to the heavenly constellations but by extrapolating graphs of quantitative indices of the resources and powers of production in which no individual human being has a distinctive role. On the other hand are those who subscribe to the heroic mythology of the leader—call him what you will—king or president, prophet or seer, statesman or philosopher. This mythology always renews itself in times of trouble. It proclaims truly enough that human beings make their own history, not abstract historical forces; it then adds that without the leadership of great personalities mankind cannot find its way out of the wilderness of contingent events. Like most easy answers, both views are oversimple without being completely false.

The myth of the hero as the savior of the tribe or nation is older than written history. Until about two hundred years ago, the hero functioned not merely as a myth or cult, but as a principle of historical explanation. His presence or absence, according to most historians, was the key to the rise and fall of countries and even cultures. It was Thomas Carlyle who summarized and popularized the notion of history as the biography of great men. (Carlyle was too hostile to women to acknowledge their historical role.) The confusions and exaggerations in Carlyle's views produced a strong reaction against them and coincided with the emergence of historical determinisms in which physical, social, and economic forces replaced individuals as the dynamic factors in the development of events.

The consequence of this conjunction has been the eclipse of the hero as the dominant historical cause of human weal or woe among scientific and reflective historians. But to the ordinary man and woman trying to understand the world, it is precisely those individuals who currently make policies or fail to make them who are responsible for the condition of the world. In our own country, for example, it is the failure of national policies to cope with our multiple problems, hard on the revelations of Watergate, that has generated the antiheroic mood of our time. This antiheroic mood is reflected in the wholesale skepticism of the voting public, in their assessment of our leadership, whether presidential or congressional, and in the emergence of a widespread cynicism among youth.

From the Carlylean point of view, there is a certain irony in the fact that our pervasive antiheroic mood has resulted from the failures of our political leadership. According to Carlyle, the hero may appear in many forms—king, prophet, priest, even poet—but since his mission is to exhibit "what of divinity is in man or nature," he can never appear in the guise of a politician. But here too Carlyle was mistaken. For every hero in history, whatever his guise, whether prophet or king, has functioned in some measure as politician or statesman. Carlyle never explained why, if there is a divine principle in man, the politician or statesman cannot be touched by its presence.

When we speak of "the antiheroic mood" of our time or "the demythologizing of the hero," the expression conceals an ambiguity. It may mean that we still believe in heroes and their important role in history, but lament their absence in our time and our place. This is presupposed when we ask where have all the heroes gone, and is implied in the answer some offer, that they have been slain by our mediocrity. It indicates a belief not only in the possibility of heroic action but in its desirability. In situations of crisis, there are very few who do not put their faith or hope in the emergence of a strong or wise leader to point the way.

There is another meaning sometimes conveyed by the term *antiheroic*. This denies that, except as models for personal conduct, there are any heroes in history. It holds that in the long perspective, it matters little who stands at the head of a country or who leads a movement. The upshot of historical development, it is claimed, does not depend upon the presence or absence of any specific man or woman. The world of today and tomorrow is the result of the growth of cities, the agricultural revolution, the industrial revolution, and the technological revolution in which no one individual, whatever his gifts, played an indispensable role. Who can believe, asks one economic historian, if Henry Ford and his confreres had not lived that our highways would be substantially less crowded today? According to this view, which I venture to say is one held by most contemporary professional historians who pride themselves on their scientific objectivity, no one man or woman is responsible for any great turning point in history, whether it was the survival of free institutions in the struggle against Asiatic despotism two and a half millennia ago, the discovery of America, the American Revolution, the French Revolution, or the Russian Revolution. Just as America would have been discovered even if Columbus's ships had foundered, so these other momentous events would have occurred, perhaps a little earlier or a little later, regardless of the personalities involved. Man proposes but something else disposes—not God as once was believed—but geography, race, tradition, the mode of production, the imperatives of technology, the compulsions of ideology, or a complex mixture of them, depending on the historian's philosophy of history. All members of this school of thought agree that when man proposes anything of historical importance, it is not man who disposes.

Finally, there is a third view of the hero which recognizes that personality is a relatively independent force in history, that great men and women have played and may still play a significant redetermining role at crucial moments in human affairs. But this view regards them as a danger in a self-governing democratic community, as aliens to any system in which the major policy decisions should rest ultimately upon the freely given consent of the governed who enjoy equal rights of citizenship. This view acknowledges the presence of movers and shakers of the world, but points out that they appeared on the stage of history mainly in the days of political absolutism. A genuinely democratic community rightfully views the hero with suspicion and is notoriously ungrateful. The mob that hails the man on horseback, the Caesars and conquering heroes, does not retain its freedoms for long. "If a Moses can lead you out of the wilderness," Eugene Debs, the great American socialist, once observed at a mass meeting, "another Moses can lead you right back again!"

There are many other usages of the term *hero*, which we may safely disregard for present purposes, for example, the protagonist of a play or novel, the man or woman of distinctive achievements or outstanding courage, or someone who is greatly admired for any reason or glorified by a public relations campaign.

Our task is not so much to discover *who* are the heroes today to whom we should pay homage, but to clarify our minds as to what we should understand by the concept of "the hero and the heroic" in a democratic society. Once we understand what we mean by "heroes," we can then ask, should we seek them? And if we should, where shall we find them?

The beginning of wisdom in any acceptable analysis of our theme is to distinguish between the historically great man (or woman) and the hero (or heroine). The distinction is fundamentally a moral one. Not all great men in history are heroes and not all heroes are historically great men or women. In popular usage it appears almost a contradiction in terms to characterize the hero as wicked or cruel or contemptible. Yet it seems demonstrable that many, if not most, great figures in history from Alexander to Napoleon, from Julius Caesar to Bismarck, from Pericles to Churchill and Roosevelt, from Constantine to Stalin and Hitler, have been judged by some historian, some defeated opponent, or some spokesman for their innocent victims as morally monstrous creatures. But such moral judgments, whether positive or negative, did not affect their historical impact. The ancient Chinese had a saying, "A great man is a public misfortune," which is reaffirmed in Lord Acton's famous observation, "Great men are almost always bad men." The validity of the judgment of their greatness, of their historical influence, of their profound impact on the lives of their fellow men is not affected in the least by the evil they have done. Indeed, if they had had less power, less influence, less historical impact, this might have mitigated their evil in the eyes of those crushed by the chariot wheels of their historical triumphs.

On the other hand, many of the men and women whom we venerate as heroes are not great historical figures. We may admire them for the risks taken beyond the call of duty, their quiet sacrifice, their fortitude in adversity, their refusal to compromise with corruption, or their independence of vision and judgment. I am thinking of the John Peter Altgelds and the Jane Addamses of a generation before my time, of the young Charles Lindberghs and Margaret Sangers of our own time, of the American prisoners of war in Korea and North Vietnam who defied their brutal torturers and returned with unbroken spirit and, noblest of all, of the medical missionaries of the world who have devoted their lives, at the risk and sometimes the cost of their own, to minister in foreign, often hostile, cultures, to the victims of plagues, to the lepers, and to the terminal cases of highly contagious diseases who have been shunned and cast out by their own communities and kinsmen.

Not to believe in heroism of this kind, even when it is streaked with some human frailty, like not believing in love, is a sign of great dullness or obtuseness. But these heroic men and women are not necessarily—indeed they are very rarely—great historical figures. They play no role in the wars, revolutions, and fateful legislative actions that constitute so much of the historical record. They are, and should be, models of personal ethical conduct. But will we find them in the seats of the mighty? It is not likely. Since "history is not a web woven with innocent hands," the weight of considered scholarly judgment in history seems inclined to strong doubt that the exercise of power in a world of evil men and wicked designs can ever be guided by the same moral principles that obtain in the face-to-face relationships of upright men and women.

In a previous chapter I have given some reasons to contest the validity of this moral dualism. It would indeed be scoundrelly to do for oneself what one must sometimes do for one's country, not because the two realms, the private and public, are governed by different moral principles but because the intentions and consequences of the actions in the two realms are different. We judge the intentions and consequences in both spheres by the same moral principles. As a soldier I may have to kill in fulfillment of my duty. If I acted in the same way to settle a personal grievance, it could be properly construed as a heinous moral offense, murder. But this would not establish the existence of two different sets of moral principles.

In politics this moral standpoint sometimes takes the form of the ethics of the lesser evil when all possible choices have evil consequences, including the refusal to choose. To some, the decision taken by President Kennedy during the Cuban missile crisis gave him heroic status because he was prepared to risk war in defense of our relatively free society. But during those crucial days, Bertrand Russell denounced him as "the most wicked man in history," worse than Hitler and Stalin, for taking that risk. And this despite the fact that Bertrand Russell himself had previously urged that atomic war be unleashed against the Soviet Union, when the United States enjoyed a monopoly of atomic weapons, if the Kremlin refused to accept the Baruch-Lilienthal proposals to internationalize all sources of atomic power.

Regardless of how we morally evaluate President Kennedy's decision, it was of great historical significance. What is the nature of that significance? Leaving aside for the moment the moral judgments, whether absolute or relative, by which we assess the great historical figures of the past and present, whether we esteem them as heroes or despise them as villains, what makes them "great"? I have sought to answer this question at greater length and detail in my *The Hero in History: A Study in Limitation and Possibility,* and I present it here in brief. The great men or women in history are those of whom we can say on the basis of the available evidence that if they had not lived when they did, or acted *as* they did, the history of their countries, and of the world, to the extent that they are intertwined, would have been profoundly different. Their presence, in other words, must have made a substantial difference with respect to some event or movement deemed important by those who attribute historical greatness to them.

Are there such individuals in history? Those who recognize the possibility of great historical protagonists must reject any overarching, monistic, and systematic determinism that forecloses major alternatives of development. They must reject all unilinear forms of social evolution and myths of inevitable social development. They deny that great men are created by the needs of the time so that if one leader fails to do "the work history has assigned him," someone else is sure to replace him. They deny that the great man is merely the carrier of the spirit of the time, or of the material forces working over and through him. They assert that for some tasks, in some periods of world history, some great men and women have been indispensable; and because there are genuine options that have been taken or missed, these men and women are blameworthy or praiseworthy.

This view must not be identified with Carlyle's fantasy of historical supermen who create the very conditions of their own effectiveness. The great historical figures face alternatives that are not created by themselves, but by the consequences of the actions of those who have preceded them and by the cumulative weight of the unsolved problems of their times.

The bane of most discussions of the role of the outstanding personality in history is easy generalization. For example, it is sometimes said that no one person, however situated in the places of power, can cause or prevent a war or a revolution. Yet I would be prepared to argue on the basis of the evidence that Woodrow Wilson could have kept the United States out of World War I, while Franklin Roosevelt or anyone else who had been elected in 1940 could not have kept the United States out of World War II had Hitler absorbed all of Europe. And with respect to revolutions, there is no individual of whom one can plausibly say, had he or she not been on the scene, the Russian *February* Revolution of 1917 would not have occurred.

But when we consider the Russian *October* Revolution of 1917, the evidence is overwhelming that if Lenin had not been on the scene, first in April to prod his party to overthrow Kerensky, then to restrain it from precipitate and untimely action in July, and finally to impel it to storm the bastions of the Provisional Government in October, there would have been no Bolshevik October Revolution. Despite his orthodox Marxism, even Leon Trotsky ultimately conceded that Lenin played this event-making role, not the economic forces and relations of production in Russia. And if there had been no Bolshevik Revolution, which split the European socialist and working class movement, it is highly questionable whether Mussolini or Hitler would have come to power.

It should be noted that I am not asserting that human history, whether it be considered with Hegel, Spencer, and Marx as the record of inevitable progress or with Gibbon as "little more than the register of the crimes, follies and misfortunes of mankind," has always depended upon the decisions of the leaders of men, whether kings, emperors, generals, presidents, or prime ministers. Actually, I believe there have been comparatively few occasions on which the imputations of such awesome causal power to any individual person is justified. But there have been a sufficient number of situations in which the role of an individual as the head of a nation may be as fateful to its destiny as the role of the head of a family, or the leader of an enterprise, or the president of a university or college, or the mayor of a city, to the survival or downfall of their respective institutions. It is false to say that "no man or woman is indispensable." With respect to some important outcome or purpose, a particular person may very well be indispensable.

Whenever we discover an individual strategically placed to influence events in history, it does not follow that such influence is a consequence of outstanding character or personality. An individual may be eventful in history, in virtue only of the position he or she occupies. The paradigm case of the *eventful* man in history is Harry Truman. He found himself in a position in which he had to decide whether to drop the atomic bomb and bring the war with Japan to a close quickly or not to drop it and risk millions of casualties on both sides in storming the beaches of the Japanese homeland. The *eventful* man is like the legendary little Dutch boy who became a hero because he stopped up the gap in the dike with his little finger until aid could come. He could have passed by. There was no extraordinary stamina or virtue required. He saved the town to be sure, but any little Dutch boy who happened by could have done it. He was a hero by happenstance. Similarly, any man in Truman's position would have had to make the decision, and either one of the two basic possible decisions would have had far-reaching consequences. President von Hindenburg was another eventful man in history. Had he not called Hitler to power in January 1933, when the Nazi popular vote was already declining, and provided him with the trappings of legality, Germany and Europe might have been spared the catastrophe of Nazi rule.

In contrast to the *eventful* individual whose accident of position gives him a choice between two mutually exclusive and exhaustive alternatives of decision, there is the *event-making* individual. He or she is the truly great figure in history. The *event-making* individual is someone who by extraordinary traits of character or intelligence or some other distinctive facet of personality has largely shaped the viable alternatives of action between which he chooses, alternatives that but for him would probably not have emerged. Such individuals are not made by events so much as events are made by them. It is not merely in virtue of their inherited position that they influence events but in virtue of exemplary will, skill, or infectious vision. These traits enable them to redirect the movements of social change against great odds, against the opposition of recalcitrant elements, and against the even more formidable inertia of traditional institutions. Peter the Great and Mustapha Kemal are instances in point, as are Lenin and Stalin. The event-making personalities in history are few in number. They are more likely to be found in periods of political absolutism in which rulers or those who seize the helm of state enjoy a monopoly of power unchecked by countervailing forces and independent of any democratic consensus.

This makes focal the difficult question: What is or should be the role of the great man or woman in a democracy? There are some who would shrug it aside as a pointless question on the ground that in our day and age it is sheer historical superstition, a vestige of religious anthropomorphism, to believe that any man or woman, however richly endowed or strategically placed, can significantly affect the upshot of the great demographical, geopolitical, industrial, and economic forces whose conjunction is shaping the future of all mankind. If my argument is sound, it is those who think this way who are the victims of what Charles Peirce called the superstition of total necessity. What must be, of course, must be; but what *will be* often depends upon what our leaders do or leave undone, and ultimately depends upon those who vote them into power.

Others will dismiss the question on the ground that the truly great historical figure is indifferent to what citizens think his role should be. He creates his own role, they say, whatever the electorate may think. His political skill may consist in making his constituents believe that he is carrying out their will or, if they have no strong feelings about matters of crucial importance, that he is furthering their welfare.

As a principled democrat, I make a crucial distinction between the "great" man or woman who imposes his will on the electorate by manipulating the sources of public opinion and resorting to other devious means of patronage and intimidation, and the democratic leader who does not flinch from following his sense of high responsibility even when it conflicts with the prejudices of the crowd but who relies only on persuasion and intelligent compromise to win their support.

There is a certain paradox in the concept of democratic leadership. A democracy delegates leadership but cannot surrender to it. A democracy—a self-governing republic of citizens with equal rights —must be jealous of the powers it delegates to its leaders; for unless power is limited by other power, it is subject to usurpation and abuse. In a healthy democracy the leader must be more than a mouthpiece of those who select him. He cannot trail after events, or in a world of dizzying change break out the flags and rhetoric of yesteryear to conceal the absence of an adequate program. He must anticipate events, devise policies for the benefit not only of the interests that supported him but for the interests of all. For where there is no vision, a people perishes—particularly in times of danger.

That is why the heroes in a democracy are not likely to be *event-making* men and women unless they subvert the democratic process. The ideal democratic leader, whatever the merits of his policy —and let us remember Lincoln's observation that "there are few things wholly evil or wholly good . . . especially of government policy"—is characterized by two traits: intellectual honesty and moral courage. He must have the courage to differ and sometimes to oppose his own supporters until he wins them over or they retire him from public life. He may console himself with the reflection that posterity sometimes redresses the injustices of his contemporaries, but there are no guarantees either in nature or history that truth will prevail even when he has the truth or more of it than those who oppose him.

In terms of my distinction, a democracy has room and great need for moral heroes—even for heroes who fail or whose reputations are ultimately deflated—but not for great *event-making* figures who by definition do not fail. And it is because the democratic hero must be prepared to fail, that he cannot use any means to achieve his ends no matter how worthy those ends are. Whoever makes success the be-all and end-all of his policy, like the person who literally will do anything in order to survive, is building an epitaph of infamy for himself, since he will betray every principle, every value, every human being that stands in his way. The fanatics of virtue and the fanatics of vice have this in common: The consequences of the means they use imperil and ultimately undermine the values and institutions that make their own careers possible. It is this failure to understand and act on the logic and ethics of the democratic process that has led to the sorry state of affairs in recent American political history. The cardinal sin of those involved in the Watergate scandals is their treatment of *opponents* within the democratic process as if they were *enemies* of that process. What, under proper judicial safeguards, may sometimes be justifiable measures against the enemies of the democratic system in a struggle for its survival, can never legitimately be employed against one's opponents within that system without calling all the axioms of democracy into question.

Even if we were to foreclose opportunities for *event-making* personalities to emerge in a democracy, we live in an age in which the political leaders of American democracy, regardless of their personal traits, are and will continue to be, by force of circumstances, *eventful* men and women. We live in a dangerous world and in an age more precarious than any before. Our age is one in which for the first time in human history the sudden death of nations and cultures is possible. There are some who believe that the very survival of mankind has become problematic. The age not only of Coolidge and Harding but also of Roosevelt and Truman is beyond recall. A new political epoch entered the world with the development of nuclear weapons. The peace which results from a balance of terror is an unstable one. It is made more so by the proliferation of nuclear arsenals in an increasing number of nations. In a world of fanatical ideologies, of madmen in or out of uniform, a world in which the politics of absurdity have replaced the politics of sagacity, the decision that our leaders may have to make within hours, or even less, may make all the difference to that world—to its habitability and to the place of freedom in it if it remains habitable.

The danger of the antiheroic mood of our time is that in our world of increasing complexity and multiple hazards, it may result in mediocre leadership just at the time when we need men and women who are knowledgeable and compassionate at the helm of affairs. They must be firm in their loyalty to democratic first principles yet aware that they must live on the same planet with those who live by other principles. They must have a global perspective free from the twin faults of sentimentality and arrogance, be sensitive to ideas and aware that, because ideas are ultimately potential plans of action, they therefore have consequences.

The only antidote I know to the antiheroic mood and the indifference it breeds to the character and problems of leadership in a democracy, is an increase in intelligent political participation on the part of citizens. What is hard to understand, no less to explain, in view of the universal chorus of dissatisfaction with almost every aspect of our industrial, social, and educational experience is the failure of citizens to take a greater active interest in the political process. Almost everyone is critical of the government and most critics look to government for relief. Yet the proportion of those eligible to those who actually vote has been an open scandal for years. And the proportion of those who play an active role on any of the many possible levels of government to those who vote is lower still. Most people want to be led rather than to be leaders themselves or more importantly, to participate in the choice of leaders. And this is natural in view of the price in effort, uncertainty, and loss of privacy or anonymity that must be paid for political distinction. Unfortunately, if we are to judge by their political passivity, too many citizens seem content to be led by their noses rather than by their reflective interest.

Thomas Jefferson contended that the political life of the local ward or township "made for the perfect exercise of self-government." Inspired by Jefferson, John Dewey a century and a half later developed the philosophy of participatory democracy. It presupposes not that all citizens are equal in the capacity to govern, but that they are all equally entitled to judge those who govern them; and that the soundness of their judgment depends upon the extent to which they attend to the daily business of government as it affects them and their neighbors where they work and live. Why, then, has participation in local government as a basis for intelligent participation in the state and national political process failed? I am not persuaded that anyone knows the answer. Political parties and the federal bureaucracies have been denounced as the villains that have corrupted the pure self-governing political processes of town and municipality. This seems to me a myth. Political parties and bureaucracies developed in consequence of the failure of the local community to take care of its own needs, and at the same time to defend the human rights of all men and women regardless of local conditions and prejudices. We can no more have a decentralized equitable system of civil rights enforcement than we can have a decentralized national transportation system.

We cannot abolish political parties and bureaucracies without abolishing politics and a free society. We can, however, make them more responsive to the needs of those they presumably serve. The principle enunciated by Thomas Jefferson and John Dewey is still valid if it can be put to work in a modern context. As a beginning we must reeducate our youth to wean them away from the strange notion that what is public, what belongs to all, is what belongs to no one—one of the sources of the shameless vandalism that disgraces so many cities. They must learn that whatever is public belongs to us, that public money is our money, public parks our gardens, public transportation our means of conveyance, and public policy something for which, now that the voting age is eighteen, they are as much responsible as the rest of us.

Once the fires of intelligent interest in local political life are lit, they are sure to extend to the national scene if ony because so many local problems are national ones, too. This is our best hope that the choice of national leadership, of the *eventful* men and women of tomorrow, will be wisely informed. More than this we cannot reasonably expect. But anything less than this carries the threat that democracy may degenerate into a mobocracy or anarchy. If history has any lesson it is that the rule of the mob is always followed by the rule of the despot. The democratic republic that was born in this hemisphere some two hundred years ago is the only political alternative ever devised to mediate, in Lincoln's phrase, "between anarchy, on the one hand, and despotism on the other." Its prospects of survival for the future depend in some measure on each one of us.

1978

Chapter 13
The Relevance of
John Dewey's Thought

The abuse of the term *relevance* by radical ex-
tremists in educational institutions might justifiably have set up an
allergic reaction in the minds of critical readers to its use. Nonetheless, if we recall that *relevance* is a relational term, the question,
"Relevant to what?" is one whose legitimacy cannot reasonably be
disputed. To the extent that the demand for relevance by educational revolutionaries was intelligible in recent stormy years, it
referred to the bearing of studies on the acute social and political
issues of the day—a bearing that was foolishly elevated to the sole
criterion of an educational curriculum appropriate for modern man,
and then degraded by tying it to the "happenings" of the passing
scene.

When I speak of the relevance of John Dewey's thought I refer not
to its bearing on the contemporary crisis situations but to its bearing
on the condition of man, his problems and predicaments in war *and*
peace, good times *and* bad, whenever he reflectively axamines alternatives of action in the course of choosing a desirable way of life.
John Dewey wrote millions of words on the topical issues that arose
during the three quarters of a century that spanned his adult life. But
it is not for that reason that his ideas have relevance today. They are
relevant to areas of thought and action in which our basic intellectual and practical interests are still involved—education and ethics,
culture and politics, social philosophy in the broadest sense. In some
of these areas his views are emerging once more; in others, events

and institutional change are giving an *actualité* to positions that seemed utopian if not unrealistic at the time he enunciated them.

As one familiar with the whole corpus of Dewey's writings would have expected, the basic educational ideas and ideals that pervade them have been foremost among the rediscoveries of his thought. Addressing the American Association for the Advancement of Science in 1909, Dewey affirmed the central importance of science in the curriculum of the schools long before his post-Sputnik critics sought to reconstruct the American school system to overtake Soviet technological achievements and developments. But by the study of science Dewey does not mean the acquisition of a miscellaneous store of information of facts, laws, theories, and interesting correlations that constitute the subject matter of so much of the science curriculum of the schools. He means the understanding of what it is that confers scientific validity upon a particular conclusion or "the knowledge of the ways of which anything is entitled to be called knowledge instead of being mere opinion or guesswork or dogma." It is this kind of knowledge which for him is of most worth.

Long before the critics of "scientism" appeared on the scene Dewey warned against the view that any specific method in the particular sciences—whether it was physics, biology, or psychology—could define the pattern of rationality. When Dewey criticized the traditional humanistic education of his days, his analysis was directed against the formal study of languages and literature that gave a narrow training in certain techniques that constricted the imagination and emotions instead of liberating and humanizing them. For him the humanities were not merely subjects to be taught, they were the means of affecting liberal and humane minds, what he sometimes called "the production of a social and socialized sense." They were preeminently the field in which the qualities of value were revealed and their interrelations explored. A half century before Snow's superficial book on *The Two Cultures* appeared, Dewey had defined the problem facing reflective citizens concerned with education as "how we are to effect in this country a combination of a scientific and a humanistic education."

Dewey's conception of this combination was profound, not superficial, because he was aware of a third culture—the social or cultural —that embraced the "two cultures" and without reference to which humanistic training was in danger of becoming precious, if not snobbish, and scientific training harnessed to barbaric goals. The very distinction between the humanistic and scientific disciplines presupposes an overarching cultural or social dimension expressed in institutions, basic habits and some hierarchy of value choices that make up the quality of life or the distinctive character of civilization at any given time. An education that seeks to make its students imaginatively aware of those dynamic forces in society that ultimately affect the direction of both scientific and humanistic activity must stress the understanding of its basic social and economic structure, the problems and conflicts of the encompassing cultural milieu, and the alternatives of development or retrogression always open to it.

This is required particularly in a democratic society where every adult citizen theoretically counts as much as any other in determining the ultimate direction of its policy. That is why the abstract celebration of moral values—dignity, integrity, happiness, serenity —is insufficient to tell us what changes in social institutions are required to give them a concrete embodiment in the life of most human beings. Similarly, without the assessment of the effects of science and technology upon our social life and upon the quality of the resulting experience, we run the risk of adapting our ideals to the unplanned and unintended consequences of the applications of science rather than organizing its resources in the responsible service of man. Neither humanistic nor scientific education traditionally conceived, because of their failure to understand the encompassing third culture of social, economic, political, and historical studies, can tell us when to produce, what to produce, and why.

This suggests an even more fundamental area of thought in which Dewey, albeit much misunderstood, anticipated some very recent intellectual developments, namely, in the very conception of philosophy itself. Many have been the conceptions of philosophy that have prevailed in different societies, and these differences are present within our own. Dewey continuing the Greek tradition has maintained that philosophy is a quest for wisdom, but as distinct from ancient, medieval, and almost all other modern thinkers, he has rejected the attempt to identify or ground wisdom with or on some metaphysical or transcendental (ultimately religious) insight or with the purely descriptive knowledge of the natural sciences. Wisdom for Dewey is a moral term "and like every moral term refers not to the constitution of things already in existence, not even if that constitution be magnified into eternity and absoluteness. As a moral term it refers to a choice about something to be done, a preference for living this sort of life rather than that. It refers not to accomplished reality but to a desired future which our desires, when translated into articulate conviction, may help bring into existence."[1]

1. John Dewey, "Philosophy and Democracy," *University* [of California] *Chronicle* 21 (1919): 43; reprinted in *Characters and Events*, ed. Joseph Ratner (New York: Henry Holt and Co., 1929), 2:841–55.

This makes a philosophy a *normative analysis* of the basic value conflicts of the culture of which it is a part. It is a conception of philosophy which is both a historical interpretation of what philosopy has been and a proposal of what it should be and do. It makes the philosopher a moralist but not a moralizer or social reformer. It faces certain difficulties which I have attempted to meet elsewhere.[2] But what is significant for present purposes is that this conception, derided or ignored for many years by most American philosophers who have regarded philosophy either as a quest for a reality beyond the reach of scientific methods, or as an analytic explication of scientific methods, or as a linguistic analysis of basic concepts whose ordinary and peculiar uses when not properly distinguished gave rise to intellectual confusion, has now strongly emerged on the philosophical scene and is moving more and more to the center of current philosophical concern. Unfortunately not all who are now concerned with normative analysis of values in their social bearing have understood Dewey's conception of the vocation of the professional philosopher as distinct from the activity of the citizen. They seek to politicalize philosophy by harnessing it to some specific controversial political program rather than to the analytic functions of clarifying the alternatives of social action and their consequences.

To some readers this will suggest that Dewey's thought has been an anticipation of the certain themes in later-day existentialism. This would be more false than true. The existentialists have been concerned like Dewey with moral choice, its phenomenology and psychology. But their irrationalism, their contention that no grounds can be given for our basic choices, that they are all on the same level, would raise doubts on Dewey's view whether they have a right to any theory of *moral* judgment. For the existentialists a moral choice is a passion. For Dewey it is more than a passion, it is a conviction for which rational grounds can be given, that is, it is "a passion that would exhibit itself as a reasonable persuasion." A persuasion can be reasonable even if it is not logically entailed by the facts of the problematic situation in which the judgment is made. For Dewey the usual objection to the view that values or ends can be rationally determined, namely, that rationality is a quality of *means* that are adapted to achieve specific ends but that the ends themselves are a matter of arbitrary choice, does not hold. For he denies that there are any ultimate ends and contends that there is a plural means-end continuum in all problematic situations of moral choice. We never confront bare facts with pure ideals. The factual situation al-

2. Sidney Hook, "Philosophy and Public Policy," *Journal of Philosophy* 67, no. 14 (1970): 461–70.

ready includes some value commitments, not questioned in that particular context, and the pure ideal presupposes some assumption about the factual causal circumstances out of which it arose and the factual consequences to which it leads. That is why Dewey holds that "if ever we are to be governed by intelligence, not by things and by words, science must have something to say about *what* we do, and not merely about *how* we may do it most easily and economically."[3]

The typical response of some philosophical intuitionistic critics to Dewey's view that moral virtue is intelligence is that this makes the economical use of means to the achievement of *any* given end moral (for example, then the person—it is said—who discovers that cyanide is the cheapest and quickest way of destroying the victims of a genocide program would be the most moral!). But Dewey's point is that he is prepared to show that the choice of that given end in the determinate historical situation is unreasonable or unintelligent. Despite the denial by emotivists and existentialists that ends and goals are beyond rational evaluation, that it is unintelligible to speak of them as being "rational" or "irrational," "foolish" or "wise," the facts of ordinary experience, as well as of ordinary language, give this position the lie. We are continually discussing the reasonableness or unreasonableness of pursuing specific goals, ends, objectives, or ideals.

It is not enough to vindicate the cognitive validity of value judgments today. More important than the acceptance of beliefs about the good and the better is the way in which the beliefs are held. Despite widely held opinions to the contrary, it is not from ethical skepticism or even from subjectivistic relativism we suffer most. For at their worst they make for an indifferentism that the exigencies of practical choice often reveal as merely a conventional pose. And at their best they make for an initial tolerance toward expressions of difference that may broaden the spectrum of choice. The major threats to democratic political and social life stem not from relativism or skepticism but from fanaticism. We live in an age of true believers whose self-righteous absolutisms brook neither contradiction nor delay in bringing about the promised land of their faith. Disagreement is automatically attributed either to immeasurable stupidity or to unmitigated venality. Some of these fanaticisms are on the side of the angels, like absolute pacifism whose consequences often embolden aggressors like Hitler to believe that

3. Dewey, "Science as Subject-Matter and as Method," *Science*, n.s. 31 (1910): 217; reprinted as "Science and the Education of Man," in *Characters and Events*, 2:765–75.

they can make armed moves, and ultimately, war with impunity. The fanatical social revolutionist equally with the fanatical reactionary or standpatter holds his beliefs in such a way that nothing that occurs can disconfirm them. The less fruitful and effective those beliefs are, the greater his impatience, the more intense his conviction of their truth. Only too often he ends up proclaiming that the evil system that defeats his demands—demands so clear, so obvious, so eminently reasonable—must be destroyed "by peaceful means if possible, by any means if necessary." In a few short strides the utopian idealist becomes a guerrilla warrior, an arsonist, or even a bomber—still self-righteous and full of moral indignation and completely unaware of the way in which the means he has used have corrupted both his ideals and his characater.

In practice the fear of failure may curb fanaticisms except of the messianic varieties that border on the psychotic. But Dewey is interested not in the techniques of frustration or repression but in an intellectual approach that would prevent or at least hinder the emergence of fanaticism. To this end he believes that the cultivation of a historical sense is essential. Whether it is peace or justice or freedom or welfare that we have made the end-all and be-all of our social or political program, "the gist of rationality" in striving for them is "temporal perspective," for in human affairs, in contrast with pure logic and mathematics, our decisions are based on judgments of "more or less" rather than on judgments of "either-or."

This historical perspective on human affairs is wedded to a lively sense of the pluralism of values exhibited in such affairs. It is not that Dewey denies the validity of a moral stance that at some point stakes one's life, honor, and fortune on a position and digs in behind the declaration: "Hier stehe Ich. Ich kann nicht anders" [Here I stand. I can do no other]. The question is: On what am I standing? On my conscience or on a platform of reason? For Dewey, conscience has no moral authority unless it is the result of a rational conscientiousness. And if it has moral authority, it necessarily requires taking note of the plural values of experience and their interrelatedness, and of rationally assessing the consequences of one's stand upon them. Especially today when "conscience" is often and sincerely invoked as an organ of ultimate and superior insight into one's moral duty—and not only as an easy pretext of avoidance of one's duty and responsibility, for betrayal of cause and country—it becomes necessary to point out that those who with a righteous pride affirm that they are preapred to take some action "in complete disregard of consequences," are immoral fanatics. For morality is always an affair of consequences. If we are prepared to say, let justice prevail though the heavens fall, well and good—provided we understand that the fall of heaven also means the death of love, the loss of freedom, the end of happiness, and the euthanasia of all other human values. And if these are rationally grasped as the true consequences of pursuing or realizing absolute justice, of what use or good would such justice be? We can ask the same questions of any other single value-term substituted for *justice*. The interrelatedness of values and the consequences of the means used to achieve one value or the constellation of values of which it is a part, makes the sharp disjunction between "merely" instrumental values and "pure" intrinsic values untenable.

Occasionally it is asserted that survival is the truly ultimate value which in cases of moral conflict always has an overriding validity. Reflective human behavior does not always square with the assertion. Sometimes the worst thing we can know of a human being is that he survived under the conditions laid down for survival—that he torture and destroy the innocent, betray friends, family, cause, and country.

For Dewey each situation has its own unique good discovered by intelligent analysis of the factual situation and of the competing value claims. No formula can guide our resolution. Sometimes we must give heed to the overriding imperatives of justice; sometimes we must subordinate the claims of justice to the overriding need of human welfare; sometimes both justice and welfare may temporarily be sacrificed to the requirements of security and survival. "This is opportunism," jeers the absolutist. To which one can legitimately retort that if opportunism means "the seeking of immediate advantage with little regard for principles or ultimate consequences," this is decidedly not opportunism, since regard for consequences is of the very essence of this approach. On the other hand, an absolutism that disregards fruits and consequences is the very quintessence of fanaticism, and often leaves no alternative where absolutes conflict except war, so that in the end sheer might determines what prevails in human affairs.

There is another generic sense of opportunism which stresses the intelligent application of principles to new occasions. In this sense, the social philosophy of Dewey is as opportunistic as scientific medicine. Those who issue the same prescription for all medical affairs are quacks. Social absolutism can be regarded as a kind of quackery in human affairs despite the high-mindedness and personal sincerity of its exponents. Sincerity is always a desirable trait in politics but unless accompanied by intellectual humility, by a consciousness that one may be wrong in an area in which claims to certainty reveal a severe limitation of intelligence, it can express itself in monstrous form. Hitler did not lack sincerity.

Long before the misleading slogan of "participatory democracy" was sounded by the spokesmen of the so-called New Left, Dewey had developed the idea, expressed in germ in Jefferson's later writings, that democracy was not only a political form of government but a way of life, that it "must begin at home, and its home is the neighborly community."[4] The nature of community requires more than mere physical contiguity. It involves face-to-face relations and direct communication among citizens so that joint undertakings can be initiated. Individuals sharing ideas and emotions lose the feeling of being dwarfed by social forces moving behind their backs, of the impersonality of the political process and the anonymity of large numbers and organizations with their inescapable bureaucracies. This explains why Dewey welcomed grass-roots movements and was quite critical of the functioning of purely formal mechanisms of political rule.

How then does Dewey differ from the gurus of the New Left who would justifiably repudiate any suggestion that he has inspired their thought? First by his acceptance of the principle of majority rule. For him this is a necessary but not sufficient condition of democratic community decisions. The New Left is contemptuous of majorities if they do not agree with the program of the leadership of the moment. Despite its rhetoric, it is elitist in conception and character. Second, Dewey's conception of participation does not entail the view that all individuals are capable of doing everything, that all political functions are interchangeable, and that responsible leadership is incompatible with democratic accountability and control. The New Left professes that all leadership other than its own must end in a cult of leadership. In an attempt to conceal the character of its actual elite control of organizations, meetings, and assemblies that flaunt the slogans of participatory democracy, it becomes manipulative. Every group that shouts "All Power to the People" not only has no mandate from the people to speak in its name but is at the same time engaged, under the skillful direction of its ideologues and managers, in frustrating the decisions of the larger majority of the people among whom it is agitating whenever the popular judgment runs counter to the predetermined goals of the shouters. Thirdly, for Dewey the survival and expansion of democracy depends upon its use of scientific method or creative intelligence to solve its problems. For the New Left and its congeners, "science" and "reason" are suspect tools of the Establishment used to fashion

4. See Dewey, *The Public and Its Problems* (New York: Henry Holt and Co., 1927), pp. 212–13.

rationalizations in behalf of the *status quo.* This is a kind of primitive Marxism that mocks the genuine insights of Marx himself.

We must now confront a profound difficulty in Dewey's political philosophy which to the extent that he solves it requires the introduction of a faith that in the eyes of some may seem to transcend his commitment to the scientific attitude. The difficulty arises from the conjunction of a series of positions each of which appears to be well-grounded. Dewey believes that our reflective behavior as well as the conclusions of analysis commits us to a cognitive theory of ethics according to which judgments of good and bad, right and wrong, can legitimately be called valid or invalid, true or false. He also is aware of the growth and complexity of government and that most of the tasks of government are administrative, requiring specialized and expert knowledge in the manifold technologies of the industrial arts and sciences. Why then, one asks, does not Dewey draw the conclusion that the likelihood of good government depends upon entrusting political rule to those who have the expert knowledge? Scientific judgment and truths do not depend upon the vote of majorities or even upon the participation of individual citizens in the scientific process. If scientific knowledge, as Dewey believes, is the only reliable method of reaching conclusions in human as well as in natural affairs, why not entrust the political destiny of the community to those who possess this scientific knowledge? And if we do, how can we still be loyal to the spirit and letter of democracy?

This is another way of asking Plato's question: If we do not elect the pilot of a ship to whom we entrust our lives and goods, why should we elect the pilot of the ship of state whose decisions may determine our collective lives and estates? We cannot make the easy answer of the emotivist: We elect pilots on the basis of their knowledge and craftsmanship to take us to our destinations but the pilots have no authority to determine what our destination should be; for a choice is expressive of an attitude or wish or preference and not dependent upon any knowledge, scientific or other. Dewey cannot make that answer, for, as we have seen, he believes that the relevant scientific knowledge can help "form the social and moral ideas for the sake of which it is used," and that "science must have something to say about *what* we do [and *where* to go], and not merely about *how* we may do it [and *how* to get there] most easily and economically."

Dewey is quite aware of the objections that can be made to the Platonic view, shared by Santayana and other honest totalitarians, that knowledge and knowledge only gives incontrovertible authority to rule. And in writings spanning his entire life he has voiced these objections incisively and vigorously—that history shows that the dictatorship of the wise becomes corrupted by its monopoly of power into the rule of vested interest, that it is not necessary to be an expert to judge or evaluate the recommendations of experts, that those who actually wear the shoes know best where they pinch and therefore have the right to change their political shoes in the light of their political experience.

But these rejoinders of Dewey are not enough to justify the democracy of a *self-governing* community. For they could be accepted by an elite to justify a nonparticipating democracy in which the electorate passively registers its approval or disapproval of executive or legislative decisions but does not engage in the multifarious activities of joint association that Dewey regards as the *sine qua non* of democratic health and vitality. Intelligent decisions in a democracy require extensive participation by the citizenry on all levels. Has the common man the capacity as well as the willingness to make intelligent decisions? And if he does not possess them now, can he be educated to acquire them? If his education is not sufficient to enable him to acquire political sophistication and some expertise, has he the wit and gumption to learn from experience? Dewey answers all of these questions affirmatively, despite his awareness of the fact that the powerful mass media of press, radio, and television are hardly geared to the educational needs of an enlightened commonwealth. On what then do his beliefs rest? On the same faith that underlay Jefferson's faith in the success of the American experiment, namely, that most human beings who have access to relevant information can learn from their own experience, including their mistakes and defeats, and can discover what they really want, what they must do to achieve it, and what price must be paid for its achievement. They can learn this better than exalted rulers or leaders who claim to have superior knowledge of what is really good for those whom they rule or lead. It is a double-barreled faith—they *can* learn it, and they *will*.

It is interesting to observe that something like this faith was held by Marx, too, not about the people as an undifferentiated mass but about the idealized working class. At a time when democratic political institutions had not yet been introduced into Western Europe, when, since peaceful reforms were seemingly impossible, revolutionary action seemed necessary to those who experienced conditions as morally unendurable, Marx sought to assess the prospects of ultimate victory for the working class in the aftermath of a series of shattering defeats.

The proletarian revolutions . . . criticize themselves constantly, interrupt themselves continually in their own cause, come back to the apparently accomplished in order to begin it afresh, deride with unmerciful thoroughness the inadequacies, weaknesses and paltrinesses of their first attempts, seem to throw down their adversary only in order that he may draw new strength from the earth and rise again, more gigantic, before them, recoil forever and anon from the indefinite prodigiousness of their aims, until a situation has been created which makes all turning back impossible, and the conditions themselves cry out: *Hic Rhodus, hic salta.* [5]

What is this but a colorful account of how the working class presumably learns from experience, suffused with an expectation and hope that it will eventually triumph? Dewey writes with much greater sobriety than Marx, not about the workers but about the public or organized citizenry, faced not by one task or challenge that is finally mastered but by a succession of them, working not under conditions of illegality and despotism but within an accepted tradition of change. Yet despite all these differences he, too, expresses the same faith in man and his ability to learn from experience that animated Marx's faith in the working class. Marx's faith turned out to be mistaken, for the workers in the Western world never espoused the cause of revolution, and the workers elsewhere supported at best revolutions from above engineered by a small group of professional revolutionists. The workers of the Western world did learn from experience, however, but it was a lesson that Marx did not altogether anticipate, namely, that they could realize their demands for bread and freedom more effectively and in a less costly way by working within the democratic political process, and using the tax system and welfare state to redistribute wealth more nicely and justly, than they could by guillotine and firing squad.

Has Dewey any better reason for his faith that the masses will find their way to a participating democracy, a commonwealth in which institutions function to be helpful to all individuals seeking to achieve their maximum growth as persons—through "methods of consultation, persuasion, negotiation, communication, co-operative intelligence"? [6] This faith has been sorely tried by events in the United States since Dewey died, and by the growth and partial success of movements in many areas of public life that have relied not

---

5. Karl Marx, *The Eighteenth Brumaire of Louis Bonaparte*, in *Karl Marx and Frederick Engels: Selected Works in Two Volumes* (Moscow: Foreign Languages Publishing House; London: Lawrence and Wishart, 1950), 1:228.
6. Dewey, *Freedom and Culture* (New York: G. P. Putnam's Sons, 1939), p. 175.

on the methods Dewey stressed as essential to a participating democracy but on force and violence or the threat of force and violence. It is true enough that it is very dubious that the genuine gains in civil rights, social welfare, education, and health are attributable to this violence, and a good case can be made for the contention that force and violence in behalf of good causes, by developing reactions and backlashes, have hindered them rather than helped further them.[7] It may even be true that if the democratic methods Dewey enumerates are not employed in the political process, the ideal of a self-governing participating democracy will remain a chimera. Nonetheless it remains true that despite these considerations Dewey has a right to hold this faith. Its invalidity has not been established. Like all faith it involves risk and gamble even if it be more reasonable than any other. It is a risk and gamble not only because it assumes that where fundamental interests collide men will use their intelligence to find the shared interests on the basis of which their differences can be composed, but because it also assumes that those who have the creative intelligence to discover ways of building on shared interests will have the moral courage to propound and defend them in the face of violent opposition. The behavior in recent years of the faculties of institutions of higher learning, not only in the United States but in most countries of the world, in meeting violent disruptions of the academic process show lamentably that intelligence and moral courage do not go hand in hand, that they seem to be two independent variables in the life of the mind.

Among other reasons this is why it is still an open question whether Dewey's faith in intelligence will be vindicated. Or to put it in another and more paradoxical way, it is still an open question whether events will not make it more reasonable and intelligent, given existing human propensities and their institutional contexts, to use methods of social action that Dewey himself eschewed and condemned. Despite hysteria-mongers and apologists for one or another variety of totalitarianism, the history of politically democratic societies shows that more has been won by the methods of intelligence, of peaceful negotiation, persuasion and reasonable compromise than by any other method. But the future in this respect is more problematic than the past.

It remains briefly to discuss the relevance of some of Dewey's more technical philosophical ideas to the contemporary scene. This

7. I have discussed this in two related essays: "The Ideologies of Violence," *Encounter* 34 (1970): 26–38, and "Reason and Violence—Some Truths and Myths about John Dewey," *Humanist* 29 (1969): 14–16.

may be briefly summarized by the statement that Dewey's ideas are highly relevant to some of the present philosophical concerns of contemporary professional philosophers but that the latter are unembarrassedly unaware of it. Many of Dewey's positions are widely accepted but not in the form in which he developed them. Although a leading protagonist of a naturalistic and functional theory of mind and an arch-foe of psychophysical dualism, today a more materialistic or physicalistic theory largely prevails. This is a family of doctrines that accepts some version of the identity-thesis that "mental processes are purely physical processes in the central nervous system," to use the language of one of its systematic exponents. Those who have developed this theory have done so independently of any perceptible influence of Dewey. To the extent that they believe that the true relation between the mind and the brain depends upon the findings of science, Dewey would endorse their position. He would, however, contest their apparent isolation of the mental from the social and cultural, and maintain that the categories of the physical and mental are neither exclusive nor exhaustive. He would also assert that the dimension of the social, although it has necessary physical and biological correlates, is not reducible without remainder to them.

More surprising is the seeming evanescence of the philosophy of naturalism which received one of its most significant expressions in Dewey's *Experience and Nature*. To some, naturalism is a philosophy based upon the question-begging assumption that the methods of science are the only valid ways of acquiring knowledge and that, aside from commonsense knowledge which is continuous with science, there is no reliable knowledge except scientific knowledge. This conclusion has brought naturalism not only into conflict with all varieties of supernaturalism but also with those who believe in the existence of ontological or metaphysical truths (that are neither scientific nor logical) and more recently with those who on the basis of their introspective experience of intention and choice assert the existence of a freedom of action for man that scientific methods cannot establish. The Kantian dualism has been reasserting itself according to which human life, especially man's moral life, cannot be accounted for in terms of scientific explanation. The doctrines of all of these newer tendencies are incompatible with Dewey's clear-cut rejection of psychophysical dualism.

Dewey was unsympathetic to the doctrines of logical positivism or logical empiricism that flourished in the last two decades of his own lifetime not because of its absorption in the language and methodology of the natural sciences but because of its suspected atomism, its slighting of normative ethical and social propositions,

and its emotive interpretation of their meaning. When this movement was eclipsed by the ordinary language analysis inspired by
Wittgenstein, Dewey's initial neutrality turned to hostility on the
ground that although it was true that *some* philosophical problems
arose from errors in logical grammar, most of them arose from genuine *problems* in the extension of scientific categories from one domain to another. There is a haunting similarity between some pages
of Wittgenstein and some pages of Dewey. Long before Wittgenstein, Dewey had established, by linguistic analysis of the way in
which the question was posed, that the so-called problem of the
external world was not a genuine problem and that the very use of
mental or sensory predicates, without which the question could not
be asked, already presupposed the world of physics and the environment of everyday things. Nonetheless, for most philosophical problems Dewey would deny that because they cannot be coherently
stated in their own terms that therefore they are no more than mistakes in a logical grammar or false moves in a language game. He
would maintain that they arise out of unclearly formulated scientific problems, and that philosophical analysis should go on to
attempt to state the problem in such a way that we can see what
would constitute relevant scientific and commonsense empirical
evidence for its resolution.

Since Dewey believed that central to philosophic activity should
be the normative analysis of value judgments, he is far from agreeing
with Wittgenstein that philosophy leaves the world pretty much the
same after it is through with its philosophizing. For Dewey all genuine knowledge is an implicit judgment of practice whose truth is
established by some experimental activity that literally transforms
part of the world. If there is genuine scientific knowledge of what
is morally true or false then philosophy, for better or worse, does not
leave the world unaltered. This explains why for Dewey the social
responsibility of science is not a problem which has emerged only in
consequence of modern technology. For him all knowledge involves
possible control, and when achieved, some actual change in the
world.

Dewey himself set great store by his last great work: *Logic: The
Theory of Inquiry.* This is a book not in formal logic but primarily
in the methodology and philosophy of scientific investigation. As
far as present-day logicians are concerned, it might as well not have
been written; and few are the philosophers of science who are familiar with it. Ernest Nagel, who studied with Dewey, is the only outstanding philosopher of science who reflects his influence.

Although predictions in intellectual history are hazardous there is some reason to believe that in the future Dewey's purely technical philosophical work will be rediscovered, reassessed, and developed. If his educational and social views are taken seriously by professional philosophers, they will go on to explore the epistemological and logical views that Dewey thought were bound up with them. Although they may reject a great deal, they will also find that Dewey's philosophical writings are chock-full of fruitful insights, and that although they do not constitute a finished system, they hang together in a coherent way.

Probably Dewey's philosophy will remain in temporary eclipse until the present phase of irrationalism and anti-intellectualism in American life runs its course, and reflective Americans once more seek a philosophic outlook consonant with an age in which a more adequate science of human nature serves the ideals and goals of an enlightened morality. The original inspiration of Dewey's philosophy was to find a rational basis of authority in morals comparable to the method by which claims and counterclaims in the natural sciences could be settled. This emphatically does not involve "the assimilation of human science to physical science" which represents only another insensitive form of absolutism, for it "might conceivably only multiply the agencies by which some human beings manipulate other human beings for their own advantage." This is the historical upshot of allegedly scientific Marxism in the Soviet Union and elsewhere that has betrayed both the spirit of scientific inquiry and the humanistic ideals of a responsible freedom. To the last Dewey remained true to his original inspiration. His legacy to our age is a phiosophy that would extend the area of desirable human freedoms by the arts of intelligence. Its most important corollary in social and political affairs is the interrelatedness and continuity of ends and means, of process and product.

Taken seriously, this approach to human affairs puts us on guard against shortcuts and panaceas, empty revolutionary rhetoric, and the "reasons" of the heart, blood, or passion that have resulted in intellectual absurdities and often culminated in atrocities. At the same time it does not justify, out of fear of substituting new and greater evils for the old and familiar ones, a defense or glorification of the social *status quo*. For, according to Dewey, the cumulative effect of human knowledge and the consequences of human decisions make it impossible to preserve the *status quo*. Our choices, and even our refusal to choose on basic issues, make matters either better or worse. We must take our problems one at a time, admitting that some are related to others, and that some are larger than others, and therefore require large steps that in perspective may appear revolutionary. The health of society can be achieved like the health of the individual with which in many ways it is interrelated. As Dewey himself has put it:

> The human ideal is indeed comprehensive. As a standpoint from which to view existing conditions and judge the direction change should take, it cannot be too inclusive. But the problem of production of change is one of infinite attention to means; and means can be determined only by definite analysis of the conditions of each problem as it presents itself. Health is a comprehensive, a "sweeping" ideal. But progress toward it has been made in the degree in which recourse to panaceas has been abandoned and inquiry has been directed to determinate disturbances and means for dealing with them.[8]

This invites a program of unending social improvement inspired by visions of excellence. It is a program in which the political and cultural freedoms, essential to a humane and democratic society, and on which other desirable social and economic freedoms must be built, come first. These freedoms can never be taken for granted. They can always be lost when men lose their nerve and intelligence.

To a willful romanticism that focuses only on goals, Dewey's melioristic outlook will seem prosaic. To a nearsighted realism that immerses itself only in efforts to preserve the familiar and customary, Dewey's vision of the consummatory experience that guides and tests institutional change will appear utopian, if not fanciful, too optimistic in its estimate of human potentialities. But like William James, John Dewey would have defended his right to believe in the fruitful marriage of freedom and science as warranted by the nature of man and history.

1973

---

8. Dewey, *Freedom and Culture*, p. 170.

Chapter 14
Leon Trotsky and the
Cunning of History

Although it is a proposition that Leon Trotsky himself would not have endorsed, there are good reasons to hold that the strongest intellectual case for the Communist version of Marxism has been made by him rather than by Nikolai Lenin to whom in most matters after the October Russian Revolution he deferred. I say this as one who disagrees fundamentally with both and with their radical revision of the democratic ethos of Marx. The publication of Isaac Deutscher's remarkable trilogy of the life of Trotsky* offers an occasion for an evaluation of some aspects of Trotsky's thought. This is all the more appropriate because for good or for evil —and from the prospects of a democratic socialism mainly for evil— the ideas of Trotsky exercise today a greater influence on revolutionary groups in some countries than do those of Lenin, Stalin, and Mao.

Deutscher's biography is a moving and sympathetic study of a heroic figure, a master of the deed and of the word, whose actions and ideas deeply affected the lives of millions and whose impact may still be felt in the future. For all his grave errors, both as a man and thinker, Trotsky still looms large on the horizons of historical action and political thought. History has no record of a human being

---

*Isaac Deutscher, *The Prophet Armed: Trotsky, 1879–1921; The Prophet Unarmed: Trotsky, 1921–1929; The Prophet Outcast: Trotsky, 1929–1940* (London and New York: Oxford University Press, 1954, 1959, 1963).

similarly circumstanced who fought against such odds and with such limited resources. Until he was killed by the hand of a GPU assassin, the Kremlin feared him more than it feared Hitler. The struggle was literally between one man and the regime of the largest nation on earth, but that man was a titan.

Trotsky is in no need of rehabilitation by Stalin's heirs and erstwhile supporters, either within or without the Soviet Union. Among such creatures he enjoys the hated authority of someone who has been criminally victimized. With respect to the central events described in *The Prophet Outcast*—the Moscow trials and the subsequent purges, with their multitudes of innocent victims—Trotsky was, from the outset, the accuser rather than the accused in the minds of those who cared even a little about justice and truth. As Deutscher describes the pattern of infamy which Stalin imposed on the Soviet Union, the mind reels once more in incredulity and horror. One wonders what all those liberals and progressives who endorsed the trials now make of them, how they account for the roles they so willingly played in defaming those who insisted on examining the evidence.

Deutscher's biography has many merits. He knows how to point up a story by highlighting significant detail. He makes effective use of historical analogies. He weaves together the personal and political events in Trotsky's life history so skillfully that the reader is always aware of the protagonist as a complex and suffering human being, and not merely as the arrogant incarnation of a program. Those who know Trotsky only from his political writings will be surprised at this portrait of a man with a rich and intense emotional life—a man who could be tender and sometimes foolish toward family and friends, despairing and hopeful, aware of even slight nuances in the susceptibilities of those around him. Yet this is the same man who permitted the coarse-grained but wily Stalin, whose measure he early took (although he failed to discern Stalin's capacity for growth in evil), to elbow him off the stage of history. Even sadder, this is the same man whose heart, encased in triple-plated dogmas about history, never seemed to be moved by the agonies of those whose lives he had earlier written off as part of the cost of the class struggle.

The struggle between the personal and the political pervades Trotsky's deepest emotions. The father who, in his exile, could contemplate suicide in the desperate hope that perhaps Stalin would thereby be induced to spare his son, Sergei, does not hesitate to denounce his other son, Lyova, for "slovenliness bordering on treachery" merely for the failure, through no fault of his own, to forward documents in time. Few men have exhibited such courage and devotion to principle under sustained persecution, and paid so dearly with the lives of those whom they loved. Hidden from the public eye, Trotsky's grief for his children and friends was biblical in its integrity.

What was lacking was an appropriate measure of compassion for those who had suffered when Trotsky himself had shared the seat of power. Something is wrong with a political passion which blinds one to what is universal in human experience. Most human beings sense their kinship with one another in grief and death and great suffering. In all of Trotsky's writings, despite his power of imagination, there is not the slightest expression of concern or compassion for what happened to the children of the "class enemy," to the dependents of those who on his orders were shot "like partridges" after Kronstadt, to the "wild children"—every one of them a human tragedy—or the children of the kulaks transported in cattle cars under conditions which cattle never had to endure to the wastes of Siberia.

For all its merits, however, Deutscher's biography is flawed at its heart. I am not referring to errors of fact, which are surprisingly few. (Deutscher is mistaken, though, in asserting that Trotsky never met John Dewey outside the public sessions of the International Commission of Inquiry into the truth about the Moscow trials. There was a meeting after the sessions were over.) Nor am I referring to his vindictive and sneering references to Boris Souvarine and others who, not content with criticizing the crimes of Stalin, were morally and intellectually moved to criticize the system which made those crimes possible. The principal flaw I am referring to is Deutscher's super-Marxist orthodoxy—really his Leninism—which transcends even the orthodoxy of Trotsky. And because it denies the possibility of genuine alternatives in history and derives morality from the allegedly "objective" and "necessary" laws of the class struggle, Deutscher's own orthodoxy renders his moral condemnation of Stalin inconsequential as well as unintelligible.

Trotsky himself, when not in the grip of his unexamined dogmas about historical materialism, had a flair for empirical analysis. The best illustration of this is the discussion, in his *History of the Russian Revolution*, of the role of Lenin in the October Revolution. Here Trotsky's fidelity to the facts triumphs over his allegiance to dogma. His real view of Lenin's role, at times muffled in the *History*, is perhaps more sharply stated both in his letter to E. A. Preobrazhensky, written in 1928, before the *History* was composed, and in his French diary, written after. To Preobrazhensky he wrote, "You know better than I do that had Lenin not managed to come to Petrograd in April 1917, the October Revolution would not have taken place." This is arrant heresy to orthodox Marxism, for it makes "the most important social event in human history" contingent upon a historically chance (not uncaused) event.

Deutscher is properly outraged at this doctrinal heresy and undertakes to set Trotsky right. The result is intellectually pitiful. He demands of those who accept the view that Lenin's presence was responsible for October to prove that if Lenin had not been there, it would have been impossible for someone else to have done his work. But no such explanation is necessary. On the contrary, it is up to Deutscher to show that someone else would have appeared in Lenin's absence. All Deutscher can do is declare that, "If neither Lenin nor Trotsky had been there, someone else might [sic] have come to the fore." But this "might" implies "might not." Logically, Deutscher has to prove that someone *"would have"* come to the fore rather than "might have," and he does not come within a mile of doing so.

The rest of Deutscher's discussion of this point illustrates his unfamiliarity not only with the requirements of empirical confirmation but with those of formal inference. With scornful finality he writes, "If it seems implausible to assume that the October Revolution could have occurred without Lenin, this is surely not as implausible as is the opposite assumption that a brick falling from a roof, in Zurich, early in 1917 could have altered the fortunes of mankind in this century." But the opposite of 1) "It seems implausible to assume that the October Revolution could have occurred without Lenin," is *not* 2) "A brick falling from a roof, in Zurich, early in 1917 could have altered the fortunes of mankind." The opposite of 1) is 3): "It seems implausible to assume that the October Revolution would *not* have occurred without Lenin." And if 1) is true, 3) must be false. A falling brick is not the only event which could have removed Lenin from the historical scene. An indeterminately large number of contingent events could have removed him. It is implausible that any *one* of them could have this effect. But if we consider the complex, disjunctive proposition that expresses all the possible contingent events which could have removed Lenin, then if 1) is affirmed, the disjunctive proposition is no less plausible than 1).

Unfortunately, Leon Trotsky could only occasionally permit himself a lapse from doctrinal orthodoxy. He would never admit that what the Communists were doing in the Soviet Union was what the theory of historical materialism had declared it impossible to do. He was at his worst, for example, in the Introduction he wrote to *The Living Thoughts of Karl Marx*, in which his blind application of the Marxist schema to material with which he was unfamiliar led him to make confident predictions of America's future with disastrous and somewhat comical results. Not only did he predict that the middle classes would disappear, and become "pauperized," if not "proletarianized," but that the New Deal would culminate "in ferocious capitalist reaction and a devastating explosion of [American] imperialism . . . directed into the same channels as the policy of fascism."

The fateful consequences of Trotsky's dogmatically held belief that the legal relations of production uniquely determined the character and culture of a society were manifest in his political program and pronouncements. These tied him to the support and defense of the Soviet Union as "a workers' state" even when it was invading neighboring states (Poland and Finland) and shooting down their workers and peasants. It made his appeals for democracy and freedom, which became louder as the pitch of internal Soviet terror increased, sound disingenuous. The notion of "a workers' state" which is not controlled or influenced by workers is either a deception or a flight into mysticism. Even in 1940, Deutscher admits, although the number of workers in the Soviet Union had become huge, "the workers' direct influence on political life was immeasurably less than it had been in the last years of Czarism not to speak of 1917." Yet throughout his book, Deutscher snaps at Trotsky's heels to prevent him from jettisoning this fetish of a "workers' state," which at best could only become a state *for* workers administered by Communist shepherds who, of course, know better what is good for the sheep than the sheep themselves.

By refusing to make a functional analysis of terms like "state," "property" and "workers' state," and therefore refusing to judge the character of the state by *what* it does, *how* it does it, and for *whom*, Trotsky was hampering his own opposition to Stalin. For he was refusing to extend the basis of that opposition by embracing elements outside the Party, even if they were Socialists and workers, or elements outside the working class, even if they were peasants. Consequently, his plea for democracy was not a plea for the democratic rights of *all* workers and peasants, nor a plea for the democratic rights of *other* working-class parties; it was only a plea that his own *faction*, rather than Stalin's, be given the power to administer the dictatorship of the Party. Anyone who challenged the dictatorship of the Party was as much a class enemy to Trotsky as to Stalin. However much Trotsky abominated the methods of Stalin, he was nonetheless prepared to welcome Stalin as a comrade-in-arms rather than make common cause with those who opposed not only Stalin but the dictatorship of the Party. Practically to the day of his death Trotsky could say, "Before class enemies I assume full responsibility . . . for the Soviet government such as it is today, including that government which has banished me and deprived me of Soviet citizenship." He might well have added, for that government which has murdered tens of millions of its own workers and peasants.

By making a fetish of the legal relations of production, and insisting therefore that the Communist regime, even under Stalinist terror, is historically "more progressive" than *any* other democratic society with a capitalist or mixed economy, Deutscher—even more than Trotsky, who at least harbored some fleeting doubts—is compelled to extenuate in advance any horrible crime committed by a Communist regime as a lesser evil is opposition to that evil threatens the continuity of its system of production. Since third alternatives are not viable in most situations, Deutscher would have to approve, however reluctantly, a Communist invasion of Western Europe even if most Western European workers were destroyed in the process, for the very same reasons that he ultimately approved, after first deploring, the Soviet violation of Finland's rights to self-determination as an action strategically necessary for the preservation of "the workers' state." Despite Stalin's mistakes and crimes, the logic—or illogic—of Deutscher's position would compel him to support the Kremlin in any adventure against the democratic West.

With transcendent naïveté, Deutscher assumes that the "workers' state," even if it functions like an oriental despotism, will some day generate an economy of plenty which will usher in a New Jerusalem of freedom and democracy. The assumption is plainly question-begging, as is the assumption that in an economy of material plenty all class conflicts and even the state will disappear. It also overlooks the possibility that the democratic transformation of capitalism into a welfare economy may achieve plenty more quickly than existing Communist economies without sacrificing basic political and cultural freedoms.

Deutscher does not seem willing to subject any of his predictions to empirical tests. In this respect, his procedure is characteristic. Aware that Trotsky's predictions about the development of the American economy were "a bust," he nonetheless refuses to say that Trotsky was wrong. "Whether Trotsky's prognostications . . . will look as unreal toward the end of this century as they did at its middle," he writes, "must, of course, remain an open question." But if there are any Deutschers around at the end of the century, will they not say the very same thing—namely, that it is an open question whether the predictions will not hold for the end of the twenty-first century? Apparently the predictions are not at fault—they follow from Marx's economic analysis. It is history which is at fault for its tardiness in living up to them. Deutscher's Marxism is, in reality, composed of a set of completely unverifiable hypotheses, and is thus comparable to the religious belief that God will see to it that things come out right in the end.

Deutscher, like Trotsky, is unaware that, for all his moral indignation over Stalin, he is saddled with a theory of history which made such indignation unintelligible. Although he accurately presents the gist of John Dewey's trenchant criticism of Trotsky's *Their Morals and Ours*, a brochure on the ethics of Bolshevik-Leninism, Deutscher shows that he does not understand it. He impatiently dismisses Dewey's argument as neither new nor original. In the context of revolutionary literature, though, it was new, original, and *valid*. Trotsky had protested that the charge of Bolshevik immoralism came only from those who believed in a world of eternal and absolute moral truths, in transcendent ends that could have no commerce with the means used to achieve them. Dewey accepted Trotsky's profession of (ideal) utilitarianism. He declared himself willing to sanction the use of appropriate political means to further desirable ends in concrete historical situations. But Dewey then showed that, in specific historical situations, Leninists do *not* justify the use of their own political means by reference to their actual effects on human welfare. Nor do they justify their use of political means with its full panoply of terror as more likely to achieve their professed goals than other alternative means.

The good of man is inadequately described by Trotsky as the "increase of man's power over nature and decrease of man's power over man." The responsibility for the use of *any* means is then thrust on the so-called "law of the class struggle," and is therefore not taken by the human actors themselves, who are aware of what they are doing. This "law of the class struggle" is conceived as an ineluctable force compelling events toward the inevitable triumph of the revolutionary Party. But the actual decisions concerning means are always made by historical agents. In the case of the Communists, these decisions are made not by considering the *actual* effects of means on ends but, at most, on the prospects of victory for their Party. Any means are justified if they lead to the victory of the Party! But whether the victory of the Party, achieved by these means, will *in fact* lead to the declared or professed ends is never considered.

If it turns out that taking hostages, deceiving others, violating one's pledged word, and framing political opponents are necessary to win victory, then it is *history* which is cruel, the iron law of the class struggle which is truthless toward its victims—and not the Communists, who are merely the human instruments by which the historically inevitable comes to pass. The notion that some kinds of victory may not be worth winning is completely foreign to them. It is history which casts human beings into its dustbin, not Lenin or Trotsky. Only when Trotsky found himself cast into the same historical dustbin that he had cast others was his faith in the logic of history somewhat disturbed. At that point it is not the logic of historical events that has "betrayed" the revolution but Stalin. He does not realize that on his own theory of history the concept of "betrayal" is unintelligible.

Again and again, one gets the impression that the Communists, in commenting on their actions, seem to stand outside the realm in which personal moral decisions are made. They describe their actions as if they were merely natural events, determined by an objective law of the class struggle which they discover but do not create. The logical and psychological analogy with the religious fanatics who believe they are doing the work of the Lord is exact. Only the metaphysics differ. In both cases, the good is what the Lord commands or what History demands; the Church or the Party is the only authorized interpreter of the Divine Command or the Historical Need. One does not need to accept Dewey's own ethical view, which stresses the continuity between ends and means, to recognize that his criticism of Trotsky's position is definitive and annihilating.

Trotsky was a thinker of far greater intellectual power than Lenin, who was a master of political improvisation with a perfect sense of timing, though crude and inept in handling fundamental ideas. Yet for all his daring, Trotsky never considered challenges to the apocalyptic economic mystique of Marx, or to the dialectical materialist ontology of Engels. He was like a great medieval scholar or Talmudist whose brilliant insights, imaginative reach, and logical ingenuity were brought to bear on secondary matters. When it came to analyzing contemporary political events where the empirical data were controlling and the terminological pieties about the underlying forces and inevitable goals of history were irrelevant, he was without peer.

Trotsky subscribed to a theory of history which excluded the possibility of heroic, event-making men in history. Yet together with Lenin, and despite his theory which stressed "the ripeness is all," he showed that indeed sometimes "the readiness is all." While his common sense told him that the revolution had been "betrayed," his theory of the Soviet Thermidor attributed that betrayal to factors beyond Stalin's control and therefore made his use of the term *betrayal* absurd. For all his reflections on the past, he kept his eyes tightly closed to the fact that his critique of the Leninist revision of Marx (written long before he had become a Bolshevik)—which substituted a monolithic party dictatorship *over* the proletariat for

Marx's concept of the dictatorship of the proletariat—both predicted and explained what transpired in Russia after October. The greatest irony of all, the views that he fashioned in defense of the Soviet dictatorship against the critical revolt of his own disciples, may yet save the Soviet Union from the very grave into which its guardians hurled him by the hand of an assassin.

Leon Trotsky's personality dwarfs his ideas, as large and important as these ideas are. Whatever else the Marxist theory in any of its versions explains, it leaves unexplained the grandeur and the tragedy of his life. It is a life to whose dimensions only a great poet or dramatist can do justice. As a biographer, Deutscher's achievement is highly creditable.. But it falls short of greatness because it lacks a touch of the sacred fire which burned so fiercely in its subject.

1964

Chapter 15
Toynbee's City of God

One of the noteworthy things about Toynbee's *A Study of History* is the uncritical character of its reception in England and the United States. The explanation may simply be that it has been more widely bought than read. But even among those who give evidence of having read it, few have been able to move from under its overwhelming bulk and survey it as a whole. And yet despite its many praiseworthy adornments, never has such an imposing architectonic synthesis rested on such spindly theoretical foundations. In comparison Spengler's fancy-ridden *Decline of the West* is a model of solidity.

As if to shock his readers into reappraising his as yet uncompleted magnum opus, Toynbee now publishes *Civilization on Trial* *—a slight book of essays in which he discusses the important issues of our own civilization *in extremis*, and reaffirms more boldly than ever the theological assumptions that underlie his historical writing. One turns eagerly to its pages to discover what the remarkably learned historian and analyst of all the great cultures of the past has to say about the problems to which *we* must make a successful response or perish—the unification of Europe, the attack of Soviet communism against the West, control of economic and scientific technology, a viable form of international government. The keener the anticipation, the greater the sense of dismay with which one reads these irrelevant and graceful commonplaces that do not rise,

* (New York: Oxford University Press, 1948).

except in some erudite asides, above the level of a good newspaper editorial.

The explanation can be found in Mr. Toynbee's own explanatory categories and in the absence of any verifiable hypothesis about the nature of the historical process. His impressive achievement is to have transcended Augustine's parochial conception of human history and embraced all the known cultures in his historical ken. But he has retained almost in its entirety the whole set of Augustine's parochial theological dogmas in terms of which he attempts to decipher the meaning of human history. Because he has widened the range of his historical inquiries he deludes himself into believing that his approach is more empirical than that of Spengler. It is only more Christian.

Toynbee is writing history fundamentally as a poet and moralist and not as a scientific historian. When he writes illuminatingly about the past, as he often does, it is for the same reason that we find Dante and Santayana suggestive in their historical judgments. The sense of significance which the reader finds in *A Study of History* arises from Toynbee's genuine psychological and moral insights which are completely independent of his evangelism. For example, the whole pattern of challenge-response and ever-differentiated response to fresh challenges which Toynbee presents as the key to the growth of civilizations is a partial *psychological* truth which enables us to distinguish between individuals who can cope with a changing environment and those who cannot. Applied to cultures it is a convenient metaphor that conveys an edifying moral truth and enhances our awareness of what we already know, namely, that the successful life is a continuous succession of problems met and solved. Unless we can define what constitutes a successful response, unless we can say in advance what kind of unsuccessful response to what kind of problem spells disaster for a culture, unless we can formulate a hypothesis concerning the determinate conditions under which a creative response will or will not be made, we have hardly made a beginning toward a scientific study of the rise, growth, and decline of cultures. It may be that we do not know enough to speak confidently about laws that hold for cultures as a whole. But we do not know more when we resort to myths or to capricious intrusions of the creative spirit to account for what at the moment we cannot explain.

One might start with quite another psychological or biological insight, and with Toynbee's erudition one could compose, out of selected historical materials, an entirely different interpretation of cultural development and decline. For example, Charles Peirce says somewhere that all development takes place through the limitation of original possibilities. Goethe's remark that the secret of all great achievement is limitation and Veblen's observations about the frustrations of trained incapacity by overspecialization are corollaries. With Toynbee's imaginative and dramatic flair one could find myriads of historical illustrations of these principles. Our own problems could be presented in a way to disclose the operation of these "laws." We could "prove" that the disastrous consequences of overreaching power always result from an attempt to realize incompatible possibilities. Our whole account could serve as an argument for a kind of Leibnitzian cultural pluralism or "compossibility" in international affairs. Provided, of course, we already believed in it.

To take this as anything more than a poetic or prophetic excursion in order to amplify the *meaning* of a vision is to confuse historical illustration with historical proof. Toynbee systematically falls into this confusion wherever he ventures beyond the discussion of a specific problem such as, say, why Monophysite Christianity survived in Abyssinia. Before a historical illustration can be considered part of a historical proof of the principle it illustrates, it must be shown that it follows logically from the principle and that alternative principles cannot explain it more adequately. And if ever the truth of the illustration is successfully challenged, the validity of the principle itself must henceforth be questioned. Mr. Toynbee's empirical "laws," however, are so vague that it is hard to see what kind of empirical evidence could possibly refute them. Many of the historical illustrations he cites could have been otherwise and still serve as historical illustrations of the thesis, for example, that "schism in the soul" is at the heart of the "schism in the body social" which is a necessary phase of social disintegration. He nowhere comes to grips with the view that the spiritual crisis of our time, as of other times, is a consequence of profound dislocations in economic and social institutions, and that the cure of the business cycle will affect the incidence of neurotic anxieties over salvation much more decisively than spiritual therapy will affect the business cycle.

Toynbee's conception of historical proof, and of the truths it can establish, is expressed in one of the most revealing sentences any historian has ever written: "Christians believe—*and a study of History assuredly proves them right*—that . . . the brotherhood of Man is impossible for Man to achieve in any other way than by enrolling himself as a citizen of a *Civitas Dei* which transcends the human world and has God himself for its King." (*A Study of History,* Vol. 5, p. 585, my italics; cf. also Vol. 6, p. 167.) If History can prove that, it can prove anything. Note that Mr. Toynbee is ostensibly not writing the quoted lines as a Christian but dissociates himself for the moment from Christians as an objective historian, who adds his testimony to theirs. It is not surprising therefore that hard upon this he proclaims that anyone aware of what the study of history proves "will feel certain *a priori*" that Marxism or any form of socialism which is not Christian is bound to fail. What is surprising is that on the basis of the failures in the past a self-proclaimed empirical historian should be so confident about the *only* way the brotherhood of man can be reached in the future. And no less surprising, all the historical evidence is blandly ignored which shows that in those communities, like thirteenth-century Christendom, where men have come closest to universal citizenship in the City of God, they suffered more torture, exploitation, terror, and wars of extermination than in many other communities before or since.

The great merit of Mr. Toynbee's new book is that it makes his theological assumptions so explicit that they cannot be dismissed by reader or critic as quaint anachronisms. His honest self-portraiture shows how focal they are to his reading of history and at the same time how cruelly deceived he is in his notions that they are supported by an empirical analysis of the facts of the past, or that they support in any way the concrete proposals he makes to his fellowmen in the present.

The following are among the more modest of Mr. Toynbee's theological beliefs. Civilization has a goal. The goal is "the communion of saints on earth." "No known civilization has ever reached the goal of civilization yet." Only a truly Christian civilization based not merely on the brotherhood of man but on "the Christian doctrine of the Trinity" can realize the goal of history. The community of saints on earth is not the Kingdom of Heaven on Earth. For the tincture of original sin will always cling to imperfect creatures; that is why the church, even when it triumphs over all secular institutions, will have to stand forth "armed with the spear of the Mass, the shield of the Hierarchy, and the helmet of the Papacy." "On this showing, the victorious Church Militant on Earth will be a province of the Kingdom of God." Even before that blessed victory, "the state of eternal felicity in the other world" can be won by Christian souls in this one. Indeed, "the Christian soul can attain, while still on earth, a greater measure of man's greatest good than can be attained by any pagan soul in this earthly stage of its existence."

One could have foretold on the strength of these beliefs why Mr. Toynbee would find psychologically plausible, in advance of his study of history, two further propositions which have a familiar ring. First, that Western civilization took the path of disintegration, not only spiritual but social and economic, when it surrendered its Christian faith for secularism, humanism, and naturalism. And second, that social welfare and progress can be most effectively achieved only through the "replacement of the mundane civilizations by the world-wide and enduring reign of the Church Militant on Earth."

It does not seem to have suggested itself to Mr. Toynbee that insofar as he is interested in the brotherhood of man, democracy, peace, cooperation, economic security, all of this theological baggage is completely superfluous. For not a single one of the concrete proposals he makes for social change follows from his theological assumptions. The latter, whether true, false, or meaningless, are compatible with any state of social affairs. As a decisive test of this let us take Mr. Toynbee's recommendations in answer to his own question, "What shall we do to be saved?" He replies, "In politics, establish a constitutional cooperative system of world government [through the U.N.]. In economics, find working compromises between free enterprise and socialism."

Precisely from what theological assumptions do these—or any other—political and economic directives necessarily follow? What dogmas of Christianity are incompatible with free enterprise or with collectivism or with the varied alternatives to constitutional world government? What could be clearer than that Mr. Toynbee's theology is neither a necessary nor a sufficient condition for his own proposals for a better world? Not necessary because many non-Christian Chinese, Hindu, Moslem, and Jewish public figures advocate them just as firmly as Mr. Toynbee. Not sufficient because many of Mr. Toynbee's coreligionists, whose theological sincerity and orthodoxy he would be the last to dispute, are bitterly opposed to them.

The point is very elementary but its implications have such a devastating significance for Mr. Toynbee's view on the relation between theology, the good life, and world order that it is necessary to underscore it. Once it is firmly grasped, the utter irrelevance of religious revivalism for any kind of social reform becomes apparent. We will then be free to explore the mischievous psychological and political consequences of insisting upon a return to religious foundations as a prerequisite to social reform. And by religion I mean here what Mr. Toynbee and most people who have called themselves religious mean—belief in theological dogmas as revealed to an authoritative church.

Some may feel that Mr. Toynbee, whose piety and good will are deeper than his theological acumen, is a weak representative of the general position. Consider for the moment, then, the case of M. Maritain whose apologetics for the Christian basis of politics and peace does not lack subtlety. In one of his books on scholasticism and politics, M. Maritain develops the importance for human society of the theological distinction between "the individual" and "the person." In the course of his analysis he relates, not without a certain sly satisfaction at the benefits conferred by a Catholic education, a story of a visit paid by Georges Duhamel, François Mauriac, and himself to Dr. Salazar, the philosopher-dictator of Portugal:

> Duhamel, who is a confirmed individualist, asked how could a dictatorship—even of a non-totalitarian type—be combined with the free development of individual beings, which alone makes human life tolerable. "Ah," answered Dr. Salazar, "in order to explain this to you, I would have to speak of the distinction between the individual and the person." Mauriac fully enjoyed this philosophical answer, addressed by a dictator to a novelist.

Here is not the place to go into the niceties of the distinction. Briefly the individual is man as a natural organism whose existence is contingent on the behavior of a material system in space and time, while the person "subsists entirely in the very subsistence of his spiritual soul." The point of the story is that M. Maritain, accepting the distinction made by Dr. Salazar, disagrees with him about its compatibility with dictatorship. Mr. Maritain is a democrat; Dr. Salazar decidedly is not. Yet they both believe in the intrinsic dignity of the subsistent person. *But conceived in their terms there is no known logic by which it can be established that such persons require one or another form of political life for their development.* It is highly significant that M. Maritain is careful not to charge Dr. Salazar with being a bad Catholic or tax him with inconsistency. Yet this is what he should have done if the transcendental dogmas of Catholic theology necessitate belief in the democratic society rather than in the hierarchical corporative state.

Since Mr. Toynbee is not a theologian one would gladly overlook a certain fuzziness in his discussion of these matters despite his insistence upon their central importance. But one cannot overlook what must be called his theological imperialism. For that is what it means to say that there is little hope that constitutional world government and peace can be established until the peoples of this planet, or their regimes, accept both the theology and the authority of the Church Militant upon earth. As if it were not sufficiently difficult to win people of different religious and political faiths to agreement on empirical matters necessary to insure their survival as well as the survival of their different faiths! Mr. Toynbee would add to our tasks the conversion of all the peoples of the world to one parochial variant of one religion, universal in intent, but parochial in origin, organization, and dogma. But can we dismiss so easily the evidence that for all their religious differences many groups at different times have found it possible to work out a viable civic life together *without* agreement on first or last things?

If Mr. Toynbee has seriously explored any other way of solving our problems save by "enrolling ourselves as citizens of a *Civitas Dei* of which Christ Crucified is King," there is no evidence of it. The nearest he comes to it is in his discussion of what he characterizes as "a purely this-worldly view," which for him embraces every variety of secularism, humanism, and naturalism. "On this view," he writes, "the individual human being is nothing but a part of the society of which he is a member. The individual exists for society, not society for the individual." And so on in a succession of horrendous *non sequiturs*. The upshot of his remarks is that the this-worldly view culminates in totalitarianism to which the only genuine alternative is Christian supernaturalism. To this end he is compelled to depict the system of pagan superstition, which Christianity overthrew, as this-worldly in outlook. Nothing could be more mistaken. The triumph of Christian over classical culture was not a triumph of other-worldliness over secularism but rather a triumph of one species of other-worldliness over another, of one mystical religion over a series of magical cults with mysteries imaginatively less adequate. We are dealing here not with contradictory beliefs but with contraries: Both could not be true, but from the point of view of a genuine this-worldliness, both would be considered false.

This-worldliness in philosophy does not entail the belief that the human being is *nothing but* a physicochemical system, or *nothing but* a part of society, as Mr. Toynbee would have it. It recognizes the presence of whatever distinctive human qualities emerge in experience, insisting only that these qualities modify organisms which have natural histories. It rejects not only Mr. Toynbee's transcendental myths—when they can be given a determinate meaning—as false but also the syntactical nonsense about individuals existing *for* society. Individuals exist *in* societies but only *for* other individual beings or for themselves. They serve their own purposes and interests or other people's purposes and interests—sometimes consciously, more often unconsciously. The sense behind the nonsense of the phrase "existing *for* society" is that it makes it easier for some individuals to impose their purposes upon others, whether the social institutions in question are the Party, the State, or the Church. Because secularism refuses to worship Christ Crucified as King, although prepared to learn from him as a man of great but not perfect moral vision, it need not worship as divine either the Roman Emperor or Stalin and Hitler. Yet the assumption that if one does not worship God one must worship some man as God is central to Mr. Toynbee's position.

The basic form of other-worldliness is the fetishism of abstractions. Such fetishism may be clothed in the language of secularism as well as that of religion. A genuine this-worldly philosophy, on the contrary, far from worshipping abstractions uses them to understand and control the problems of human existence. It does not bow down to institutions of the visible or invisible Kingdom but evaluates them only as instruments for the enrichment of human experience, whose centers and carriers are always persons. Its data in any culture are the needs, as well as the limitations, of human natures as they have developed in history, the possibilities of material and social production, and the values tested by time and intelligence which have contributed to human experience. It can see no guide to human perplexity, no hope for the oppressed and anguished, no spur to moral freedom in the alternative position of Augustine, whose words are echoed with approval by Mr. Toynbee: "What gives happiness in life to a human being is something which does not proceed from human nature but which is above human nature."

In *A Study of History* there are many pages of illuminating historical detail which are in no way related to the author's theological prepossessions. But, unfortunately, in his *Civilization on Trial* this bias obscures recognition of where the real center of gravity lies in the issues which constitute civilization's trials. This is manifest in Toynbee's discussion of the conflict between the United States in which "an undiluted [!] regime of private enterprise still prevails," and the Soviet Union. The totalitarian despotism of the Soviet Union is presented as a kind of Christian heresy, a historical hangover from the Greek Orthodox Christendom of the Byzantines. Western democracy, despite and because of its secularism, is a degenerate expression of Christianity. With sublime faith he assumes that the expanding dynamism of Soviet communism can be contained within the U.N.—provided, of course, the secular "superculture" of our culture is rebuilt on religious foundations.

There is no indication whatsoever that Toynbee is familiar with Stalinist doctrine and organization, which he uncritically identifies with Marxism. He speaks as if the United States were expanding in the same way as the Soviet Union—gobbling up territories and people against their will. To him the defense of the Western world against the Stalinist crusade is a struggle between free enterprise and collectivism rather than between representative democratic institutions, which permit nations to choose freely the degree of collective control they wish to introduce into their economy, and a worldwide totalitarian police state. He sees rightly that a Persian conquest would have destroyed completely the civilization of the Greek city-states but he has no realistic conception of what would happen to Western civilization if it came under the Soviet yoke. He suggests that a mildly socialistic Western European union might mediate the conflict between the United States and the U.S.S.R. despite the evidence that there is little which Stalin detests more than an independent *democratic* socialist movement.

The reason for this uncertain, fumbling touch to all the great questions of the time has already been indicated. Toynbee believes that the downfall of civilizations provides the great opportunity for a universal religion to bring salvation to the individual soul. The worse the chastisement, the greater the likelihood of spiritual rebirth. Although he heatedly denies the allegations of Gibbon and Frazer that Christianity contributed to the decay of Roman civic virtues, his own theological approach to politics, which leaves no room for any great passion except the passion for spiritual redemption, illustrates the unwitting support piety may give to brute power as it moves to crush free minds and free institutions. Although he does not say so explicitly, Toynbee has, in effect, written off Western secular and humanist civilization—a civilization which, with all its imperfections, still holds the possibility of rebirths and renewals of freedom in the only world we will ever know.

Were Toynbee consistent, he would pray for the conversion of the Alarics, Generics, and Clovises of our time—Stalin, Tito, and Beria —since what troubles him most profoundly about them are not their acts of political commission but of spiritual omission. If we can imagine such a prayer to be answered—and it is not excluded that we may some day see a confessor in every concentration camp —the existence of a *Pax Sovietica,* based possibly on heretical but certainly not on secular foundations, would save us the trouble of imagining what Tertullian's Hell would be like on earth. As it is, the extension of Stalin's regime, even without benefit of clergy, is too great a price to pay either for peace in this world or the promise of salvation in the next.

1948

Chapter 16
A Talk with
Vinoba Bhave

When I went to India, I knew very little about Vinoba Bhave, except that he was continuing the Gandhian tradition and had initiated a mass movement in the villages which gave land gifts to agricultural laborers. But it was impossible to read the newspapers or discuss the contemporary situation in India without running up against his name and influence, and the hopes and doubts he inspired. And so when Jayaprakash Narayan, leader of the Praja Socialist party, upon learning that I planned to attend the meetings of the Indian Philosophical Society at Ahmadabad, suggested I visit Vinoba for a talk, I accepted with alacrity. Narayan made arrangements for me to be met at the airport, which I reached from Bombay by an early morning flight. Narayan had preceded me by rail the night before and had gone ahead by train to within a few miles of Vinoba's encampment. I, however, had to traverse the entire distance of almost sixty miles, first to Mehtana and then to the village of Walim, by car. It was the roughest ride I ever took, with the possible exception of the journey from Pagan to Chouk in Burma. It also took four hours with a Fiat, which was used as if it were a jeep or small tank.

The driver of the Fiat was an amazing and attractive personality. He was the representative of the Praja Socialist party in Ahmadabad, a great admirer of J. P. Narayan and at the same time an organizer for Rotary. A geologist by training, he had visited the United States briefly. He was extremely sympathetic to the West, and at the same time a veritable encyclopedia of the shortcomings in the program of Western aid to India. Like many other Indians, he was very knowledgeable about the details of India's Five-Year Plan and its multiple difficulties. But unlike most Indians, he had a very optimistic, almost a bravura personality. The difficulty was that he carried it over into his driving. Wherever he saw a thin wisp of a trail, he assumed it was a road in being; and wherever he came to a fork, instead of studying the lay of the land, he made a lightning quick decision on the basis of his years of accumulated driving in India at a time when "the British built no roads" and he used an old Ford to get around. The result was a bone-breaking, jolting ride over gullies, eroded fields, scrub, and brush, which had never been traversed by automobile.

One way of describing the difference between the United States and India is to say that the roads of India are inhabited. In crossing the country I have never seen a horizon devoid of human beings, cattle, or signs of their habitation. And on this trip, too, we seemed always in sight of some living thing. But nothing prepared me for the spectacle of 30,000 people (a rough estimate made by someone in Vinoba's entourage) clustered in and around the quarters of the village where Vinoba was resting when I arrived. They had come from several villages, I was told. There was an air of excitement, as if a religious festival or carnival were in progress. Most of the adults and children seemed to be in holiday dress, despite the weekday. Although there were few shoes in the crowd, clouds of dust were kicked up by the milling throngs. A stand had been prepared in a field several furlongs away from the whitewashed hut which Vinoba occupied, and already people were sitting there awaiting his afternoon talk.

We were met by Narayan, and together with Mrs. Narayan and one of the organizers of Vinoba's trips, we adjourned to another building, which served as a center for the teaching of crafts to a specially selected group of trainees from various villages. My repast was frugal—fruit and boiled water which I had brought along in a thermos jug. My hosts seemed amused at my Spartan meal, but they, too, ate sparingly of the Indian meal prepared in the huge cauldrons under the open sky. While I made a tour of the simple buildings which had been taken over by the training center, Narayan took his afternoon nap. When he awoke, he accompanied me to Vinoba.

The following account of our conversation is based upon notes written the same evening upon my return to the Government Circuit House at Ahmadabad. Though I will not swear that every word was uttered, I am confident that it is substantially accurate, particularly since on the drive back Narayan and I discussed in great detail Vinoba's answers and my rejoinders. Vinoba had asked that I write some questions out. I had written out many but at Narayan's suggestion pruned them down to essential principles. The political and factual questions he could fill me in on himself. Vinoba's answers to my questions were taken down in shorthand by a young man and woman who worked alternately, and there must be a record of them. But when I spoke, they merely listened with poised pencils waiting for Vinoba's reply.

Vinoba's building was about thirty yards away from ours, but a way had to be cleared for us through the dense throng which stood shoulder to shoulder around the ramshackle gates which set off the enclosure. When we entered, Vinoba was seated on the floor on a cushion or coverlet, reading. He seemed oblivious to our approach, until Narayan, slipping down beside him, said, "Here is our visitor, Professor Hook."

Everyone has seen a picture of Vinoba—thin, slight, and ascetic looking. When he looked toward me, I saw a benign, grandfatherly person with a rebellious curl at the end of his little white beard. He reminded me of a mild-mannered rabbinical scholar who had been interrupted in his reading. His voice was firm and his English was good as he welcomed me and made inquiries about how I had come and from where. To my surprise, he invited me to remain and walk with him the next day and made me feel, when I explained that my schedule prevented it, that I lacked seriousness. "Ah! It is a pity that you are too busy to talk with me." I protested feebly that my presence showed, on the contrary, how eager I was. "I mean you are too busy to walk with me despite the distance you have come. You would learn more about our work that way." At this point, Narayan said something in Hindi which I assume referred to the fact that I was scheduled to return to Ahmadabad for the meetings of the Indian Philosophical Society. Vinoba then turned to my questions—reading them aloud and then answering.

My first question was whether he believed that any religious commitment or doctrine is essential to his program of land reform and social reconstruction, or whether moral values or a purely ethical commitment without any religious overbeliefs constitutes a sufficient base.

"To me there is no difference between religious values and ethical or moral values," he replied. "However, it is true that in the Indian tradition, religion is not only a matter of moral values but of the Dharma, which involves certain beliefs in another existence. But these do not enter into my discussion of the important questions, and it is not required that anybody hold them to judge the worth of our proposals. Anyhow, religion is important in history and society because it expresses moral values."

My second question was, assuming he believes in the relevance of religion to the problems of social change, how he explains the failure of traditional religion to come to grips with the problems of man and society in the past and present.

"To the extent that religion has failed in the past, it can be attributed to two general causes. First, religion has not been sufficiently universal. Religions in the past have emphasized their differences from each other, and these differences often became the source of conflicts which made conditions worse. Secondly, religion in the past was not scientific. It taught things which were not true, which ran counter to scientific evidence. The main thing always is truth. Any belief which is untrue in the end is bound to fail."

I confess I was startled by these unexpected answers to my questions. I said that as a humanist and rationalist I heartily agree with him, especially if no religious doctrines are to be given credence if they cannot be substantiated by the same kind of evidence we accept in scientific affairs. I wanted to know, however, if the ethical views which are common to all religions are enough to solve our problems. Aren't they too vague and general? Don't we find that in many situations of conflict both sides appeal to them with equal fervor? How can they be a guide in a strike or on differences in national policy, where conflicts of interest are involved? Shouldn't the emphasis fall first upon the objective study of the facts of conflict and the exploration of alternative solutions?

To this, Vinoba said several things. It is a question of sincerity. If there are differences, despite the profession of agreement, it might mean that one or both parties are not sincere—are not interested in the truth. If they want to find the truth, they would make all the investigations that are necessary. Existing conditions in any given place or time must be carefully studied, and when we understand them we can rely upon human intelligence to find the right way. It is not enough to talk about science, industrialization, and modernization in relation to society as a whole. They have to be brought down to where people live here and now. For example, most people in India live in the villages. Industrialization has to start with the local unit so that there will not be too sharp a break with their way of life, which would uproot them.

These ideas were not developed consecutively by Vinoba but as comments. He returned to my written questions. The next one was: What in general is your conception of a good society?

"A good society," he replied after some hesitation, "is one in which there are no conflicts of interest among men, in which men live according to their obligations to each other." I objected that I could not conceive of such a society so long as men are men and not angels, and that I have doubts about angels. In any society there would be conflicts about some things, and I gave a few illustrations. He then qualified his answer and said that the absence of conflict is an ideal which can be progressively approached. A society with fewer conflicts would be a better society. I raised the question whether social development depends upon conflicts of interest and whether it would not be more fruitful to conceive of the good society in terms of procedures rather than of goals, as a society in which all conflicts of interest are resolved by intelligent inquiry, the give-and-take of democratic process.

Vinoba did not reply to this directly. He answered that the important element in a good society is the absence of any coercion, the use of nonviolent methods. "The fundamental values of the good society are Truth, Compassion, and Love. It is only by relying upon and following them that we can achieve either a good life or a good society in which violence has no place." He went on in this vein and quoted in Sanskrit from the Sutras to illustrate the perennial wisdom of the Indian tradition.

I had two difficulties with this, and we had a warm and friendly exchange that lasted for almost a half hour, until it was time for Vinoba to speak to the assembled crowds. First, I asked him why he assumed that Truth, Compassion, and Love are always compatible. The facts of moral experience show that sometimes they *are* in conflict with each other. To which he replied that the value of Truth is primary. But sometimes, I persisted, out of compassion we do not tell the truth, or the whole truth, in our personal relations to others. Sometimes the truth is a weapon in the hands of the cruel. It is not enough to establish a scheme of values, for each situation seems to have its own good which requires that we choose or mediate between values that are deemed absolute. In other words, I do not see how any value can be regarded as absolute, except possibly intelligence, which in contradistinction to all other values is the judge of its own limitations.

Vinoba seemed puzzled by all this, but nonetheless persisted in his view that one cannot ground the necessity of nonviolence in human affairs unless one accepts the trinity of Truth, Compassion, and Love. If they are not absolute values, then nonviolence is not an absolute value. I asked whether he recognized any distinction between the scope and validity of the values of Truth, Compassion, and Love, and its corollary, nonviolence, in personal relations, on the one hand, and social life on the other. He replied in the negative and implied that to recognize any such distinction would be to introduce an element of insincerity into our moral experience, that it is this divorce between personal and social morality which seems to him at the root of many social evils. I agreed but said that I was afraid of all absolutes, and have found that in the field of personal morality his trinity of values must sometimes be breached. We cannot always be kind when we are truthful and truthful when we are compassionate—and in the field of social morality we cannot always be nonviolent because of our love and compassion for others. He objected to this as one of the oldest illusions in human relations and the source of the ever-recurrent cycle of evil being combated with evil means.

I asked him whether out of compassion for certain victims of a determined and wicked aggressor I would ever be justified in using violence to restrain the aggressor and, if necessary to save the lives of his innocent victims, to kill him. He answered firmly in the negative. I gave him one graphic illustration after another, from Hitler to a pyromaniac about to destroy hundreds. Each time he replied that one must be prepared to lay down his life to save the lives of others, but not to take life. I pressed the matter and pointed out that this assumed we could save the lives of others by sacrificing our own. But the conditions of the problems I put before him—and they were not artificial problems but arose again and again in the struggle for freedom and human dignity—assume that it is the case that the *only* way we can stop the slaughter of the innocents is by using violence against those who are about to employ it. "To stand by," I said at one point, "and watch the slaughter of those for whom we have the love and compassion you enjoin on us, when by our actions we could save them, is to share the responsibility for the evil done them. One must be more than human or less than human to live by the creed of nonviolence in such a situation."

I shall never forget the answer with which he brought the discussion of this issue to a close. He said: "In such case if you used violence I would find it in my heart to forgive you."

Narayan had joined the discussion when I asserted that, as I understood Gandhi, not even he had made an absolute fetish of nonviolence in all circumstances. Narayan countered that Gandhi had said that cowardice is worse than the use of violence, that if one refrains from using violence against an aggressor about to commit some horrible and despicable crime only because one is afraid for his own skin, it would be better to fight for the victim even with violence. If one remains rational and unafraid, ready to die if need be to prevent evil, then one cannot breach the absolute rule against nonviolence. (Later, on the way home, we continued the discussion with whose earlier outcome Narayan had been unhappy. He had understood me to argue for a general philosophy of violent resistance to evil, as if it were simply an either-or question. I explained, however, that all I was concerned with was to avoid the *fetishism* of nonviolence on the basis of a philosophy of nonviolence. Unless extreme or limiting situations are recognized, in which we can make an *intelligent* use of force against those who are embarked on a policy of total terror, we would be turning the world over to sadistic monomaniacs like Hitler and Stalin and to jolly gangsters like Khrushchev.)

Toward the close of our discussion, I observed that I found his position quite compatible, except for the danger of fetishizing nonviolence, with scientific humanism. Vinoba replied that I had overlooked a central point. "There is something operating in experience completely beyond the realm of ethics and science. That is the self, or better, the 'I.' After all, it is *we* who must know, it is *we* who decide or choose. But what is it that knows? When we strive for self-knowledge, what is the object of that knowledge? Here is something that cannot be grasped by any scientific knowledge, something which is the source of all values. It is the 'I'—and it is the gateway to religion." I raised some difficulties with this. I asked whether the nature of the "I" does not depend upon the biological, social, historical, and psychological contexts of experience, whether the consciousness of self-identity is anything more than memory of continuities in the stream of events. He implied that it is something over and above all these. I then asked how he distinguishes between true self-knowledge and false self-knowledge and argued that since our knowledge of others and others' knowledge of us are sometimes more accurate than the deliverances of self-knowledge, the self cannot be understood as something independent of its history or total behavior in space and time. It seems to me that the word "I" is either a term of mere reference or a shifting symbol of a complex of histories and experiences with a locus in a given body. I do not see how, without some involvement in matter or energy or history, one "I" can be distinguished from another "I." When I said this, Vinoba and Narayan exchanged smiles and the former replied, "Perhaps they cannot." The camel's nose of Indian metaphysics had gotten into the discussion, but the exigency of time kept it tethered.

Two other questions I recall putting to Vinoba. One was whether he thinks he can achieve his program of social reconstruction in India without organizing a political movement. He replied that if he were to attempt to develop a political movement, he would divide his followers, that he wants to transcend all the political differences and organizations in India with an attitude and program whose spirit would influence existing groups. Later, Narayan explained that Vinoba is already a political force to be reckoned with, even though he is waging his struggle for the betterment of India with spiritual weapons. Testimony to Vinoba's political influence was the fact that a man like Nehru took time from a busy political life publicly to visit and consult with Vinoba, to be seen with him, and to impress the Indian masses that he is sympathetic with what Vinoba stands for. When I was at Ahmadabad, I was told that when Vinoba visited the city he drew a greater outpouring of people than India's popular prime minister.

The other question to Vinoba was whether in addition to Gandhi he had been inspired by other social or religious figures. He replied, with the only touch of asperity I detected in his remarks, that he is not concerned with tracing his indebtedness to any other figure, incouding Gandhi, and that it is not personalities that should inspire belief and action, but ideals and ideas.

When I left, I walked to the field through a passage made by cordoning off the bystanders. Thousands of eyes stared at me as if some of Vinoba's *charisma* had rubbed off on me. A few minutes later, Vinoba followed, walking with amazing swiftness, and was preceded by shouts and hails that rippled like waves through the crowds. Vinoba mounted the platform while the audience kept shouting, *"Jaya Jagot"* ("Victory to Mankind"). It hushed when he arose. His voice even over the loudspeaker seemed frail and reedy. He spoke in Gujerati, one of the many Indian languages in which he is at home. Narayan told me he was not making a plea for Boodan (the gift of land by one individual to others) or Gramdan (the gift of land by an individual to the community), but for the "People's pence," to support the men and women in the Boodan movement who had dedicated their lives to work in the villages.

I do not know enough of India to make an intelligent assessment of Vinoba Bhave's influence on the shape of future events. He has obviously captured the imagination of the villages, not merely as a successor of Ghandi but in his own right as a holy man. He seems to me to be more intelligent and more learned than Gandhi, but not so shrewd. No movement can succeed in India which sets itself against him. His ethical socialism makes it possible for all sorts of people to cooperate with him. He is a purely Indian phenomenon. His like could not exist in the Soviet Union, Communist China, or even in the United States. He is on the side of freedom and self-government. But in international affairs, India's policy in the future will in all likelihood be determined by others rather than by this barefoot, lovable sage.

1959

Chapter 17
Bertrand Russell and
Crimes Against Humanity

A few months ago Bertrand Russell, the nona-
genarian but still vigorous English philosopher, issued a call for an
international tribunal of justice to put on trial "the war-criminals—
Johnson, Rusk, McNamara, Lodge, and their fellow criminals."
Next month, on November 13, 1966 a preliminary meeting of the
group is scheduled to be held in London.

Promptly and enthusiastically endorsed by Radio Hanoi and the
Communist press throughout the world, the indictment published
by Russell accuses the American government and its leaders of
deliberate and systematic resort to the use of "concentration camps,
torture, massacre, poison gas and chemical warfare" against the
Vietnamese people. It charges the United States with behaving like
the Nazis in Eastern Europe and the Japanese in Southeast Asia "on
a scale which is larger and with an efficiency which is more terrible
than complete."

The explanation of these horrible crimes against humanity, according to Russell, is simple. The American leaders have done "all
this to protect the interests of American capitalism" and further
"their own economic interests." The people ruled by these capitalists are kept ignorant of the facts by a lying press; they are unaware
that they, too, are being exploited by the war criminals and industrial overlords: "66 million Americans live at the poverty level. The
cities of America are covered with slums. The poor carry the burden
of taxation and the fighting of colonial and aggressive wars."

Russell holds out hope, however, that the rule of these "greedy and brutal men" will be overthrown just as soon as Americans understand the connection between the crimes perpetrated in Vietnam and the poverty of the American masses. "The Negro struggle in Harlem and Watts—the resistance of American students" are encouraging signs. The War Crimes Tribunal, by providing "the most exhaustive portrayal of what has happened to the people of Vietnam," will contribute to this end.

What is curious about this document, issued in the name of one of the most distinguished minds of our century, is the simplism of its thought and the virulence of its language, matching the crudest Communist propaganda leaflets. The only charge absent from its litany of crimes is that of germ warfare, the standard Communist canard during the Korean War that was laid to rest at the cessation of hostilities.

In view of Russell's declaration that the tribunal is to provide "the most exhaustive portrayal of what has happened to the people of Vietnam," perhaps a more important omission is the lack of any reference to the tens of thousands of Vietnamese men, women, and children murdered and mutilated by Vietcong terrorists. These, apparently, are not regarded as crimes against humanity. Nor is there reference to Ho Chi Minh's bloody purges, whose excesses have been admitted by Hanoi and which caused almost a million refugees to flee South. The Vietcong is mentioned only where Russell denies that it is Communist controlled. It is merely "a broad alliance, like the popular fronts of Europe"—presumably something like the movement headed by Leon Blum in France.

Because of its extremism, some observers have doubted that Russell himself is author of the statement, despite the use of the first person pronouns in it. Some sentences, such as the assertion that American capitalists "send American soldiers to Vietnam as company cops," are written in an American idiom untypical of Russell. Elsewhere, the document reads as if someone were trying to imitate Russell's style. None the less, there can be little doubt that it expresses his sentiments. He has broadcast the substance of it on the Hanoi and Vietcong radios. He has earlier charged that American soldiers in Vietnam were using their bayonets to rip open the bellies of pregnant women—a charge last laid, not against the Nazis in Eastern Europe, but against the German soldiers in Belgium during World War I. The historical irony is that Russell came into public limelight by deriding these and other atrocity stories about the Germans.

Still, a case can be made for an objective investigation of the conduct of the Vitnamese war, as of any war. All wars spell death and suffering, which are always evil even when necessary in defense of a good cause. Sometimes the death and suffering are unnecessary and therefore doubly evil. It is absurd, however, to say that all wars are equally inhumane. A war in which prisoners and wounded are murdered after being tortured is worse than a war fought under the Geneva conventions. A war in which noncombatants are destroyed by the planting or hurling of bombs, or deliberately subjected to bombing from the air, is worse than one in which the noncombatant population is spared and only military forces and installations attacked.

Some day when conditions permit, an investigation into the way the war has been conducted in Vietnam, into its crimes as distinct from its accidents, may be perfectly in order. An "exhaustive portrayal of what happened to the people of Vietnam"—if honest and objective—could be instructive to all the peoples of the world. While it would not abolish war, it might powerfully affect the way it was fought. But whoever conducts such an investigation must not be a party to the conflict or violently prejudiced against either side. He must not be so precommitted to an antecedent conclusion that he weighs the evidence unfairly. He must not have previously condoned the type of "crimes" to be investigated.

How well does Bertrand Russell pass these tests? How "objective" is this searcher for objective truth? Does he come into court with morally clean hands? How trustworthy and reliable are his reports? How much confidence can any fair person, informed of the past, have in "the *bona fides* and authenticity" of any tribunal he organizes?

Note that to begin with Russell proclaimed in the most unmeasured terms the guilt of President Johnson, Secretary of Defense McNamara, Secretary of State Rusk, and other American leaders — and then he proposed to sit in judgment on them. Having pronounced the verdict of guilty, he is now, like a character out of Gilbert and Sullivan, arranging for the trial. He and his selected associates have set themselves up to play the roles of judge, juror, and accuser all at once.

This objection to "trying" people declared guilty in advance has been raised by many critics of the tribunal, and it apparently has stung Russell and his associates. In a letter in the *New York Times* of October 6, he defends his tribunal as a grand jury considering prima facie evidence in order to bring an indictment. But Russell has *already* drawn up the indictment. Further, he seems unfamiliar with the fact that the grand jury which indicts is not the same jury which sits in judgment at the trial to resolve the issue of the truth of the indictment. He also mentions the Dewey commission, which fairly examined the evidence of Stalin's purge trials in the 1930s.

That commission, which I helped organize, was first of all an inquiry into "evidence" already introduced in the Moscow trials. It gave Trotsky a hearing denied him by the Moscow courts that convicted him without indicting him.

The analogue to the Dewey commission would be a commission of inquiry to examine the evidence to be introduced (or not introduced) before the Russell tribunal. By announcing that only the alleged crimes of the American government will be judged and not those of the Vietcong and the Hanoi regime, the Russell tribunal is more likely to function like the Moscow tribunal than like the Dewey commission. So resentful is Russell of the criticism of his procedure that he suggests that those who make these criticisms are also responsible for the crimes against the people of Vietnam. He writes, "I suggest that those who raise procedural points in objecting to the International War Crimes Tribunal would be better occupied in assessing their own responsibility for the horrendous acts against the people of Vietnam."

This sounds more like Andrei Vishinsky than like the author of *Justice in War Time*. This is exactly the way English superpatriots spoke of Russell when he questioned the stories about German atrocities in Belgium in World War I.

The charge against the American "war criminals" is indiscriminate warfare against the Vietnamese people. If this were true, North Vietnamese centers of population would long since have been destroyed. But in any event, Bertrand Russell has no moral standing in the court. He has justified indiscriminate warfare against a whole people. He was an eloquent defender of a preventive atomic war against the Soviet Union when the Kremlin refused to accept the American and UN offer to internationalize the sources of atomic energy. Clearly, atom bombs are a much greater menace to civilian populations than pinpoint bombing with conventional weapons. To condone one and condemn the other is like starting a forest fire and becoming hysterical over the danger of a campfire.

Morally, Russell's position is further weakened by the fact that he urged a preventive war on purely ideological grounds. Johnson in Vietnam, like Truman in Korea, whatever the wisdom of their decisions, intervened to repel actual aggressions—to counteract actions that unleashed war. But Russell urged preventive war to destroy communism in the Soviet Union and elsewhere. He anticipated that the Kremlin would refuse to yield to any ultimatum to internationalize atomic energy and coldly, if not cheerfully, accepted the consequences of inevitable atomic war. In such a war, he wrote: "I have no doubt that America would win in the end, but unless Western Europe can be preserved from invasion, it will be lost to civilization for centuries [since the Communists would seize Western Europe and we would have to bomb it too]. Communism must be wiped out, and world government must be established." (Written in 1948, this was published in the *Saturday Review* of October 16, 1954.)

The "American capitalists and their political and military servants," apparently more humane than Russell, refused to employ their monopoly of atomic power to destroy the Russian people in order to get rid of communism. Instead, they offered Communist countries Marshall Plan aid and sought to reach an accommodation on the principle that the political status quo should not be altered by outside foreign forces. Far from being blindly anti-Communist and going to war for ideological reasons, as Russell urged, the United States has even aided some Communist regimes to preserve their independence at tremendous costs to the American taxpayer. This policy has had greater support from Main Sreet than Wall Street. The chief errors in United States policy may be traced not so much to the fear of native Communists coming to power by legitimate political means as to mistaken appraisal of the involvement of foreign Communists regimes as in the Dominican Republic, and their efforts to impose their will on neighboring peoples by invasion or subversion.

Obviously, Russell is not sufficiently free from violent bias against either side in the Vietnam war to assess fairly the respective guilt of the combatants. Indeed, there is a good deal of evidence to show that he has become almost pathologically anti-American, not against individual Americans, but against the American nation—its leaders and policies, and its people to the extent that they support these leaders and policies. Perhaps the most emphatic expression of Russell's hostility to the United States—not without its humorous aspects—occurred at the time of the Cuban missile crisis. Russell had by that time swung from a political posture in favor of preventive atomic war to one of nuclear disarmament. When President Kennedy announced the discovery of Soviet nuclear missiles in Cuba, positioned to fire at the United States, Russell taxed the president with lying. He denied that there were such missiles in Cuba and dismissed the photographs as fakes. He denounced the American heads of state as "worse than Hitler" and as the crisis deepened, wrote: "You are going to die because rich Americans dislike the government Cubans prefer. Do not yield to ferocious and insane murderers."

When Khrushchev finally admitted the presence of Soviet missiles in Cuba, Russell was not embarrassed in the least. As a founder of the Ban-the-Bomb movement, one expected at the very least that he would condemn Khrushchev for smuggling nuclear weapons into Cuba, thus precipitating the crisis. Instead, he *praised* Khrushchev for his forbearance. Russell's attitude and sympathies were clearly expressed in the text of two telegrams. The first was to Kennedy.

YOUR ACTION DESPERATE THREAT TO HUMAN SURVIVAL NO CONCEIVABLE JUSTIFICATION CIVILIZED MAN CONDEMNS IT. WE WILL NOT HAVE MASS MURDER ULTIMATUM MEANS WAR I DO NOT SPEAK FOR POWER BUT PLEAD FOR CIVILIZED MAN END THIS MADNESS.

The second was to Khrushchev, who had dispatched the missiles and whose adventurism was subsequently criticized by his own comrades.

MAY I HUMBLY APPEAL FOR YOUR FURTHER HELP IN LOWERING THE TEMPERATURE DESPITE THE WORSENING SITUATION YOUR CONTINUED FORBEARANCE IS OUR GREAT HOPE WITH MY HIGH REGARDS AND SINCERE THANKS.

Apparently Russell's high regard for Khrushchev was unaffected not only by Khrushchev's role in the Cuban missile crisis but by the butchery of the Hungarian Freedom Fighters, carried out on Khrushchev's express orders.

One might interpret Russell's blatant anti-Americanism, his shrill denunciation of America's foreign policy, and his uncharacteristic servility to Khrushchev as a kind of subconscious compensation for his earlier espousal of a nuclear preventive war against communism. But this can hardly explain the tone and substance of his criticisms of American domestic policies and conditions in recent years. Far from recognizing the great, if incomplete, strides made toward the elimination of poverty and racial discrimination, Russell writes of the United States as if its minorities lived under a perpetual reign of terror organized against them by the federal government, and as if the American working class was still suffering the throes of hunger and unemployment. About the time the FBI arrested and jailed John Kasper, the white racist rabble rouser, for encouraging violation of a federal court order, Russell wrote of conditions in America:

"Members of the FBI join even mildly liberal organizations as spies and report any unguarded word. Anybody who goes so far as to support equal rights for colored people, or to say a good word for the UN is liable to a visit by officers of the FBI and threatened, if not with prosecution, at least with blacklisting and consequent inability to earn a living. When a sufficient state of terror has been produced by these means, the victim is informed there is a way out; if he will denounce a sufficient number of his friends, he may obtain absolution."

These and other fantastic statements, unmatched even by the worst drivel about America broadcast by Radio Moscow or Peking, brought forth an indignant refutation by Norman Thomas, the veteran Socialist leader, and a more consistent opponent of war than Russell. His "Open Letter to Bertrand Russell" [*New Leader*, January 7, 1957] refuting these falsehoods left Russell unmoved. Russell's fury against the United States has reached such a pitch that despite his claims to have returned to his earlier pacifism, he has recently appealed to Premier Kosygin of the Soviet Union to send the Soviet Air Force to combat the American planes in Vietnam—thus inviting the very global war he professes to fear.

In his latest characterization of the United States, Russell speaks of the American welfare state as if it were an economic-military dictatorship ruling over a brainwashed and poverty stricken population. He ignores the fact that the standard of living of the American working class, despite pockets of poverty, is not only the highest in the world but is currently the highest in American history. He ignores the progress the Negro, the Puerto Rican, and other minorities have made with the help of all three branches of the American government. He ignores the fact that most principled and consistent opponents of Communist aggression are not the American capitalists—many of whom wish to do business with the Communist countries, including Communist China—but the organized American labor movement.

One does not have to approve of American foreign policy in Vietname or elsewhere to be appalled by the virulence and hatred of Russell's caricature of America's culture and economy. When he shifted from the advocacy of appeasement of fascism in the thirties to resistance, he never spoke of Nazi Germany in comparable terms. What explains his transition from a staunch opponent of communism—we were premature anti-Communists in many battles together!—to a role more appropriate to Lord Haw-Haw than to Lord Russell?

I am assuming, and I think it is true, that Russell is still in possession of his remarkable faculties—that he is not a pitiable old man blindly signing statements drawn up in his name by those upon whom he has become physically and mentally dependent. One reason for believing that he is responsible for what he has written is that he has recorded large portions of it for Radio Hanoi for transmission to American servicemen in South Vietnam.

There are some who contend that Russell's transformation from a fanatical anti-Communist—prepared to destroy communism almost at any cost including nuclear war—into a fanatical anti anti-Communist and anti-American, is a consequence of the humiliations he suffered in the United States in 1940–42. At that time he was unjustly denied an opportunity to teach at the City College because of his views on sex and marriage—views that are widely held today. Later he was rudely and arbitrarily dismissed from his post at the Barnes Foundation which had been procured for him by John Dewey.

This shocking treatment left him with a justified resentment which still burned fiercely when I last met him in the fall of 1953. But it does not explain the shift of ground. For although he was very critical of the United States at the time, asserting with typical exaggeration that the United States had become a police state under McCarthy, he was even more critical of communism.

The real reasons for Russell's conversion say more for his motives than his judgment. When the Soviet Union acquire the full panoply of nuclear weapons, Russell became convinced that their proliferation would in all likelihood lead to a world war which would destroy the whole of civilization, perhaps all human life. He was aware that the West, particularly the United States, had officially declared its willingness to accept general and complete disarmament provided it was universal and multilateral, subject to strict international control in order to prevent totalitarian countries, unhampered by a free press or a free public opinion, from launching atomic Pearl Harbors. At first Russell thought that the Soviet Union would accept such controls, since they were in everyone's interest. But when it became clear that the Communists would not permit effective inspection on their territory, Russell's views underwent a profound change. He declared, "I am for controlled nuclear disarmament but, if the Communists cannot be induced to agree to it, then I am for unilateral disarmament even if it means the horrors of Communist domination." In effect, to avoid the risks of war Russell was willing to settle for peace at any price.

The foolishness of such a position is apparent, since it can only harden Communist intransigence. It offers the premium of total victory for stubbornness and unreasonableness in negotiation. It expects those who enjoy the reality of freedom and independence, however limited, to surrender them out of fear of a problematic world disaster. Freedom and independence are still precious values in the Western world. Even Russell was once prepared to sacrifice half a billion lives if necessary to prevent the triumph of communism. Not many years before his current slogan "Better red, than dead," he wrote, "Terrible as a new world war would be, I still for my part should prefer it to a universal Communist empire" (*New York Times Magazine*, September 27, 1953).

The logic of Russell's new position, the emphasis on peace at any price, compelled him to downgrade the importance of the values and institutions of freedom in the open societies of the West. He began to refer to the West and especially the United States as the "so-called" free societies—which he did not do when, less free than they are now, they were struggling against fascism—and to play down the evils of Communist dictatorship in the Soviet Union, China, and North Vietnam. If the United States is a dictatorship of the capitalists and their military henchmen under a formal veneer of rhetoric about democracy, the talk about freedom is hollow and hypocritical. Since the choice is between one kind of dictatorship and another, according to Russell's political logic, we may as well stay alive. Instead of resisting Communist aggression by war, which may destroy everyone, it is wiser to yield. "The horrors of Communist domination" will not last forever. Kublai Khan, after all, followed Genghis Khan.

It is thinking of this sort which explains why Russell has declared that West Berlin and West Germany are not worth defending, that India was more at fault than China after China invaded, that the intervention of North Vietnam into South Vietnam is not aggression. It explains why he refuses to speak of the deliberate murder of tens of thousands of South Vietnamese by Vietcong terrorists in connection with what he purports to be a "most exhaustive portrayal of what has happened to the people of Vietnam," and why he plays up as deliberate American atrocities the unfortunate accidental loss of civilian lives incurred by the efforts of American military forces to help the South Vietnamese repel the incursions of North Vietnam and its partisans.

Bertrand Russell is no more a Communist today than he was during the many years he denounced its terror. But his desperate fear of war has made him the willing ally of the Communist cause. Even in 1938 when he was pleading that the best defense of England and Denmark against Hitler was "their very defenselessness," and that in the event of a Nazi invasion and takeover "the consequences both to ourselves and the world would be infinitely less terrible than the consequences of war," he did not speak up for the Nazis or defend their actions or pretend that they represented the forces of peace and liberation. Today, however, Russell has willingly accepted the role of spokesman for the Communist cause in Vietnam. Last June 11 he sent two separate messages to the Vietcong and to Hanoi informing them that he was organizing a war crimes tribunal to bring Johnson, McNamara, and Rusk to justice. He concluded his message with these words. "I extend my warm regards and full solidarity for President Ho Chi Minh and for the people of Vietnam. I convey my great wish that the day may not be far off when a united and liberated Vietnam will celebrate its victory in a free Saigon."

Bertrand Russell's place in the history of modern philosophy is as incontestable as the place of Richard Wagner in the history of music. Neither the anti-Semitism of the latter nor the anti-Americanism of the former can alter that fact. But they prove that when great men err they err greatly.

One final question remains. Bertrand Russell may be wrong in his unmeasured indictment of the position of the United States. But this does not establish the validity of the American policy. What moral justification, if any, can be offered for American intervention in South Vietnam? Perhaps the strongest defense of the official position of the United States was actually made a long time ago by John Stuart Mill, the godfather of Bertrand Russell. In an essay on "Non-Intervention" (*Fraser's Magazine*, 1859), which reads as if it were written only yesterday, Mill wrote: "To go to war for an idea, if the war is aggressive not defensive, is as criminal as to go to war for territory or revenue; for it is as little justifiable to force our ideas on other people, as to compel them to submit to our will in any other respect."

None but ideological fanatics would dispute this. Mill then states what is required of a foreign policy, grounded in an intelligent morality, in situations like that of South Vietnam. "*The doctrine of non-intervention, to be a legitimate principle of morality, must be accepted by all governments.* The despots must consent to be bound by it as well as the free states. Unless they do, the profession of it by free countries comes but to this miserable issue, that the wrong side may help the wrong side but the right may not help the right. Intervention to enforce non-intervention is always right, always moral, if not always prudent. Though it may be a mistake to give freedom [or independence—S.H.] to a people who do not value the boon, it cannot but be right to insist that if they do value it, they shall not be hindered from the pursuit of it by foreign coercion." (Italics mine—S.H.)

No one can reasonably question that South Vietnam values its independence, and that it is right for the United States to endorse its claim. But whether what was right was also prudent, whether anything which is imprudent on a large scale is also right, are questions not so readily answered. It may have been imprudent originally to become involved in South Vietnam. But it seems even more imprudent to withdraw from South Vietnam without negotiating a peace. For this would abandon the South Vietnamese to enslavement and decimation by the vengeful Vietcong and thus encourage further Communist aggression. I believe that Adlai Stevenson spoke for the reflective conscience of America when he said, on the very day of his death: "My hope in Vietnam is that resistance there may establish the fact that changes in Asia are not to be precipitated by outside force. This was the point of the Korean War. This is the point of the conflict in Vietnam."

If this point gets across the sacrifices will not have been in vain, since they will have prevented further sacrifices. If it does not, then since the United States cannot be active everywhere, prudence may dictate greater caution in the future concerning when and where to engage the enemies of freedom and national independence.

1966

Chapter 18

The Scoundrel in

the Looking Glass

Lillian Hellman enjoys a wide reputation: students pay her homage, reviewers praise her books. A recent play on the McCarthy era presents her as a martyred heroine, radiant in the glow of the spotlight. She is also a brilliant polemicist, skilled in moralizing even at the expense of truth, honor, and common sense. And she has spun a myth about her past that has misled the reading public of at least two countries.

Let us imagine the following case.

A woman of some literary talent and reputation who, although not a cardholding member of the Nazi German-American Bund, which flourished in the 1930s, is the mistress of one of its leading figures, and hobnobs with its political leaders in the circles in which she moves. She signs denunciations of the victims of Hitler's purges and frame-up trials as "spies and wreckers" whose degenerate character has been established, and characterizes the Nazi holocaust as a purely internal affair of a progressive country whose "policies have resulted in a higher standard of living for the people." She attacks a commission of inquiry, headed by a noted American philosopher, to discover the truth about juridical affairs in Nazi Germany. At every political turn as Hitler consolidates his power and screws tighter the pitch of his terror against his own people and those of other lands, she lauds his rule. She plays a leading role in organizing cultural front organizations as transmission belts for the Nazi party line. When Berlin launches a phony peace conference, she serves as a keynote speaker denying its true auspices and savagely assailing its critics. When artists and literary figures rally to provide relief for the victims of Nazi oppression, she sabotages their efforts by insisting that charity begins at home. She visits Nazi Germany four times and returns without uttering a single word of criticism of its *gleichgeschaltet* culture, and its concentration camps.

Disturbed by the growing influence of the German-American Bund and other political groups controlled by foreign governments, Congress authorizes one of its committees to investigate their activities and the sources of their plentiful funds. The legitimacy of the inquiry is upheld by the highest courts. It turns out that many members and sympathizers of the Bund are found in the entertainment industry. By this time because the true nature of the Nazi regime has been discovered by many, and because the United States is virtually at war with Hitler, some witnesses subpoenaed and under oath, and therefore subject to penalties of perjury, testify truly about their past involvements and experiences. Some refuse to testify about their membership, invoke the First Amendment, and risk being jailed for contempt. Others invoke the privilege of the Fifth Amendment on the ground that their truthful testimony would tend to incriminate them. Some like the woman in question invoke the Fifth Amendment not on the ground that their truthful testimony would tend to incriminate *them* but that it would tend to incriminate *others*—which really constitutes an abuse of the Fifth Amendment. Some who publicly claim to have been falsely identified as members of the Bund, when invited to confirm or deny the charge, nonetheless invoke the Fifth Amendment.

Much of the interrogation appears, and indeed is, irrelevant or foolish. Some of the committee members are interested in making headlines and (in the changed climate of hostile opinion to Germany) political capital out of the investigation. Nonetheless, considerable evidence is uncovered of penetration by members and sympathizers of the Bund into various areas of American cultural life, especially the entertainment industry. Partly out of conviction and partly out of a sense of guilt at the shabby way they earned their swollen salaries in Hollywood, members and fellow travelers paid large sums of money into the coffers of the Bund. Some of them were well enough organized to place obstacles in the way of outspoken critics of Nazi causes who sought employment.

The entertainment industry is run for profit. Its moguls are exceedingly sensitive to what affects public favor and box-office receipts. Not surprisingly, owners and producers became fearful of employing those identified under oath as members of the Nazi German-American Bund, or who invoked the Fifth Amendment, lest any film, play, or program with which they are associated become the target of a public boycott. An informal blacklist developed and some racketeers sought to exploit the situation. Some economic hardship resulted. Blacklisted writers peddled their scripts under pseudonyms. However, in a few short years, the wartime hostilities with Germany having been forgotten, those who suffered temporary economic hardship resumed their prosperous careers.

What would one think of the woman in this parable who, in 1976, strikes the pose of a heroine who defied the congressional inquisition and empties the vials of her wrath on anti-Fascists in the intellectual and literary community who allegedly stood idly by when she was questioned about her involvement with leading Nazi members and organizations? What would one think of this woman who now lamely asserts that her only fault was being a little late in recognizing "the sins" of Hitler—despite all the evidence that had accumulated over the forty years from the time she had endorsed the first of Hitler's mass purges?

For the Nazi German-American Bund in the above hypothetical account substitute the Communist party. For the woman in question—Lillian Hellman who in her book *Scoundrel Time* [1] seems to have duped a generation of critics devoid of historical memory and critical common sense.

When Lillian Hellman was subpoenaed to appear before the House committee, the United States was in effect at war with two Communist powers—North Korea and China. The threat of involvement with the U.S.S.R. loomed large in popular consciousness. The leaders of the Communist party had declared that in case of conflict with the Soviet Union they would not support the United States. The record of Communist actions, at home and abroad, had generated fear in the American people—and not only among them—of forcible Communist expansion. It began with the violation of the treaties about free elections in Eastern Europe; followed by the revelations of Igor Gouzenko (the code clerk in the Russian embassy in Ottawa) of massive Soviet espionage in Canada and the United States by domestic Communists; the Communist take-over in Czechoslovakia; the arrest and conviction of Klaus Fuchs, Allen Nunn May, Harry Gold, the Rosenbergs, David Greenglass, and other atomic spies; testimony of Communist penetration into some of the most sensitive areas of government; the trials and conviction of Alger Hiss; the Communist blockade of Berlin; the hazardous and costly Berlin airlift; Communist support of rebels in Greece and Turkey; the invasion of South Korea (June 1950). Whatever one

1. (Boston: Little, Brown & Co., 1976).

thinks of the wisdom of congressional investigations—and despite Lillian Hellman's contention to the contrary, their methods and areas of investigations were *often* criticized by liberals!—they did not create the climate of concern about Communist aggression abroad and Communist penetration within. That was a consequence of historical events. CIO trade-unionists and NAACP Negro leaders were barring Communist-controlled locals from their organizations; leading figures in Americans for Democratic Action and the Socialist party (notably Arthur Schlesinger, Jr., and Norman Thomas) as well as independent anti-Communist liberals, even when criticizing the excesses of the investigating committees, were exposing the unscrupulous behavior of Communist cells in every organization they joined. The concern on the part of the public with security was quite legitimate. One of the great spokesmen of the liberal tradition, Walter Lippmann, even advocated outlawing the Communist party; fortunately it was never done. Certainly the public had a right to know who was financing the Communist party—why nothing had been done to counteract the infiltration of members of its underground apparatus into sensitive government agencies—and what ostensibly neutral organizations, political and cultural, that party had established in order to penetrate the structure of American life.

That Lillian Hellman should have been called as a witness before a congressional committee investigating Communist organizations and activity in the entertainment industry (even if she had not been identified in sworn testimony as present at a meeting organized by Communist party functionaries to enlist prominent writers as members-at-large) was to be expected. The record of her activity as a participant and defender of Communist causes was notorious.

During the 1930s she defended all the Moscow trials, attacked the John Dewey Commission of Inquiry for trying to establish the truth about them, worked hand-in-glove with the party fraction in organizations like the League of American Writers and the Theatre Arts Committee. She went along with almost every twist and turn of the party line. During the Soviet-Finnish War when a theatrical relief committee for the victims of Soviet aggression was organized, it was attacked by Lillian Hellman (among others in the Theatre Arts Committee) on the grounds that "charity begins at home," and that it was a disguised form of intervention abroad—this from the very persons who had been conspicuously active in organizing or supporting committees for Communist relief causes all over the world!

Throughout her self-serving book Lillian Hellman fails to distinguish between two types of witnesses charged with membership before the congressional committees—those who were truly identified as being members of the Communist party, and those who were falsely so identified. To her all investigation of Communist activity was a witch-hunt. One could argue (and many liberal anti-Communists did) that congressional inquiries into education and culture would have a chilling effect upon teachers and other professionals, and that whatever abuses and misconduct by Communists existed in those fields—and there were plenty!—could be dealt with by the practitioners in these fields themselves, without bringing in the state or government. Some took the same position with respect to Communist infiltration in the fields of labor and religion (see, for example, the editorial in the *New Republic* for 20 April 1953, "Communists in the Churches"). But this is not at all Miss Hellman's view. She is opposed to any investigation of members of the Communist party under any auspices. She fiercely attacks any attempt by congressional committees to identify members of the Communist party, even in the most sensitive posts of government, who had slipped through defective and often nonexistent safeguards of the security system. She dismisses the evidence against Alger Hiss in passages that betray her ignorance, really indifference, to the evidence.

According to Miss Hellman the only evidence against Hiss was contained in the documents secreted by Whittaker Chambers in the famous pumpkin. And of these she says that "the only things that had been found in Chambers' pumpkin were five rolls of microfilm, two developed, three in metal containers, most of the frames were unreadable, none of them had anything to do with the charges against Alger Hiss." She could not be more wrong. A great deal of the evidence against Hiss had nothing to do with the contents of the pumpkin (namely, all of the papers that were typed on the Hiss Woodstock typewriter). The two developed microfilm rolls of the five in the pumpkin consisted of photographs of memoranda from State Department office files to which Hiss had access and of mimeographed copies of cables from abroad that were initialled by Hiss. The other three microfilms—which were not introduced in evidence at the trials—contained unclassified material. (Espionage agents never know what the home office already has or might find useful.)

Miss Hellman's reference to the Hiss case is characteristic. On crucial matters, whenever her testimony can be checked by the record it turns out to be misleading or false. The two rolls of developed microfilm bore directly on the charge against Alger Hiss.

Roger Baldwin (the founder and long-time head of the American Civil Liberties Union, and a consistent critic of some of the techniques of congressional investigations) once observed, "A superior loyalty to a foreign government disqualifies a citizen for service to our own." Miss Hellman would have us believe, despite the oaths and pledges that Communist party members took during those years to defend the Soviet Union, that they were no more of a security risk than any others. To be sure membership in the Communist party did not mean that given the opportunity, all members necessarily would be guilty of betrayal of their trust. One may ask, "Are there not some who would refuse to play this role?" The best answer to this question was made by Clement Attlee after the Pontecorvo affair in Britain, "There is no way of distinguishing such people from those who, if opportunity offered, would be prepared to endanger the security of the state in the interests of another power."

Of course there can be no reasonable comparison between the capacities and opportunities for mischief of Communists in sensitive posts in government and Communists in the field of education and culture. Had Miss Hellman recognized this her position would be a little stronger. But her unqualified contention that the investigation of Communists any time and anywhere was a witch-hunt—a subversion of freedom of thought, a persecution of mere heresy rather than of conspiracy and underground secrecy wherever Communist cells functioned—testifies to the faithfulness with which she has followed the official Communist line. She does not regard it as conceivable that one could sincerely oppose *both* the Communists and Senator Joseph McCarthy—the Communists for what they truly represented, the existence and extension of the Gulag Archipelago—and McCarthy for making their work easier by his irresponsible accusations and exaggerations.

Individuals identified as members of the Communist party, and who did not deny it, fell into three main groups—1) those who told the truth, 2) those who refused to answer questions about their membership on grounds of the First Amendment, and 3) those who invoked the privilege against self-incrimination of the Fifth Amendment. In all such cases the motivations for testifying, or not testifying, were mixed; but to Miss Hellman this needlessly complicates matters.

She refers to those who told the truth about their past as "friendly witnesses": These are the "scoundrels." She refuses to believe that anyone who told the truth could have been genuinely disillusioned with Communist behavior or, as the record of Communist penetration and deception unfolded, that they could be shamed by a sense of guilt at having abetted the Communist cause at home and Communist regimes of terror abroad. To her the only "honorable" persons were those who refused to testify if their truthful testimony required that others be implicated. The "betrayers" were only those who did testify regardless of the consequences to others and themselves. But these terms are narrowly defined to fit only the Communist cause.

When the director of the Ku Klux Klan of the state of Alabama was sentenced to jail for refusing to produce Klan records of membership before a grand jury, he pleaded that he was bound by a sacred oath of secrecy, and that to reveal the names of the members would be an act of betrayal. Miss Hellman never raised a murmur against his conviction, and it is not likely that she would characterize his actions as "honorable." She scoffs at the notion that members of the Communist party—even their hardened functionaries—in defending the political and cultural terror of the Soviet regime and its satellites were actually "betraying" the ideals of human freedom and of their own country. Even those like Eric Russell Bentley, who disapproved of the congressional inquiries, wrote apropos of the *Miller* case:

I object . . . to the assumption that what is involved is the question of honor and betrayal with "honor" always meaning the protection of Communists and "betrayal" always meaning the revelation of Communist activity. For after all, there is also such a thing as betrayal of the United States and honorable refusal to betray the United States. Who has been betraying whom? [*New Republic*, 10 September 1956]

Since writing this and other pieces in a similar vein, and at the time in personal letters to me, Eric Bentley has reversed himself. In his *Thirty Years of Treason* (New York, 1970) he praises both Arthur Miller and Lillian Hellman for the stand they took, and out-McCarthys McCarthy by identifying the position of liberal critics of McCarthy—who attacked McCarthy when Bentley remained silent —with the position of "McCarthyism."

Not only is Lillian Hellman altogether unreliable in describing the "friendly" witnesses before the congressional committees, she does not tell the truth about the liberal and socialist anti-Communists of the time. She gives the impression that with hardly any exceptions they were either sympathetic to the investigations or silent out of fear of losing the perquisites of the high positions they occupied. She states flatly, "No editor or contributor of *Commentary* ever protested against McCarthy." The truth is that several editors and contributors protested at his vicious exaggerations not only in the relatively uninfluential pages of that publication but frequently in the *New York Times*.

The first call for the organization of a national movement to retire McCarthy from public life was published in the *New York Times* (3 May 1953) by a contributor to *Commentary, Partisan Review,* and the *New Leader*—at the height of Senator McCarthy's power. The best book on the subject during that period, *McCarthy and Communism*, was published by James Rorty and Moshe Decter in 1954 under the auspices of the American Committee for Cultural Freedom, and received the encomiums of liberal figures like Reinhold Niebuhr and Elmer Davis.

The manner in which Lillian Hellman refers to these anti-Communist liberals shows that what she cannot forgive them for is not so much their alleged failure to critize McCarthy but (despite her belated—in 1976!—acknowledgment of Stalin's "sins") their criticism of the crimes of Stalin and his successors during the forty years in which she apologized for them. Her reference to these anti-Communist liberals also betrays the priggishness of the unconsciously would-be-assimilated 100 percent American whose ancestors had reached American shores a few boatloads ahead of other immigrants. Of these intellectuals she writes that

many of them found in the sins of Stalin Communism—and there were plenty of sins and plenty that for a long time I mistakenly denied—the excuse to join those who should have been their hereditary enemies. Perhaps that in part was the penalty of nineteenth-century immigration. The children of timid immigrants are often remarkable people: energetic, intelligent, hardworking; and often they make it so good that they are determined to keep it at any costs.

What she conceals from the reader is that those she criticizes did not wait for the emergence of McCarthy to combat Stalinism at home and abroad. They began in 1933 when Stalin did his bit to help Hitler come to power. She also conceals the fact that McCarthy was elected with the support of the Communist party to the Senate in 1946, defeating the incumbent liberal anti-Communist Robert La Follette, Jr., who had opposed the treaties of Teheran and Yalta. It took McCarthy four years to become an "anti-Communist crusader" of the nationalist, isolationist variety. She conceals the facts that when McCarthy was riding high, like Congressman Martin Dies before him, he lumped together welfare-state socialists and liberals with Communists; that what contributed to McCarthy's influence (before he did himself in by attacking the army) was the spectacle of scores of Communist witnesses remaining silent, or invoking the Fifth Amendment, as the picture of Communist penetration in American life unfolded; that American reactionaries (who were criticized by those whom Lillian Hellman attacks) seem to have agreed with her that these children of immigrants were the "penalty" for America's past immigration policy; and that few, if any, of these anti-Communist liberals and socialists ever "made it so good" as

Lillian Hellman. Indeed, had they been as much concerned with "making it" as she, they would not have taken an open anti-Communist position when Miss Hellman and her Communist associates were running rampant in Hollywood and elsewhere and trying to bar "Trotskyite-Fascists"—as all anti-Stalinists were then called—from getting work or getting published.

Lillian Hellman pictures herself as a heroine defending intellectual and cultural freedom against her inquisitors. But she actually had nothing to fear from them. She claims that she was never a cardholding member of the Communist party. If true she could not by her testimony identify on the basis of her own knowledge anyone else as a member. Anything else would merely be hearsay. She herself was never clearly identified as a member but only as "present" with leading Communists at a meeting fifteen years earlier—a meeting she cannot recall as having taken place. Since she has denied that she ever was a member of the Communist party, to any question about *any other* person's membership she could have truthfully responded that she did not know. The person who placed her at the meeting had admitted his own membership—she certainly could not have hurt him. Two days before her appearance she wrote the committee that she was prepared to answer all questions about herself; but, if questioned about others, she would invoke the Fifth Amendment because she did not want to bring "bad trouble" to anyone else. She claims that she was the first witness to brave the wrath of the committee with this defiant position.

The official records of her interrogation reveal that her entire present account is a compound of falsity and deliberate obfuscation. First of all, it is not true that she was the first of the witnesses to have taken the position that only if she were not questioned about others would she answer questions truthfully about herself—a condition that no court or committee of inquiry can grant. Communists who were identified as members of the party by the sworn testimony of former members had taken precisely the same approach, and Miss Hellman was merely following the pattern with minor variations. For example, on 19 May 1952 (the very day she wrote her letter and two days before her own appearance) a University of Buffalo teacher of philosophy refused on grounds of the Fifth Amendment to answer the question whether he had been a member of a Communist party cell at Harvard during the late 1930s. He, too, had offered (in a letter to the committee earlier in the month) to testify concerning his own "past associations and activities" but not about others.

The reason why members of the Communist party took this tack should be clear. If they refused to answer any question on the

grounds of the First Amendment, they risked an action for contempt. If they denied membership (as some members of the Communist party had done in previous investigations in local areas like
New York) they risked an action for perjury, if two witnesses who
had been former members identified them. By invoking the Fifth
Amendment as the ground for their refusal, they escaped answering
any questions with impunity. In their case the admission of membership in the Communist party might be self-incriminating under
the Smith Act—although no ordinary member of the party was ever
prosecuted under it. The first victims of the Smith Act were *Trot-
skyists* whose conviction Miss Hellman's political allies gleefully
applauded. In Miss Hellman's case, since she explicitly claims that
she was *not* a member of the Communist party—and that her refusal to say so was motivated only by reluctance to incriminate
others—her invocation of the Fifth Amendment was really illegitimate because her truthful testimony could never have incriminated
her.

Even more surprising are the details of her testimony. Some questions about her membership in the Communist party she answers
without invoking the Fifth Amendment. To the question, "Are you
now a member of the Communist Party?" She answers, "No."
"Were you yesterday?" She still answers, "No." "Were you last year
at this time?" "No." "Two years ago from this time?" "No." But to
the question, "Three years ago at this time?" she refuses to answer
on the grounds of self-incrimination. She does not explain why a
truthful answer would tend to be self-incriminating to the question
about her membership in the Communist party in 1949 but not in
1950, 1951, and 1952.

The committee was satisfied with her response and, happily for
her, took no legal action, for its apparent strategy was to convince
the country that those who invoked the Fifth Amendment had
something to hide. Technically, of course, under the law an innocent person could invoke the Fifth Amendment. A police officer, for
example, earning $15,000 a year and questioned as to whether the
$500,000 in his vault was "graft," could invoke the Fifth Amend-
ment, whether he was guilty or innocent, and stay out of jail. But,
after a departmental hearing, he could very well lose his post, unless
he could rebut the presumption of unfitness to hold a position of
trust created by his refusal to answer a question germane to his
professional responsibilities. As Jeremy Bentham pointed out long
ago the refusal to answer on grounds of possible self-incrimination
creates an inescapable presumption of guilt even if that presumption
is rebuttable.

Whether or not one agrees with his politics—which were abominable since he, too, was a committed apologist for Stalin's terror and upheld its necessity as a teacher in the party school—Dashiell Hammett's course in refusing to testify was certainly more straightforward than Lillian Hellman's. The record of her own interrogation as well as of others gives the lie to the artful reconstruction of her behavior as a morally defiant witness. She relates an incident—unreported by anyone else present (newsmen were there in large numbers)—according to which after her letter had been read by the committee's counsel, a journalist loudly exclaimed, "Thank God somebody finally had the guts to do it!" This is implausible on its face. What she did had indeed been done before, and it required no guts at all to invoke the Fifth Amendment. It was a ticket to safety.

Oddly enough, although her reason for refusing to testify truthfully about herself was that she would cause "bad trouble" to others, on the occasions when she proceeded to invoke the Fifth Amendment she could not possibly have compromised or even embarrassed them. When asked whether she was "acquainted" with Martin Berkeley she invoked the Fifth. But since Berkeley was a self-confirmed former member whose testimony had identified her as present at a meeting in his house, she could not have harmed him in the least. When asked if she was "acquainted" with V. J. Jerome (who was a member of the Political Committee of the Communist party and in charge of organizing Communist party cells in Hollywood), she also invoked the Fifth. The same for John Howard Lawson. She could not have possibly caused them trouble if, as she now assures us, she was not a member of the Communist party during that time. By denying that she was a member in 1952, 1951, and 1950, and invoking the privilege against self-incrimination for periods earlier, she creates the presumption that she told the truth neither then nor now.

Lillian Hellman is not only disingenuous, to put it mildly, about her defiance of the House committee but also about her "involvement" with the Communist movement even if she is given the benefit of every doubt about whether she was technically a dues-paying member. Throughout her book she gives the impression that she really knew little about the political doings going on around her; that the discussions she heard or overheard made no sense to her; that it sounded like gobbledygook; and that her relations with the Communist party were remote, the result of association with Dashiell Hammett, on the one hand, and her opposition to fascism on the other. Yet the internal evidence of this book, and her explicit statement about her political education in a previous book, make it extremely difficult to swallow her artful picture of herself as a rebel and a Bohemian not seriously interested in politics.

By her own account in this book she was up to her neck in politics. She played an important role in both the official and unofficial front activities of the Communist party. She met with "high officials" of the party to discuss the behavior of the party fraction in former Vice-President Henry Wallace's Progressive party. She was privately opposed (she tells us) to the Communist domination of the Progressive party although its role in organizing it was patent even to outsiders. She presents a jeering caricature of Henry Wallace as a kind of eccentric hick and skinflint at a time when the worst thing about him was his invincible political innocence. Subsequently, when he turned against the Communists and denounced them (*New York Herald Tribune*, 14 February 1952) for their "force, deceit, and intrigues," and their activities in the Progressive party, Miss Hellman taxes him with lying—that is, he knew it all along because she had told him that Communists were in the Progressive party when he had asked her about it.

But Lillian Hellman is no more just to Henry Wallace than to others. Wallace had publicly recognized the damage the Communist party was doing to the cause of genuine Progressives when he declared in a speech at Center Sandwich, N.H., in the Fall of 1948, "If the Communists would only run a ticket of their own, the Progressive Party would gain 3,000,000 votes." What Wallace did not know is what Miss Hellman did not tell him—that the Communist party had infiltrated into the strategic organizational posts of the Progressive party, and that she had the evidence of it. What she did tell him when he questioned her was that indeed there were some Communists in the Progressive party and "that the hard, dirty work in the office is done by them. . . . I don't think they mean any harm: they're stubborn men." This was not an accurate account of their role, and she knew it.

In her previous book,[2] Miss Hellman has said enough to make incredible her claim in *this* book that all the strange talk about "dictatorship and revolution" she heard in Communist circles struck her as outlandish. She says she came late to radicalism. But toward the end of the 1930s she undertook a study of Communist doctrine and embarked on an intensive

kind of reading I had never seriously done before. In the next few years, I put aside most other books for Marx and Engels, Lenin, Saint-Simon, Hegel, Feuerbach. Certainly I did not study with the dedication of a scholar, but I did read with the attention of a good student, and Marx as a man, and Engels and his Mary became for a while, more real to me than my friends.

2. *An Unfinished Woman* (Boston: Little, Brown & Co., 1969).

If she could read Hegel we can be sure that she had no difficulty with the catechismic texts of Stalin although she curiously omits his name. Nor did she stop with reading. She checked her knowledge against the superior knowledge of Dashiell Hammett whose Communist political orthodoxy, despite any private doubts, was sufficiently reliable to qualify him for teaching at the party school. "I would test my reading on Dash, who had years before, in his usual thorough fashion, read all the books I was reading and more."

Therefore, when she tells us in her most recent book that precisely during and after this period of intensive study "the over-heated arguments, spoken and printed about dictatorship and repression puzzled me"—as if she were a Marilyn Monroe who had fallen among Marxists—she is singularly unpersuasive. Miss Hellman may or may not have been a member of the Communist party but until Stalin died she was not only a convinced Communist but a Stalinist; and for all her posturing about not really knowing what "dictatorship" means she may still be a Communist. She is no longer a Stalinist but it is not clear when she ceased being one. Communists ceased defending Stalin only after Nikita Khrushchev's revelations at the Twentieth Congress of the Communist party of the Soviet Union in 1956.

Lillian Hellman's most valuable contribution to the Communist cause was her activity on behalf of their front organizations. A few months after the Progressive party imbroglio she was called upon to serve as a keynote speaker at the Cultural and Scientific Conference for World Peace at the Waldorf-Astoria (New York, 25–26 March 1949). This conference was a follow-up of the World Congress of Intellectuals for Peace at Wroclau-Breslau in Communist Poland (25–28 August 1948) and was preparatory to the World Peace Conference in Paris (20–23 April 1949). The Waldorf meeting was held at the height of the Zhdanov purge of Soviet intellectuals. It barred from its program anyone who was critical of Communist party dogma of the class nature of science (including this writer who had, at first, been accepted by a rather careless program committee). The foreign-policy line the conference took was identical with that of the Kremlin: to wit, the United States was the chief enemy of peace and the instigator of the Cold War against the peaceful and freedom-loving Soviet Union. It even refused to give the platform to the Reverend A. J. Muste who was prepared to blame *both* the U.S. and the U.S.S.R. for the Cold War. Lillian Hellman valiantly defended the conference against its critics—whose chief point of protest was the refusal of the conference to speak up for the dissenting or nonconforming intellectuals who were being martyred in Communist countries (although the conference adopted resolutions condemning the court proceedings against Communist leaders under the Smith Act as "heresy trials of political philosophies and attempts to limit and destroy the right of association"). To serve as spokesman for a conference of this kind was a very strange role indeed for a self-denominated life-long "rebel" against organization—at a time when the location and character of the slave-labor camps in the Gulag Archipelago had become public knowledge.

Throughout her book Miss Hellman claims to be aware of "the sins of Stalin," acknowledging only that she was a little late in seeing them. It is only natural to wonder at what point, or when, she saw them; and what she did after she saw them.

It is reasonable to assume that whenever she became aware of them, even if she remained a critic of the sins of her own country, she would not have endorsed measures and organizations that extended the sway or influence of the sinful Stalin and his regime. For otherwise it would have betrayed a degree of hypocrisy and deviousness hard to reconcile with her celebrated forthright nature—so quick to anger when she is bamboozled or pushed around. Nor is it unreasonable to expect that after endorsing in her ignorance so many of "the sins of Stalin"—a curious phrase for "political crimes" since Miss Hellman does not really believe in sin—when she realized their true nature, she would in some way at some point make some public acknowledgment of her discovery. This has been the history of many idealistic Communists and Communist sympathizers who became alienated by some particularly vile outrage or betrayal of the cause with which they had been publicly identified. Certainly, if some former Nazi fellow-traveler were to write in 1976 that, although late, he had become aware of "the sins of Hitler," we would be curious to know when he learned about them, and what he had said or done on making the discovery. (Even Albert Speer has given us thousands of pages of details.)

The record of what Lillian Hellman has written—and not written—makes it clear that she did not know about the political crimes of Stalin during the purges and Moscow frame-up trials of the thirties, the deportations of the peasants and the resulting famine in the Ukraine; the Nazi-Soviet Pact; the invasion of Poland and the destruction of the Baltic States; the Soviet attack on Finland; the surrender of German Jewish Communists who had fled in 1933 to the Soviet Union by Stalin to Hitler in 1940; the liquidation of the anti-Fascist Jewish leaders, Alter and Ehrlich, by Stalin as "spies for Hitler"; the Katyn massacre of the Polish officers; the mass executions and deportations of returning Russian prisoners-of-war after World War II; the overthrow of the democratic Czechoslovak government in 1948; the Zhdanov purges and executions; the Berlin blockade; the Communist invasion of South Korea; the suppression of the German workers' revolt in East Berlin and East Germany in 1953.

Until Stalin died there is not a particle of evidence that Lillian Hellman regarded any of his actions as sinful or politically criminal. Even after Khrushchev's revelations in which he more than confirmed the findings of the John Dewey Commission of Inquiry, denounced by Miss Hellman twenty years earlier, did she by so much as a word signal her awareness of the nature of Stalin's crimes. She remained mute.

Nor did she speak out when Khrushchev sent in Red Army tanks to crush the Hungarian Revolution of 1956. Nor has her voice been heard in criticism of "the sins" or political crimes of Stalin's and Khrushchev's successors—the construction of (and the shootings at) the Berlin Wall, or the renewed persecutions of Soviet dissenters and their incarceration in insane asylums. After all, Miss Hellman visited the Soviet Union in 1937, 1944, 1966, and 1967. But not a single word of criticism of what she saw or heard or of disavowal of her past tributes to the Soviet Union appeared. Not even the brutal invasion of 1968 by Soviet tanks in Czechoslovakia moved her to public protest. By this time even the American Communist party, the most supine of the Kremlin's pensioners, had shown enough independence to make a feeble protest against Soviet anti-Semitism.

Writing in 1976 she expects us to accept without question her assurance that she had long seen through the horrors and systematic oppression of the Communist regimes. It is hard to do this if only because, as this book reveals, she *still* regards those opposed to the extension of Communist influence as greater enemies of human freedom and the decencies of political life than the Communists ever were. Of the Communists she writes with sadness and pity: of the liberal anti-Communists she writes with virulent hatred. By her attack on them she seeks to distract attention from the many years she faithfully served as an acolyte in the "personality cult," Khrushchev's euphemism for the total terror under Stalin. In this she is banking on the absence of historical memory on the part of most of her readers.

This absence of historical memory is illustrated in the introductions to both the American and English editions of the book by Garry Wills and James Cameron.

The introduction by Wills, reprinted as an appendix in the English edition, goes further than the most extreme of the revisionist positions on the Cold War. According to him, Truman (despite his opposition to the House Committee on Un-American Activities and to McCarthy) was the true architect of the Cold War. The Communists abroad were blameless, and the Communists at home were merely victims of a reaction to Roosevelt's enlightened policies. Indeed, the Cold War was inspired by domestic considerations. Wills flatly states that "Truman launched the Cold War in the Spring of 1947 with his plan to 'rescue' Greece and Turkey." All unprovoked, of course. There was nothing, or no one, to rescue them from. "We had a world to save with just those plans," he goes on to say, "from NATO to the Korean War." It appears, then, that Truman's plan, with which all of America's Western allies readily agreed, as early as 1947 envisaged the invasion of Korea in the summer of 1950. Wills must believe that either Dean Acheson's declaration that Korea was beyond the sphere of American national interest was a deliberate provocation by the State Department to lure the North Koreans into invading South Korea or that South Korea at the instigation of the United States invaded North Korea. Presumably the United States intimidated the United Nations to support the defense of South Korea. Wills has unconsciously reconstructed the Kremlin's propaganda line. The only omission is the failure to charge the United States with the guilt of conducting germ warfare in North Korea. Wills's account of the domestic political scene in the United States during this period is no more accurate than his flyer in foreign-policy demonology.

It is not likely that Wills will find many credulous readers who are old enough to remember the past. But among them we must number James Cameron who has written the introduction to the English edition. He confesses that he does not know Lillian Hellman, and it is clear that he does not know the United States, its recent history, and the details of the period he writes about with such sublime indifference to the record. He even believes that "Scoundrel Time is come again" in America although he leaves unclear who the scoundrels are this time: The John Deans whose testimony, bartered for immunity from prosecution, helped convict the Watergate defendants? Or those convicted? He is also unclear about the British scene. He asks: "Why did our society never have the McCarthy trauma? Because we were too mature . . .? Because our constitution, being unwritten, was too flexible? Because we produced no paranoic like McCarthy? Perhaps—but also because we had too few Lillian Hellmans."

But why should the presence of more Lillian Hellmans generate McCarthyism? Is Cameron saying that if there had been as many Communist fellow-travelers, guilty of the same hypocrisy and duplicity in British cultural and political life as in the United States, the reaction would have been the same? The British Communists, except for those recruited by the Soviets as espionage agents, were never as conspiratorial as the American Communists and were not instructed to penetrate government agencies.

Nor does the English constitution have anything to do with it. If anything its flexibility could lend itself to even greater abuse since there is no Supreme Court to nullify or overrule Parliamentary legislation. English courts have never made absolutes of any right, or tolerated abuses of the privilege against self-incrimination. Actually, in Britain from 1947 on, not only were members of the Communist party completely barred from secret work but also all persons associated with the party in such a way "as to raise reasonable doubts about their reliability." After the defection of Guy Burgess and Donald Maclean the recommendations of a White Paper by Privy Councillors were accepted by the British government in 1956. It reaffirmed the basic principle on which earlier security measures were based that "the Communist faith overrides a man's normal loyalties to his country," and extended them to embrace the much wider circle of "sympathizers" and "associates." These are vague and ill-defined terms, and they required good sense and a genuine dedication to liberal values and individual liberties to apply them without miscarriages of justice. The procedures of American security boards were in some respects much fairer than their British counterparts. Civil servants in Britain who were under investigation were never told of the evidence against them; they were denied rights of legal counsel and even of representation at hearings. They had no right of appeal from the verdict of the tribunal to a higher administrative body or to a court.

Nonetheless, the American procedures worked more hardships and injustices because they were, as a rule, administered by Democratic and Republican party regulars who were politically ignorant of the wide spectrum of beliefs different from their own and who, as I once put it, "found the distinctions between member, sympathizer, front, dupe, innocent, and an honestly mistaken liberal as mysterious as the order of beings in the science of angelology."

Even before Joe McCarthy appeared on the scene, public identification under sworn testimony had been made of individuals occupying the following posts in the American government: 1) an executive assistant to the president; 2) an assistant secretary of the Treasury; 3) the director of the Office of Special Political Affairs in the State Department; 4) the secretary of the International Monetary Fund; 5) the chief of the Latin American Division of the Office of Strategic Services; 6) a member of the National Labor Relations Board; 7) the chief counsel of the Senate Subcommittee on Civil Liberties; 8) the chief of the Statistical Analysis Branch of the War Production Board; 9) a United States Treasury attaché in China; 10) the Treasury Department representatives and adviser in the Financial Control Division of the North African Economic Board in UNRRA, and at the meeting of the Foreign Ministers Council in Moscow in 1947; 11) the director of the National Research Project of the Works Progress Administration.

What would the public reaction in Britain have been if individuals of similar government rank and influence had been identified as members of the Communist party after the Klaus Fuchs case? Probably not as virulent as the American reaction, but it is not altogether excluded that even James Cameron might have been more perturbed than he seems to be. He would have to recognize the difference between nonexistent witches and Communist subversives.

It was in this atmosphere that demagogues like McCarthy seized their opportunity. Ritualistic liberals played into their hands, not by deservedly criticizing their excesses and irresponsibility, but by denying that Communist party infiltration into government existed. The Communists and their sympathizers contributed to eliciting public support for the investigative committees by invoking the Fifth Amendment, even when it was unnecessary, thus generating the impression that the conspiratorial activity was on a vaster scale than it actually was.

The greatest damage done by Senator Joseph McCarthy—whom Miss Hellman never faced—was to the American Foreign Service. His irresponsible charges against a few who may have been guilty of political naïveté—the Chinese Communists were, after all, not mere "agrarian reformers"—tended to inhibit critical independent judgment of American policy among their colleagues. McCarthy headed the Permanent Subcommittee on Investigations which should not be confused with the Subcommittee on Internal Security of the Committee on the Judiciary whose proceedings, in comparison with McCarthy's committee as well as those of the House Committee on Un-American Activities, were fairly meticulously conducted. There is no need to deny, as Miss Hellman does, that the disclosures before the House committee about Alger Hiss and other key figures named by Whittaker Chambers were genuine. But they would not have been necessary had responsible security officers quietly acted on information which they had long before the hearings. The aura of the Hiss case kept the House committee going for a long time, but it hardly compensated for the vigilantism, cultural irrationalism, and national distrust generated by its successive chairmen and leading members who exploited their roles for cheap political publicity. Their excesses made intelligent criticism of the communism of that period—the heyday of Stalinism—more difficult.

For someone like Lillian Hellman, who loyally cooperated with members of the Communist party in all sorts of political and cultural enterprises for almost forty years, to impugn the integrity of liberal anti-Communists like Lionel Trilling and others of his circle is an act of political obscenity.

The criticisms made by anti-Communist socialists and liberals during these years have been vindicated by events. They insisted on the central distinction between "heresy" whose defense is integral to a free society and "conspiracy" whose secrecy is inimical to it.

This distinction was often ignored by the investigating committees and sometimes by their critics. A heretic is an honest defender of an unpopular idea. A conspirator is one who works stealthily and dishonestly outside the rules of the game. Our moral obligation is to the toleration of dissent, no matter how heretical, not to the toleration of conspiracy, no matter how disguised or secret. When that secrecy is combined with loyalty to a foreign power dedicated to the overthrow of free and open societies, a power that manipulates the activities of conspirators wherever they operate, the pitiless light of publicity must be brought to bear on the situation. Whatever may be the case in these polycentric days, during the years Miss Hellman writes about the evidence is overwhelming that Communists, even though their party was legal, were organized secretly in parallel underground organizations under assumed names working for political objectives framed by the party fraction. To be sure, they sometimes did other things as well, some of them worthy and all of them under deceptively high-sounding phrases, but only to increase their influence in furthering their underlying political purposes. Those who wittingly helped them, even if they paid no party dues, were morally as guilty in the deceptions they practiced. They were engaged in helping to destroy the open society whose benefits and freedoms they enjoyed.

1977

Postscript

SINCE THE ABOVE was written, Lillian Hellman dramatically confirmed the double-dealing nature of her political judgment, its use of double standards and convenient invention.

In the course of a colloquy with Dan Rather of the Columbia Broadcasting Company, Lillian Hellman was asked about the charge that she could see what was wrong with McCarthy and that whole era but failed to see anything wrong with Stalinism. After all, if considered from the point of view of loss of human life, deprivation of freedom, torture, and suffering of innocent human beings, Stalinism was infinitely worse than McCarthyism.

To which she replied: "I happen never to have been a Communist for one thing, which is left out of this story. I didn't quite understand the argument, I mean I don't really know what has one thing to do with another. I was not a Russian, I was an American." To which Rather responded: "You can't see that the basic argument here is that you applied a double standard? You applied one standard to McCarthy and the United States and another standard to Stalin and the Soviet Union." "No," replied Lillian Hellman, "I don't think I did. I was injured by McCarthy for one thing. I was not personally injured by Stalin, which is not a very high class reason but it's a very—it's a good practical reason."[3]

Lillian Hellman is an eager but unaccomplished liar. She was not German. Nor was she personally injured by Hitler. But she protested vigorously his terror regime. She was not Italian. Nor was she personally injured by Mussolini but she joined liberals in denouncing him. She was not Spanish. Nor was she personally injured by Franco but she was very active in the defense of the Loyalist Spanish cause. Only when called upon to protest against the infamies of Stalin and Stalinism did she suddenly discover that she was not Russian and that as an American she had no business abroad. But then if the fact that she was not Russian and suffered no injury at Stalin's hands exonerates her from failure to criticize Stalin's crimes, why then did she *defend* them, especially the monstrous Moscow frame-up trials, and defame those who, like John Dewey, sought to establish the truth about them?

Lillian Hellman's shabby justification for her sustained role as minnesinger of Stalin's regime is so transparent that it is perhaps needless to point out that "personally" she was never injured by McCarthy (whom she never even confronted) or by the House committee before which she testified.

3. Excerpts from the transcript of the interview with Dan Rather as published in *The New York Post* March 23, 1977.

Chapter 19

The Case of Alger Hiss

It has been claimed that the case of Alger Hiss is to contemporary American history what the Dreyfus affair was to modern French history. This seems to me a gross exaggeration. The Dreyfus affair provoked acute public disorders, divided and weakened the French nation, precipitated at one point a change in government, resulted in the decline of French military influence in public life and contributed to the separation of church and state. The Hiss case had no comparable impact on national American life. Nonetheless it had serious political consequences whose indirect consequences are still perceptible. Its chief significance has been threefold. It discredited the American liberal establishment of which Hiss was a shining figure and from which his most zealous defenders came. It generated more than any other single event a climate of opinion that gave an initial credence to the demagogic exaggerations of Senator Joseph McCarthy until he overreached himself. It divided for many years American liberal opinion.

It would not be an overstatement to say that more often than not, depending upon a person's belief in Hiss's innocence or guilt, one could predict his or her beliefs about the origin, nature, and justification of the Cold War between the Western democracies and the Soviet Union and its satellite Communist regimes. Those who are more critical of the United States than of the Soviet Union are more likely to believe in Hiss's innocence and conversely. Unfortunately even the assessment of the specific evidence on the rare occasions when it is discussed depends often on an antecedent political commitment. Sometimes the discussion of the Hiss case loses all relevance to the pertinent facts when reference to Richard Nixon is made. Political animus and political apologetics vie with each other. It probably is true that if Richard Nixon had disappeared from the public scene after Hiss's conviction, the dust would have settled on the Hiss case as it has on the Dreyfus affair, with no serious doubts about the justice of the verdict. Every controversy in Nixon's stormy career seems to have reawakened doubts in the minds of those whom he infuriated about the case in which he first won national prominence as a member of a congressional investigating committee.

It may sound old fashioned to say so but the guilt or innocence of Alger Hiss depends not on one's position towards the Cold War or the degree of one's antipathy to Richard Nixon but solely on the evidence. That is why the publication of Professor Allen Weinstein's work[1] is a noteworthy contribution, of interest to any reader more concerned with the truth than with who would be politically comforted by it.

Only someone who is relatively expert on the details of the Alger Hiss trials and on the climate of opinion prevailing at the time in the United States can appreciate the scope of Weinstein's labors and the immensity of his achievement. The size of the book, the multiplicity of the themes considered, the weight of the converging lines of evidence, the fact that at the outset of his research Weinstein believed that Hiss was probably innocent make his concluding sentence, despite its understatement, all the more impressive: "The body of available evidence proves that [Hiss] did in fact perjure himself when describing his secret dealings with Chambers, so that the jurors in the second trial made no mistake in finding Alger Hiss guilty as charged." Hiss was, in effect, although not formally (because of the statute of limitations), found guilty of espionage. His continued denial of his guilt indicates that he has perjured himself for thirty years and that he will probably go to his grave protesting his innocence.

The very fact that Hiss has persistently denied his guilt has puzzled some observers who find it psychologically difficult to understand how a guilty man could play the role of absolute injured innocence so long—"absolute" innocence, because Hiss insists not only that he was never a Communist or even a left-winger in politics but that at the time he knew Chambers he was completely unaware that Chambers was a Communist.

Hiss's persistence has been more than puzzling. It has been convincing to some who admit that the evidence alone, presented in a

1. Allen Weinstein, *Perjury: The Hiss-Chambers Case* (New York: Alfred A. Knopf, 1978).

trial characterized by Hiss's own attorneys as fair, established his guilt beyond a reasonable doubt. Philip Nobile, writing on "The State of the Art of Alger Hiss" in *Harper's* (April 1976), concludes his article with the following:

> My argument, perhaps naïve and sentimental, turns on psychology. I cannot conceive of a sane person perpetuating a quarter century [now closer to thirty years] of deceit, jeopardizing the welfare of family and the reputation of friends, in a doomed attempt to reverse what that person knows to be the truth.
> And Hiss is not crazy. Instead he is serene.

However, as we shall see, there is a simpler explanation of Hiss's behavior and serenity.

Others besides Nobile may not be convinced by Professor Weinstein's book. I am not referring now to those so emotionally committed to Hiss that they would not believe him even if he were to confess his guilt. Nor am I referring to those fanatical political partisans, at heart unreconstructed Stalinists for all their belated admission of Stalin's "mistakes," who have set the cause of the party higher than the cause of truth, and for whom the very concept of "objective truth" is suspect. Just as there probably will always be right-wing extremists in France with the mentality of members of the *Action Française*, who are convinced that Dreyfus was guilty, so the same type of mind among Communists will believe that Hiss is innocent regardless of the evidence. I am referring rather to those who, in the light of the shady pattern of events in the Watergate case and of Richard Nixon's early role in the hearings before the House Committee on Un-American Activities at which Hiss was publicly identified as a secret member of the Communist party, have simply refused to assess the evidence. They have turned an issue of fact into one of symbolic allegiance; and there is no arguing with symbolic allegiances. It is as if one were to refuse to believe that Winston Churchill in 1918 was in favor of military intervention in the Soviet Union in order "to strangle Bolshevism in its cradle" because of his wartime alliance with Stalin and his unstinting praise of the defenders of Stalingrad. None the less, if those who approach the Hiss case with this bias can bring themselves to read Weinstein's careful analysis of the actual record, they will find he is no friend of Nixon. He takes a critical approach to Nixon's claims to resoluteness in helping unearth the truth about Hiss. But they will also find that far from being "Nixon's first victim," Hiss was a victim of the facts; more specifically, the documents presented by Whittaker Chambers when Hiss challenged him to air his charges against him without the protection of privileged testimony.

What are the chief achievements of Allen Weinstein's five years of research and of his perusal of tens of thousands of pages of formerly classified FBI and Justice Department records? Leaving aside the comprehensiveness and dramatic effectiveness of the exposition of events, they are three.

1. First, he establishes firmly and exhaustively the credibility of Chambers's own story of his involvement in the Communist underground assigned to collect information from strategic sources in the United States government of possible use to the Soviet regime. He does this in various ways. He uncovers the many roots and tendrils of the underground Communist movement both before and after Hiss's involvement. Particularly engrossing is his account of the activities of Alexander and Elaine Ulanovski[2] and what it reveals of the atmosphere and organization of the Communist underground in the early 1930s. Even more significant, because it indirectly involved Hiss, is his discovery in the Hiss defense files and those of the FBI of additional evidence of the existence and purposes of the Ware group. Of special significance is the testimony of the novelist Josephine Herbst, given to Hiss's defense attorneys—but refused to the FBI—that her husband, John Herrmann, had been a member of the Ware group, that she had known Chambers under his underground name of *"Karl,"* that she was aware of the purposes of the Ware group, and that she had discussed with Karl the importance of Hiss's membership in it. And for the first time we have a trained historian's interview with Maxim Lieber and other Communists who knew and sometimes befriended Chambers and to whom Chambers had appealed in vain in his book *Witness* to come forward. Of special interest is his interview with Karel Kaplan, a Czech defector who had fled with thousands of pages from the secret archives of the Czech security police and who had worked hand-in-glove with the Soviet KGB. According to Kaplan, who had read through the interrogations between Noel Field (under arrest in Prague on suspicion of being a double agent) and the Czech security police, Field had named Alger Hiss as a fellow-Communist underground-agent in the United States State Department. He explained his refusal to return to the United States to resume work because of his fear that he would be involved in the Hiss case since he, Field, had already been mentioned by Hedda Massing, a former Soviet operative, in the second Hiss trial as someone she tried to recruit.

In several cases the new witnesses whom Weinstein had induced to speak to him about the Hiss case were former or present Communists—sympathetic to Hiss—who expected Allen Weinstein

2. Allen Weinstein, "Nadya—A Spy Story," *Encounter* (June 1977).

to vindicate Hiss when he published his book. No sooner had Weinstein's book appeared than a corps of researchers coordinated by Victor Navasky of the *Nation* checked out its every line. In an effort to discredit Weinstein's scholarship, Navasky charged (*Nation*, 8 April 1978) that he had deliberately misquoted and misstated six key interviews, and he cited repudiations from those interviewed. Maxim Lieber whom Chambers had failed to induce (despite his eloquent appeal in *Witness*) to come forward and tell what he knew gave the case away in his remarks to a reporter of the *Washington Post*, 16 April 1978. "Weinstein came to see me under false colors, representing himself as friendly to Hiss. I never would have said a single word to him if I'd known he was friendly to Chambers. I may have said things I wouldn't have said under different circumstances."

Probably Weinstein was still inclined to doubt Whittaker Chambers more than Alger Hiss when he interviewed Lieber; what he heard from Lieber, among other things, inclined him the other way. But the crucial question is whether Lieber told Weinstein what Weinstein reported him as saying in his book, or whether as Lieber now contends, "Weinstein made all these things up out of whole cloth." Unfortunately for Lieber, Weinstein recorded his remarks on tape. Two others of those interviewed by Weinstein have recanted what they said in whole or in part. They are Sam Krieger who (according to Chambers) recruited Whittaker Chambers into the Communist party; and Karel Kaplan (who simply denies that Noel Field admitted Hiss was delivering United States classified documents to the Kremlin—something Weinstein never asserted). They are also on tape. Of the three other recanters—Paul Willert, Ella Winter, and Alden Whitman—Weinstein claims in substantiation of his quotations, "I have not only the notes of my interviews but also letters from them, defense file memos, FBI records, and other interviews that corroborate their statements" (*New Republic*, 29 April 1978).

In the attempt to discredit Professor Weinstein those who have recanted have clearly overplayed their hand. Sam Krieger, who does not conceal his loyalty to the Kremlin, now claims that Chambers was never really in the Communist underground at all, that he was expelled from the Party and never reaffiliated with it. Krieger admits that one of his party aliases was "Clarence Miller" but denies that he is the same "Clarence Miller" who, as a defendant at the Gastonia trials in 1929, fled bail to the Soviet Union. Weinstein may well have been mistaken about the true identity of the Gastonian "Clarence Miller"; it bears not at all on the evidence of the case. Krieger acknowledges he was interviewed by Weinstein and that he permitted himself to be taped. At the time apparently he was under the impression that Weinstein was friendly to Hiss and intent upon exonerating him. Somewhat later he must have heard that the evidence had swung Weinstein the other way. For he claims to have contemplated legal action against Weinstein to recover the tape. As Warren Hinckle of *Ramparts* fame, to whose credulous ears Krieger confided his story, relates (*San Francisco Chronicle*, 4 May 1978), "At one time he [Krieger] was contemplating suing Weinstein for the interview but Alger Hiss, whom he had just met, talked him out of it."

This is passing strange. How did Krieger just happen to meet Hiss in 1975? Krieger, still a fanatical Communist and proud of it, would be the last person whom Hiss, were he as innocent of any Communist connection as he professes, would want to meet. Krieger insists that until *Perjury* was published he had no notion what line Weinstein would take. If this were the truth why would he be getting in touch with Hiss?

Despite these efforts to undermine Professor Weinstein's research, his reconstruction of Chambers's life before, during, and after his political experience has a compelling authenticity about it. It coheres with what every person who knew Chambers (and is now outside the Communist orbit) recalls. If one accepts Weinstein's biographical sketch of Chambers in its essentials, what plausible explanation can anyone have for his identification of Alger Hiss, among others, as a member of the Communist underground, especially in the light of the documentary evidence, save its truth? Hiss himself denies that there were any homosexual overtones in what he insists was only a casual acquaintanceship between himself and Chambers. This rules out the malice of a rejected suitor as a motive on Chambers's part. Why, then, should Hiss's outright denial of any involvement with Chambers and the Communist underground be believed?

If one looks away from the evidence—and we must remember that Hiss was convicted not on Chambers's word but on the hard evidence of documents written in Hiss's hand and typed on the Hiss Woodstock typewriter—the only reason that could be offered for believing Hiss's denials was his credibility as the darling of the American Establishment—Hiss was the clerk of Mr. Justice Oliver Wendell Holmes, the protégé of Professor Felix Frankfurter, the president of the Carnegie Endowment for Peace, the man who stood next to the president of the United States at the opening of the United Nations Conference in San Francisco. All one need do, Mrs. Eleanor Roosevelt observed in one of her newspaper columns at the time, is to "look at the two men" to tell who was speaking the truth. Alas! in the world of espionage, especially ideological espionage, appearances may be quite deceptive. Given Hiss's role, his background in the eyes of those who recruited him constituted a remarkable protective coloration. It made him all the more valuable.

2. The second of Allen Weinstein's indisputable achievements is that he destroys the credibility of Alger Hiss by showing that he lied persistently and consistently about one of the key pieces of evidence in the case, namely, the Woodstock typewriter on which the copies of the stolen classified United States State Department documents were typed. The type of the documents matched the type found in the letters the Hisses had written. It was established that both the documents and the letters had been typed on an office model Woodstock. But where was the machine itself? Without it, the government's case would be less persuasive. Consequently, the search for the missing typewriter. For a long time it was a search in vain. Questioned about its whereabouts, Hiss professed complete ignorance. He repeatedly affirmed this to the FBI and to the grand jury then deliberating whether to indict him—or Chambers, or both—for perjury.

None the less, the records in Hiss's own defense files show that he had previously telephoned one of his attorneys (on 7 December 1948) asking him to check on an old machine he remembers giving to Pat, the son of Claudia Catlett, who used to assist the Hiss families with their housework. Yet "on three separate occasions" between 10 December and 15 December, he affirmed to the grand jury that he had no recollection of what had happened to it, whether it was given away or destroyed. By that time, the machine had become "hot" since Hiss's own experts had determined that the stolen Baltimore documents—produced by Chambers when Hiss sued for libel —and the Hiss private letters, used as technical standards of mechanical comparison, had been typed on the same machine. During the frantic search for the Woodstock typewriter, Hiss (as well as his brother Donald) knew where it was all the time! Only when the FBI began questioning the Catletts who had received and disposed of the Woodstock machine and who, out of loyalty to the Hisses, persistently lied to the FBI, did Hiss's defense recover the "smoking gun" to get credit in potential jurors' eyes for bringing in the evidence.

3. The third major achievement of Allen Weinstein's book is to knock into a cocked hat, among other speculative fantasies, the notion of Hiss and his defenders that he was the "victim of a plot" by the House Committee on Un-American Activities (HUAC), the FBI, and the Department of Justice to frame him by forging the Woodstock typewriter. The classified documents released to Weinstein, after he won his court action under the new United States Freedom of Information Act, showed that J. Edgar Hoover went into a tantrum

over the failure of the horde of his FBI men to find the Woodstock typewriter. In the light of the continued lying by the Hisses and the Catletts, and especially the misleading hints by Priscilla Hiss that she disposed of the machine either to a second-hand typewriter store or junk shop or the Salvation Army—which sent squads of agents off on fool's errands—the ineptitude of the FBI seems somewhat mitigated. Even so, it appears that they were closing in on the Catletts when the Hisses beat them to it.

Much more devastating to the notion that Hiss was the target of a conspiracy are the official documents which show that despite all the incriminating evidence produced by Chambers, and despite the evasiveness and shiftiness in Hiss's testimony, there was a real struggle going on between HUAC and the Justice Department concerning which of the two men was to be indicted. HUAC naturally had a vested interest in Chambers. Were he to be indicted, its own revelations about Hiss—the crowning point of years of investigation—would be impugned. The Justice Department and the FBI were acting in concert with an administration whose chief officer, the president himself, had declared the Hiss case to be a "red herring." To indict Hiss was to embarrass Harry Truman; not in his own eyes (since nothing could embarrass him) but in the eyes of the country.

Whittaker Chambers and J. Edgar Hoover seem to have mutually despised each other (albeit for different reasons). Actually, until the conclusive finding was made, shortly before the completion of the grand jury's term, that the Baltimore stolen documents and the Hiss standard letters had all been typed on the same Woodstock acknowledged to have been owned by the Hisses, there was a much greater likelihood that Chambers would be indicted for perjury than Hiss because Chambers had previously *denied* under oath that Hiss had been guilty of espionage. Even after the conclusive evidence was in, as Weinstein reveals, Chambers was not in the clear.

On December 15, the last day of the Grand Jury's term, Deputy Attorney General Peyton Ford phoned Assistant FBI Director Ladd to advise "that he thought it possible that an indictment might be returned against Hiss." Ladd asked Ford "if he had forgotten the charges of perjury against Chambers," to which Ford replied that "the Department wanted to see if they could obtain a conspiracy indictment for espionage first and thereafter they had in mind still considering perjury charges against Chambers."

The whole notion that there was a conspiracy against Alger Hiss was born out of his despairing response to the grand jury on the day of his indictment. Confronted by the evidence that it was on *his* typewriter that the stolen government documents had been transcribed, he opined that Chambers must have sneaked into his home and typed the incriminating documents. The suggestion was greeted with some hilarity by members of the grand jury. What they did not know (and what Hiss must have known) was that two of the *defense* document examiners had already reported to Hiss's attorneys, on the basis of comparisons between samples of Priscilla Hiss's typing and the stolen Baltimore documents, that *she* had probably typed them. Had this been pointed out to him at the time, it is hard to conceive what retort Hiss could have made—other than telling the truth—save that Chambers by some paranormal means had taken possession of Mrs. Alger Hiss's spirit. In a twenty-page appendix devoted to *"Forgery By Typewriter—The Pursuit of Conspiracy, 1948–1978,"* Weinstein presents a masterly analysis of six different and incompatible conspiracy theories advanced by Hiss partisans. He shreds them into absurdity.

It may be instructive to the reader unfamiliar with the record to note that even if Whittaker Chambers had been indicted for perjury, at the same time or after Hiss, his conviction would be possible only on the evidence that Hiss was guilty of espionage. This apparent paradox is easily explained when it is recalled that, *originally, in order to spare Hiss,* against whom he had no personal animus, Chambers had denied both to HUAC and the grand jury that Hiss had engaged in espionage. (Actually, Chambers had told the truth about Hiss and others almost a decade earlier to A. A. Berle, Assistant-Secretary of State, almost immediately after the Stalin-Hitler Pact, in expectation that those he named who had fed him classified information would be retired from sensitive government posts only to find that instead they were being promoted!) When Chambers, driven and harried by Hiss's attorney, William Marbury, at the libel hearings, reversed himself and introduced the documentary evidence to support his charge of espionage, he admitted that his former explicit denial of Hiss's espionage role was perjurious. Had he been indicted and convicted for that perjury, the jury would have had *to be convinced that Hiss indeed was guilty of espionage* and that Chambers was lying when he denied it.

Some of Hiss's partisans who have characterized Chambers as "a self-confessed perjuror" and inferred Hiss's innocence on the basis of it, seem blithely unaware of the illogic of their position. For the only perjury to which Chambers confessed was his statement that Hiss was *not* an espionage agent for the Kremlin. Whatever else we may believe about Whittaker Chambers, if we believe that he was in fact perjuring himself in denying Alger Hiss's espionage activities, then we must believe in Hiss's guilt.

It does not detract in the least from Weinstein's magnificent achievement to say that it still remains true that the logic of the evidence introduced at the trials was more than sufficient to establish Hiss's guilt beyond a reasonable doubt. What Weinstein has added increases the weight of the evidence against Hiss by exposing his calculated effort to conceal the whereabouts of the crucial typewriter, and by uncovering more of the root-structure of the Communist party underground. There is no need to rehearse the details of the evidence that convinced twenty out of twenty-four jurors that Hiss was in effect a traitor to the United States on behalf of the Soviet Union. His guilt rested not on a linked chain of evidence all dependent on one premise or assumption but on a cable of intertwined strands of unequal length and strength. The legal logic of the case has already been stated and evaluated with admirable clarity by Judge Irving Younger.[3] But there was one particular piece of evidence whose extraordinary significance has been overlooked by those who are politically uninformed or unsophisticated about the history of the Communist movement.

Among the purloined materials produced by Chambers at the Baltimore hearings were four handwritten notes of classified cables. Three of them contained military and diplomatic information of great importance to the Soviet Union but which were outside the scope of concern of Hiss's section of the State Department, then headed by Francis B. Sayre. These original cables also contained information that *was* highly relevant to Sayre's international trade section but which, oddly enough, was not summarized on Hiss's handwritten memoranda. A fourth cable by Loy Henderson in Moscow sent to Secretary Cordell Hull referred to "the Rubens case."

A. A. Rubens was a Latvian Soviet secret agent (with an American-born wife) who had been recalled to Russia. He was arrested during the great Stalin purges in 1937 and charged with being "a Nazi spy." The couple was traveling at the time with two sets of false American passports made out to "Rubens" and "Robinson." Mrs. Rubens (*nee* Ruth Boergers) in distress told her story to some American newsmen in Moscow and solicited their help. Before long she too was jailed; but the story had already made headlines in the United States.

At the time, I was very much interested in the "Robinson-Rubens" case because the news reports indicated they had recently been in Yucatan, Mexico. This seemed to me vaguely suspicious. The John Dewey hearings on Leon Trotsky and the truth about the Moscow trials had just been completed in Coyoacán, Mexico. Herbert Solow, who had helped organize the Dewey Commission of Inquiry, was the first to sound the alarm and aroused concern about

3. Irving Younger, *Commentary* (August 1975).

the likelihood of another Moscow trial at which the Rubenses would testify to discredit the work of the Dewey commission. We, therefore, followed events with interest. Subsequently, it was learned that Chambers knew Rubens under the name of "Ewald" and in his articles on Soviet espionage in the United States (written at the bidding of Solow) Chambers referred to the very document Hiss had copied and to other cables Loy Henderson had sent after interviewing Mrs. Rubens in prison. The document Alger Hiss had handcopied was the text of a cable from the wife of a former United States intelligence agent identifying Rubens and cautioning against involvement despite Mrs. Rubens's American citizenship. The Kremlin was intensely interested in knowing what the United States government was going to do about the arrest of a native-born American citizen since the episode had caused considerable friction between the two governments. Apparently, judging from Chambers's account, the Russians were completely aware of the contents of all United States communications about the couple and were greatly relieved when the State Department accepted Mrs. Rubens's request to drop her case.

Weinstein quotes from Chambers's chilling recital of the interview between Mrs. Rubens and the United States chargé d'affaires in the presence of a Soviet intelligence officer, which shows that the latter was aware of the contents of the cable Hiss had copied! Nothing has since been heard of Rubens and his wife.

There was no plausible reason for Hiss to copy the cable about Robinson-Rubens. This was confirmed by his State Department superior, Francis Sayre; nor did Hiss offer any reasons for his transcription. He simply denied that the transcription was in his handwriting. According to Weinstein: "[Hiss] stuck by this in discussion with his own attorneys until the Spring of 1949 when FBI laboratory experts and *Hiss's own handwriting experts* confirmed that he had transcribed Henderson's cable." [My emphasis]

Hiss's explanations of the summaries of the three other cables were lame enough. He had no explanation of the fourth one. Even if he had not given it to Chambers and it had been transmitted by one of Chambers's other sources of information, the very fact that Hiss had made a copy of it was of damning significance.

There remains to assess the only consideration which has been raised to dispute the authenticity of Whittaker Chambers's story.

On several occasions Chambers gave as dates of his break with the Communist party and its underground "late 1937." Later he put the date in 1938. All of the documentary material was dated in 1938. If Chambers really broke in 1937, how could he have had the documents dated 1938? The discrepancy is more apparent than real. One does not break with the Soviet Communist party underground apparatus overnight. In every case it is a long drawn-out process, from the first doubts to the final irretrievable action. Especially is this true when one possesses dangerous knowledge involving the safety and even the lives of others.

In Chambers's case, we know that he had been ordered to report in person to Moscow. In those years this was often tantamount to a death sentence. Open refusal to return was dangerous. I have no doubt that in his own mind Chambers had firmly decided to break without fuss or feathers already in 1937. He had begun, so to speak, to run for his life even then, without making an overt hostile act. He had probably heard about what happened to Ewald (A. A. Rubens) and Julia Stuart Poyntz. And it was quite natural that he should begin carefully to squirrel away compromising stolen documents so as to have something to bargain for, and with, if it came to the crunch. Chambers had already come under suspicion because of the public political activities of some of his old, now anti-Stalinist Left-wing, friends with whom in violation of party and underground practices he maintained personal relations. They were active in the movement to establish an international commission before which Leon Trotsky could plead his case against the charges broadcast at the Moscow trials that he had plotted from the very beginning of the October Revolution to destroy the Communist regime. I myself recall that toward the end of 1937 Professor Meyer Schapiro, the distinguished Columbia University art historian, informed me that Chambers was getting ready to "break with the Stalinists."

Professor Meyer Schapiro, still teaching at Columbia University, was a friend of Whittaker Chambers (1901–61) over many decades. When Colonel Boris Bykov took over the GPU control chair of Chambers's Soviet secret intelligence unit in New York, he asked for a number of presents to be given to loyal collaborators. Chambers had objected to money, but consented to expensive presents—and he was asked to purchase a number of Bokhara rugs, one of which was to go to Alger Hiss in Washington. Bykov instructed Chambers to explain that "these rugs had been woven in Russia and were being given to them as gifts from the Russian people in gratitude to their American comrades."

As it happened, Chambers, although a cultural historian of some merit, knew nothing about rugs, Oriental or otherwise, and he turned to his old friend Meyer Schapiro for advice. Dr. Schapiro arranged the purchase with a rug dealer in New York. Chambers made the delivery to Hiss. Hiss and his wife admit having had the rug in their Washington apartment, but claimed it was given them in partial payment of the rent of their apartment by their paupered acquaintance, "George Crosley." They professed to have received the rug in 1935 but the documents of sale prove that the four rugs were purchased by Schapiro on 23 December 1936; additional evidence shows that the other three rugs were delivered in 1937, the same year in which Chambers asserted he gave Colonel Bykov's present to the Hisses. The Hisses' maid identified the rug, testifying that it was not used but kept in a storage closet. One of the other recipients of a rug (Julian Wadleigh) testified that "the only recompense for his [underground] work was a nine-by-twelve Persian rug." Professor Schapiro still had the receipt from Touloukian in Manhattan for the four rugs. A rug expert, acting on behalf of Hiss's attorney, inspected Hiss's rug in 1949, and declared it to be a Bokhara rug as indicated on the sales slip which Professor Meyer Schapiro received for the four rugs he purchased at Whittaker Chambers's request in 1936.

It was a fairly open secret at the time what Chambers was doing. I communicated the news to another old friend of Chambers, Herbert Solow, who not long after actively helped Chambers in making his break. All this, as Allen Weinstein reports, is confirmed in Solow's invaluable papers. All of us for years, and especially since the Moscow trials, have been engaged in savage polemics with the Communist party spokesmen and their literary allies, for example, Malcolm Cowley, who defended the Moscow trials. There is good reason to believe that Chambers was a marked man, that he knew this, and that both the record of the first and second Moscow trials and the public criticisms of the crudely forged tales of the defendants—all "Gestapo agents" working for Hitler—contributed to undermining his faith in the Communist cause.

Despite the overwhelming evidence against Alger Hiss, some have found it difficult to believe in his guilt because of his unwearied, continued protestations of his innocence. It is psychologically impossible, they say, for someone so fine-grained and sensitive as Hiss—to whose likable personal traits Chambers himself paid tribute—to persist in a series of monstrous lies in which he has involved so many worthy persons (in addition to the Stalinist hacks who have hewed to the party line that Soviet espionage is a complete myth). To be sure, some who have read Hiss's own book in his own defense, *In the Court of Public Opinion* (1957), or heard him speak, have been puzzled by the absence of that tone of anguished sincerity and outraged moral conviction we usually associate with innocent men crying out against an injustice. Someone observed that Hiss sounds more like a cautious Philadelphia lawyer intent upon getting a verdict of "not proven" than like an innocent victim of a conspiracy. This is a matter of style, and is inconsequential. Hiss had never been vehement about anything. It is the unyielding asseveration of innocence in the face of evidence strong enough to convict a man in any enlightened criminal jurisdiction that has impressed those who are still skeptical. It undoubtedly influenced the scandalous decision of the Massachusetts Supreme Judicial Court to readmit Hiss to the Massachusetts bar, the first United States lawyer ever readmitted following a major criminal conviction. And this despite the remark of the presiding justice, "Nothing we have said here should be construed as detracting one iota from the fact that in considering Hiss's petition we consider him to be guilty as charged."

The most plausible hypothesis that accounts for Hiss's public posture as a victim of a conspiracy by the American government involving all three of its branches is that he is still a "true believer," a species of fanatical Communist (even if formally not a member), case-hardened by his experience, sustained by the hope, and sometimes by the conviction, that someday he will be honored as a hero of the New Order when it spreads throughout the world. It is not well known that although Whittaker Chambers willingly agreed to take a lie-detector test, Hiss refused! A person sincerely convinced that he has spoken the truth, that he has nothing to hide, that the only lies that have been uttered are those of Chambers is unlikely to refuse the opportunity to be tested together with his accuser. When Hiss's devoted friend, Dr. Carl Binger, suggested that he be injected with scopaline (the "truth serum") in hopes that he would recall details of his early relationship with Chambers to undermine Chambers's story, he refused. It is significant that Hiss has refused to meet Professor Weinstein in open debate to discuss the evidence against him. If my hypothesis is true, a day may come when the Kremlin will honor its man-in-Washington openly in the same way that it has honored another valiant operative, Richard Sorge, its man-in-Tokyo, who obtained (and relayed to Moscow) the Japanese war plan against the United States. This enabled Stalin to dispatch the Siberian troops, positioned to oppose a Japanese attack, to Moscow in time to save the city.

We do not really know the full extent of Hiss's intelligence services to the Soviet Union, for the purloined documents in Chambers's possession were culled only from those delivered by Hiss over a short three-month period. Chambers could not (or would not) recall the content of the communications received during previous years. Nor is the period accounted for between Chambers's break and the time when rumors about Hiss became so thick that he was eased out of the State Department. Although we cannot now determine the extent or degree of Hiss's guilt, the fact of his guilt can no longer be contested on any rational grounds.

1978

Part Four:
Religion and Culture

Chapter 20

Religion and Culture:

The Dilemma of T. S. Eliot

In an interesting essay in the *New English Review* entitled "Notes Towards a Definition of Culture," T. S. Eliot raises some basic questions about culture, society, and religion which have provoked wide discussion on both sides of the Atlantic. The position Mr. Eliot takes on these questions challenges attention not only on its own account but as an indication that influential intellectual circles, despairing of the present and fearing the future, have turned from secular to religious solutions of the crisis of our time.

To understand and evaluate Mr. Eliot's proposals, we must begin by distinguishing the three different meanings of the word *culture* that appear in his analysis. He himself is explicit only about the first two. The first is the practice of arts and letters. The second is the anthropological concept of culture, familiar since Tylor, as a complex of institutions, techniques, and ideals—sometimes used interchangeably with the term *civilization*. The third is the normative sense of culture expressed in the adjectives Mr. Eliot prefixes to it, like "superior" or "true" in contrast with "deteriorated" or "retrograde."

The mark of culture in this third sense is its *organic* character revealed in the functional interrelation between human activities. The complete absence of organic character may spell the end of culture. But there are various kinds of organic societies which Mr. Eliot evaluates quite differently. A head-hunting community in which the crafts of design are interwoven with its economy and a heresy-hunting community in which religion is synthesized with politics are both organic. This necessitates a purer kind of value judgment to enable Mr. Eliot to choose between them. That organic society has the best culture in which great arts and letters flourish, and in which they are integrally related by certain distinctive religious beliefs to the whole complex of social institutions. Such a culture is designated by Mr. Eliot as a "total culture."

Mr. Eliot's argument is that the development of this total culture is dependent upon a common religious faith whose values and meanings unify both the workdaday and the intellectual-artistic life. The dominant social influence must be wielded by a hereditary elite, based on "transmitted aptitudes and domestic environment" and open to new recruits who meet "the sole qualification of *achievement.*" A common faith is necessary to counteract the shattering effects upon institutions and personalities of withdrawing large areas of human life from traditional religious sanctions. For past history has shown that once a binding religious faith is loosened, "the spirit of inquiry, skepticism, and innovation" corrodes the fabric of social life. Even religion, now isolated from the rest of the cultural pattern, is disintegrated by the acids of the inquiring spirit. In time the pattern itself is threatened with dissolution, which "with the advance of liberty of thought and behavior imposes a strain upon human beings greater than the majority can bear."

Totalitarianism is one pattern of unification, but Mr. Eliot rejects it as "artificial" without explaining the term further. He recognizes it, however, as a natural reaction to the disorder produced by separating religion from the rest of culture. For Mr. Eliot a total, religious culture is the only alternative to the blight of totalitarianism.

The fundamental difficulty in Mr. Eliot's position, as I see it, is that his common religious faith, which is frankly supernatural, provides no principle of direction for the intelligent control of social change. Although he insists that we must make "fresh judgments and decisions in constantly changing situations," these judgments are in the nature of the case empirical. They cannot be derived either by logic or intuition from absolute supernatural truths, which in the Christian tradition are compatible with different empirical judgments. Despite the fact that Christianity has exercised a great influence, both for good and evil, on all societies in Western Europe since the days of Rome, the principles of not a single social system can be attributed to its dogmas. It has, however, shown itself capable of adaptation to every social system, including fascism. The source of our fresh judgments and decisions in constantly changing situations must therefore be sought elsewhere. Mr. Eliot's "common religious faith" runs the risk of having no more influence on the actual sources of these judgments and decisions than the chaplain's prayer in Congress has on the subsequent proceedings.

Where a common supernatural faith does seem to bear on what appears to nonbelievers to be empirical questions like divorce, birth control, separation of church and state, the point is that such questions are decided by believers without reference to "constantly changing situations." In short, they are not treated as empirical questions at all.

This basic difficulty is almost admitted by Mr. Eliot in his further remark that a common supernatural faith must become the faith of peoples of different cultures and, "while uniting these peoples in a common brotherhood, can be contemplated in its transcendence of culture, *as well as lived in the condition of each particular culture*" (my italics). What specific directives can be supplied by a supernatural religious faith which must be thinned down to the vaguest phrases in order to be acceptable to Mohammedan, Confucian, and Hindu cultures, whose members constitute the majority of the human race? Or is Mr. Eliot thinking only of a Christian world order, and an Anglo-Catholic one at that?

I pass over Mr. Eliot's notion of a hereditary elite because of its ambiguity. It is noteworthy, however, that he conceives of accessions to his elite not in terms of blood or wealth but of excellence and achievement. But if the avenues of achievement are to be kept open, it is of the utmost importance to preserve "the spirit of inquiry, skepticism, and innovation," and if fresh judgments and decisions are required for constantly changing situations, it is even more important to extend "the advance of liberty of thought and behavior." Yet all this makes for what Mr. Eliot and the neo-Thomists call "disorder." It must be controlled by a common religious faith, or else, despite certain gains, it will have the same disintegrating effects as it allegedly had on the medieval synthesis. Such control to be truly effective demands an iron grip on the intellectual life of the community. This in turn entails the existence of an organization, more centralized and powerful than the church in the Middle Ages, to determine what threatens the unity of culture and what not. No field of thought or actcion can be permitted to develop autonomously, for although the power of such an organization may nominally be restricted to matters of faith and morals, *it alone is the judge of what concerns faith and morals.* It is a foregone conclusion that the judgments of relevance will flow not so much from supernatural dogmas—which are unanalyzable abstractions that can be filled with variable historical content—as from the special interests of an ecclesiastical elite. The upshot is a variety of the very totalitarianism whose general pattern Mr. Eliot is anxious to avoid.

This, then, is Mr. Eliot's dilemma. He is unwilling to embrace current forms of totalitarianism, but his diagnosis of the causes of their rise leads him to proposals which, if enforced, would result in some kind of ecclesiastical fascism. His own account of the new total culture sounds gentle and conciliatory enough. But it is practically certain that people like him, or M. Maritain, will not administer it.

There is another alternative to Mr. Eliot's pattern of unification. This is a worldwide common faith, of a secular not supernatural character, based upon regional and international planning in economy, democracy in political and social life, and scientific method as the highest source of authority for those "fresh judgments and decisions in constantly changing situations" whose necessity Mr. Eliot admits. Its pattern of unification differs in notable ways from that proposed by Mr. Eliot. First of all, it is far less monistic. It aims at removing the disproportions between social, economic, and legal institutions but seeks no control over the free market of ideas or over manifestations of ideal culture—art, philosophy, theoretical science, and religion. It recognizes the desirability of producing integrated persons, but aside from equitably supplying the materials and the opportunity, it leaves the achievement of integration to the individual.

In general there is too much loose talk of integration and unification, and I fear that to some degree Mr. Eliot's analysis suffers from it. Unless we carefully distinguish the levels on which we should seek unification from those on which we must avoid it, we are likely to slur over the virtues, aesthetic and moral, of a rich plurality of cultural expressions. The common faith we require is limited only to beliefs that justify the social *practices* which insure democratic, cooperative living, peace, a decent standard of living, and an open career to intellectual and artistic talents—in other words, to what makes it possible for *different* human beings to live together without the plagues of poverty, war, and cultural terror. Integration on this level can be organized by intelligent social planning. But it neither presupposes nor implies integration on the plane of ideal cultural life, although the latter will naturally reflect in divers ways the new social experience. We have the right to believe, if democracy is preserved, that art, literature, philosophy, even religion, will be less constrained in a planned social-economic order than in the unplanned order of capitalism, whose "fetishism of commodities" exerts powerful, even when indirect, compulsions on the artist and thinker.

The underlying premises, whether theological, metaphysical, or naturalistic, from which different groups justify their common democratic beliefs and practices must not be subject to integration. It is enough, so to speak, that human beings live in accordance with democratic laws: It is foolish intolerance to make only one justification of the laws legal.

Integration on the level of personality is something else again. Mental and moral hygiene since the time of Plato teaches the wisdom of achieving a balanced wholeness. Yet it is also true that the torn and sick soul, like the "morbid secretions" of the oyster, to take an example from the opposite pole of creation, has often given the world pearls of great luster. We know that some geniuses have been borderline cases of insanity. We would not hesitate to lose the benefit of future geniuses of this type if we could free mankind altogether from the curse of insanity. But neuroses are too varied, and we know too little about their causation, once we strip current theories of their mythological elements, to justify any stringent, wholesale measures to prevent their emergence. Health has too often been confused with normality. According to some notions about neurosis, firemen would have to be declared neurotic about fire: They cannot see a large blaze without wanting to put it out. According to some other notions, the creative life, save in the case of a few Olympian characters, demands an inner torment and compulsive drive that may appear queer or unnecessary to the happily adjusted. Freud himself regards neurosis as inexpugnable from life because it grows out of the Oedipus complex, which is transmitted through the racial unconscious; while his more sober followers interpret it as a conflict between the spontaneous expansion of the ego and the constricting patterns of social authority, and therefore an integral element of all social life.

My point is that however we gauge the value of wholeness of personality, the desire to achieve it and the choice of any particular pattern must be left to the individual as sacred ground on which society cannot trespass, although through education it can surround the individual with multiple options. Wholeness of personality is practically impossible of achievement, except by a few, in a culture whose social relations are discordant. Yet the presence of harmonious social relations is far from sufficient to guarantee it.

An integrated character is made, not born. It is the individual himself, *when society provides tolerably decent permissive conditions,* who plays the greatest part in the making of it. The most significant problems in the struggle for the maturity and the inward peace and freedom that define the integrated character are personal, particularly when the threat of poverty and insecurity is removed. But such problems cannot always be resolved. Who does not know individuals, some of great powers and some of small, of whom we can say with ground that in our Western society, planned or not, they will remain beset by insatiable hungers, driven by errant impulses, and lacerated by conflicting allegiances or frustrated ambitions? Nor are they all denizens of Bohemia! There is evidence that even in Mr. Eliot's total organic culture the sensitive artist and the devout Christian will continue at war with each other in his soul. For his religious faith does not well up wholeheartedly from his poetic insights, nor is it a compulsion of a mystical experience: It is the object of a deliberate will-to-believe enjoying an uneasy triumph over the scruples of intelligence.

There is no valid reason to fear that a secular, democratic, socialist order would be hostile to the development of a superior culture. Let us not forget for a moment that the racial mythology of Hitlerism and the authoritarian dialectic materialism of Stalinism are vicious *ersatz* theologies; that their political systems are more theocratic than democratic; that their socialism is nonequalitarian without the adornments of an aristocracy of virtue or talents.

Mr. Eliot asks those of us who disagree with him to reflect that "a high degree of culture in an equalitarian society can only be attained if the great majority of men can be raised to a level, and kept at a level, which has never been remotely approached in the past." After reflection I am much puzzled by this. What can Mr. Eliot have in mind by an "equalitarian society"? Surely, not a society of biological equals! An equalitarian society is a democracy in which opportunities are accessible to all and in which levels of income, as an index of standards of living, are not oppressively disproportionate for those who do productive labor and which preserves a level of human welfare for all who are able and willing to work. Is Mr. Eliot saying that before a superior culture can be achieved, not only must some people enjoy a decent standard of living, but others must be deprived of it? Why? After all, we can count on the same normal range of *biological* variation as a seedbed of cultural talent in an equalitarian society as in a stratified one. Specifically, what phase of culture is threatened by an equalitarian society? Why must "the majority of men" be raised to a historically unparalleled level for great science to develop, or great literature? How has it been in other societies which have enjoyed great cultures but in which the vast majority have been little more than beasts of burden? Why should the emancipation of the great majority *necessarily* make matters worse? Let us lay aside the parochial bias concealed in the invocation of absolute standards that eternalize the past. Once we do, there is no compelling reason to expect that in respect to cultural achievement an equalitarian society with present-day technological resources will fall short of the high levels of nonequalitarian societies.

Because for Mr. Eliot, "Man is a rational animal," is a metaphysical, not empirical, proposition, it has no relevance to his program of social reform. Taken empirically, not all men are rational; but neither are most of them cretins or idiots. Rationality is not a timeless "essential" property of man but a natural and social power, dependent upon many other things which have a career in time. That is why men may become more rational and human through intelligent control of nature, society, history, and body-mind.

Because for Mr. Eliot, "Human personality possesses a unique worth," is a theological, not empirical, proposition, he discounts the possibilities of organizing education, after a socialist order has been won, not merely to raise the level of cultural interests but to diversify creative achievements. He overlooks the fact that the so-called average man is a social category, not a biological one. To a society that plans for freedom, the notion of the gray undifferentiated masses is utterly repugnant. The truth on this point was recognized long ago even under the distorting influences of conventional class society. "The greater intellect one has," says Pascal, "the more originality one finds in men. Ordinary persons find no difference between men." William James and John Dewey have between them elaborated the systematic basis for this insight and its educational imperatives—it is an insight that is freshly rediscovered by every teacher who has found his true vocation.

In the democratic socialist culture of the future—if it has a future, a question I have completely begged—it will be the teacher dedicated to the scientific spirit and the democratic faith, and not the priest, who will bear the chief responsibility for strengthening and enriching a common faith.

1945

Religion and Culture: A Reply by Jacques Maritain

Mr. Sidney Hook's article [1] deals with an issue which is crucial for democracy and the world of tomorrow. In my opinion he supports with questionable theoretical arguments a practical solution which for quite different reasons seems to me to be on

---

1. "The Dilemma of T. S. Eliot," *Nation* 160 (20 January 1945): 69–71.

the right track. Thus, all in all, I feel in agreement—in qualified agreement—with him on this practical solution, though I disagree with him on certain important particulars, which I shall try to elucidate.

I did not read the essay by T. S. Eliot to which he refers. Yet if the way in which he understands the import of the statements contained in this essay is correct, I am afraid I would also disagree with T. S. Eliot, at least as regards the manner in which theoretical views that both of us hold to be true should be applied to our present historical situation. This is a rather paradoxical situation, which may be explained by the fact that conclusions depend not only on the major premises but on the minor as well. Since I have endeavored for many years and in many books to discuss the matters involved, I shall take the liberty of summing up my position here.

1. In the "sacral" era of the Middle Ages a great attempt was made to build the life of the earthly community and civilization on the foundation of the unity of theological faith and religious creed. This attempt succeeded for a certain number of centuries but failed in the course of time, after the Reformation and the Renaissance; and a return to the medieval sacral pattern is by no means conceivable. In proportion as the civil community has become more perfectly distinguished from the spiritual realm of the church—a process which was in itself but a development of the Gospel distinction between the things that are Caesar's and the things that are God's—the civil community has become grounded on a common good and a common task which are of an earthly, "temporal," or "secular" order, and in which citizens belonging to diverse spiritual groups or "families" equally share. Religious division among men is in itself a misfortune. But it is a fact that we must willy-nilly recognize.

2. In modern times an attempt was made to ground the life of civilization and the earthly community on the foundation of mere reason—reason separated from religion and from the Gospel. This attempt fostered immense hopes in the last two centuries, and rapidly failed. Pure reason appeared more incapable than faith of insuring the spiritual unity of mankind, and the dream of a "scientific" creed uniting men in peace, and in common convictions about the aims and basic principles of human life and society, vanished in contemporary catastrophes. In proportion as the tragic events of the last decades have given the lie to the bourgeois rationalism of the eighteenth and nineteenth centuries, we have been confronted with the fact that religion and metaphysics are an essential part of human culture, primary and indispensable incentives in the very life of society.

3. As concerns, therefore, the society of tomorrow and the revital-

ized democracy we are hoping for, the only solution is of the *pluralistic* type. Men belonging to most different philosophical or religious creeds and families could and should cooperate in the common task and for the common welfare of the earthly community, provided they similarly assent to the basic tenets of a society of free men.

For a society of free men implies basic tenets which are at the core of its very existence and which it has the duty of defending and promoting. One of the errors of bourgeois optimism was to believe that in a free society "truth," and decisions befitting human dignity and freedom, would automatically emerge from the conflicts of forces and opinions; the error lay in conceiving of free society as a mere neutral boxing-ring for all kinds of ideas in mutual competition. Thus democratic society, in its concrete behavior, had no concept of itself, and freedom lay open, disarmed and paralyzed, to the undertakings of those who hated it, and who tried by all means to foster in men a vicious desire to become free from freedom.

If it is to conquer totalitarian trends and fulfill the hope of the peoples of the world the democracy of tomorrow will have its own concept of man and society, and its own philosophy, its own faith, enabling it to educate people for freedom and to defend itself against those who would use democratic liberties to destroy freedom and human rights. No society can live without a basic common inspiration and a basic common faith.

But the all-important point to be noted here is that this faith and inspiration, this philosophy and the concept of itself which democracy needs, all these do not belong in themselves to the order of religious creed and eternal life but to the temporal or secular order of earthly life, of culture and civilization. Even more, they are matters of practical rather than theoretical or dogmatic agreement; I mean they deal with practical conclusions that the human mind, rightly or wrongly, can try to justify from quite different philosophical outlooks, probably because they depend basically on simple, "natural" apperceptions of which the human heart becomes capable with the progress of moral conscience. Thus it is that men possessing quite different, even opposite metaphysical or religious outlooks—materialists, idealists, agnostics, Christians and Jews, Moslems and Buddhists—can converge, not by virtue of any identity of doctrine, but by virtue of an analogical similitude in practical principles, toward the same practical conclusions, and can share in the same practical democratic philosophy, provided that they similarly revere, perhaps for quite diverse reasons, truth and intelligence, human dignity, freedom, brotherly love, and the absolute value of moral good. As Mr. Hook puts it, "the underlying premises, whether theological, metaphysical, or naturalistic, from which different groups justify their common democratic beliefs and practices must not be subject to integration"—let us say to socially or politically enforced integration. "It is enough, so to speak, that human beings live in accordance with democratic laws"—and, let us add, share in the common—human, earthly, temporal—democratic faith and inspiration. "It is foolish intolerance to make only one justification of laws legal."

Here, if we want to be thorough in our thought and do not fear words, we should point out that where faith is, divine or human, there are also heretics, who threaten the unity of the community, either religious or civil. In the sacral society the heretic was the breaker of religious unity. In a lay society of free men the heretic is the breaker of "the common democratic beliefs and practices," the totalitarian, the one who denies freedom—his neighbor's freedom—and the dignity of the human person and the moral power of law. We do not wish him to be burned or expelled from the city or outlawed or put in a concentration camp! But the democratic community should defend itself against him, be he materialist, idealist, agnostic, Christian or Jew, Moslem or Buddhist, by keeping him out of its leadership, through the power of a strong and informed public opinion, and even by handing him over to justice when his activity endangers the security of the state—and over and above all by strengthening everywhere the philosophy of life, intellectual convictions, and constructive work which makes his influence powerless.

On the other hand, a serious task of intellectual reexamination should be undertaken regarding the essentials of democratic philosophy. And it would be especially desirable to develop the understanding of the pluralistic principle and the technique of pluralistic cooperation—it seems to me that the free traditions and the historical setup of this country would provide special opportunities for such a development.

4. The above-mentioned considerations explain why, writing on French affairs, I often emphasized my hope that the new French democracy would spring from the cooperation between Socialists and Christians. In such a democracy, however, would the "worldwide common faith" implied find in scientific method its highest source of authority? Would "intelligent social planning" be enough to insure the integration of culture? In the democratic culture of the future—if it has a future—will it be "the teacher dedicated to the scientific spirit," "and not the priest," "who will bear the chief responsibility for nurturing, strengthening, and enriching a common faith"?

Here are the main points on which I should like to express disagreement with Mr. Hook's views. I am afraid he has been inspired in these passages by that rationalist bias whose illusory character I pointed out above (Number 2).

The very expression "common faith" which Mr. Hook uses should make us realize that democratic inspiration cannot find in scientific method its highest source of authority. This "faith" is "of a secular not supernatural character"; yet even a secular faith implies the commitment of the whole man and his innermost spiritual energies, and draws its strength, therefore, from beliefs which go far beyond scientific method. In other words, the justification of the practical conclusions which make such a "common faith" common to all is in each one an integral part of this very faith. As for social planning, even intelligent, I am afraid a culture organized by social planning alone would offer little chance for the creative powers of human personality or for the enthusiasm and happiness of the people.

The scientific spirit is of invaluable help for culture insofar as it develops in human minds, in a general way, respect and love for truth and the habits of intellectual accuracy. (This is why, let us observe parenthetically, the scientific spirit of the eighteenth-century schoolmen played so basic a part in the rise of Western culture.) Yet neither culture nor democracy lives on science alone. Science, especially modern science, deals with the means, especially with the material means, of human life. Wisdom which deals with the ends is also—and above all—necessary. And the fact remains that democratic faith—implying as it does faith in justice, in freedom, in brotherly love, in the dignity of the human person, in his rights as well as in his responsibilities, in that quality of just laws which makes them binding in conscience, in the deep-rooted aspirations which call for political and social emancipation of the people—cannot be justified, nurtured, strengthened, and enriched without philosophical or religious convictions—"whether theological, metaphysical, or naturalistic"—which deal with the very substance and meaning of human life. Here appears the truth of T. S. Eliot's emphasis on the organic character of culture, as well as the injustice of reproaching him with suggesting proposals which, if enforced, would result in some kind of "ecclesiastical fascism." For we can be sure it is not to the compulsory power of any ecclesiastical agency, but rather to the persuasive power of truth that he makes the effort toward the integration of culture appendant. The effort toward integration must not only be brought about on the level of personality and private life; it is essential to culture itself and the life of the community as a whole: an integration which does not depend on legal enforcement but on spiritual and freely accepted inspiration.

As a result, it is but normal that in a democratic culture and society the diverse philosophical or religious schools of thought which in their practical conclusions agree with regard to democratic tenets, and which claim to justify them, come into free competition. Let each school assert its belief with fullness and integrity! But let no one try to impose it by force upon the others! The reciprocal tension which ensues will enrich rather than harm the common task.

5. As for myself, who believe that the idea of man propounded by the metaphysics of Aristotle and Thomas Aquinas is the rational foundation of democratic philosophy, and that the Gospel inspiration is its true living soul, I am confident that in the free competition of which I just spoke the Christian leaven would play an evergrowing part. In any case the responsibility for nurturing, strengthening, and enriching a common democratic faith would belong no less to the priest, dedicated to the preaching of the Gospel, than to the teacher, dedicated to the scientific spirit, if both of them come to a clear awareness of the needs of our times and rid themselves of parasitical prejudices inherited from the past. If you are looking for the *chief* responsibility, I would say that as a matter of fact it would probably be that of a leadership made up of Christian laymen and the most enlightened elements of the working classes.

Finally, if I affirm that without genuine and vital reconciliation between democratic inspiration and evangelical inspiration our hopes for the democratic culture of the future will be frustrated, I do not appeal to police force to obtain such reconciliation; I only state what I hold to be true. It would be foolish intolerance to label as intolerance any affirmation of truth which is not watered down with doubt even if it does not please some of our democratic fellow citizens. I insist as forcefully as T. S. Eliot that the Christian leaven is necessary to the life and integration of our culture. From the religious point of view I would wish all men to believe in the integrity of Christian truth. From the social-temporal point of view, I would be satisfied if the Christian energies at work in the community draw on the fullness of supernatural faith in a number of men and retain at least their moral impetus in those in whom these energies still exist, perhaps unawares, but have been more or less secularized.

It is true, moreover, that supernatural faith does not provide us with any particular social or political system. In such matters supernatural faith must be complemented by sound practical philosophy, historical information, and social and political experience. Yet supernatural faith, if it is truly lived—in other words, if Christians know "of what spirit they are"—provides them with basic inspiration and vital truths which permeate their social and political systems and work for human dignity against any kind of totalitarian oppression.

Allow me to add that to consider the religious faith of a poet like T. S. Eliot as "the object of a deliberate will-to-believe enjoying an uneasy triumph over the scruples of intelligence" is perhaps the only way in which an unbeliever can explain to himself such a strange phenomenon, but is in itself perfectly irrelevant. It is no more relevant to pretend that the neo-Thomists regard as "disorder" "the spirit of inquiry, skepticism, and innovation": (or) "the advance of liberty of thought and behavior" (as disorder) if this liberty is inspired by what is true and good.

I should like to conclude by saying that I have been particularly happy to find myself this once in agreement, even qualified, with Sidney Hook, except for the points to which I just referred, which are of no little importance. Such an agreement on practical conclusions between philosophers whose basic theoretical outlooks are widely separated is, to my mind, an illustration of the pluralistic cooperation of which I spoke.

1945

Religion and Society: A Rejoinder

It would be churlish not to recognize the generosity of spirit with which Jacques Maritain responds to the position of a militant secularist whose forthright criticisms of all varieties of supernaturalism he regards as so profoundly mistaken. His response is all the more significant because the great transformation in the theoretical *political* position of American Catholicism—and it can be argued of the Church itself—can be attributed largely to his direct influence. A generation or two ago, the Catholic position in politics was expressed in Ryan and Boland's *Catholic Principles of Politics*. Based upon past papal encyclicals, it frankly asserts that in the event—admitted to be unlikely—that Catholics ever constituted a majority of the population, consistency required that freedom of religious belief and practice be denied to other confessions on the Augustinian grounds that where man's eternal salvation is at stake, error has no rights. In this respect the Catholic position was sometimes compared with the Communist position on civil rights. Just as the Communists invoked the freedoms of the Bill of Rights to agitate for and organize a society in which these very freedoms would be denied to those who dissented from communism, the traditional Catholic position invoked freedom of religious advocacy under the Bill of Rights while Catholics were in a minority but in principle could not acknowledge the same freedom to other religious and irreligious groups if and when Catholics constituted a majority.

Today this position seems happily to be a matter of history. Although the persecution of some Protestant sects continues in some South American countries, the theoretical position has been abandoned. In fact its reassertion some years ago by Father Feeny of Boston and his charge that the papacy had capitulated to the modernist heresy it once condemned led to his excommunication. The fact that in a Catholic country like Eire there is no religious persecution is a sign of the change, the election of John Kennedy to the presidency of the United States evidence of the belief in the credibility of the change among non-Catholics. One need only contrast the character of the political argument in the United States when Alfred Smith ran for the presidency in 1928 with the campaign of 1960. If any one man can be credited with responsibility for changing the theoretical position of the Catholic Church it is Jacques Maritain. When we add to this his insight into the democratic promise of American institutions and his courageous defense of the main direction of America's postwar policy against America-haters at home and abroad (Sartre), the debt of the democratic community to him grows.

Nonetheless, in the interest of the truth to which Jacques Maritain appeals, I must challenge the validity of some key points in reply. To begin with, empirical questions must be distinguished from semantic ones. The first empirical question is historical in character. Is it true that "in modern times an attempt was made to ground the life of civilization and the earthly community on the foundation of mere reason"? To answer this question affirmatively would be a strange misreading of modern history. Reason is never "mere" or wholly "pure"; it is always related to interest, passion, and desire. Is it reasonable to assert that the conflicts of interests, passions, and desires were mediated by the establishment of institutions that sought to give the widest and securest expression to democratic values? Can we justifiably say that any regime in the modern period—roughly from the English Revolution to 1914—has devised its laws of property, family, divorce, and related matters on rational ethical grounds without traditional religious influences?

When Maritain mentions "contemporary catastrophes" he is referring to the great twin evils of fascism and communism. But surely no one justly claims that the dogmas of racialism and dialectical materialism and the practices based on them could ever pass rational or scientific muster. True, traditional religion no longer rules the world but some of its worst features have been embodied in the ideology and practice of twentieth-century totalitarianism. They have functioned in a way to justify reference to them as political religions.

But what of nontotalitarian societies—whether democratic or not? Can their existing political and social mess be attributed to the consistent attempt to follow rational policies? It would require considerable hardihood to assert this. Although democracy is celebrated on holiday occasions as a moral faith, has it been consistently and reasonably applied in practice to the social, economic, and political institutions of our culture? To what extent have the laws set up to govern human behavior been derived from enlightened jurisprudential considerations? To what extent have religious influences still operated in the field of sexual behavior, marriage, divorce, birth control, the position of women, crime and punishment?

Jacques Maritain stresses the "all-important point" that the "philosophy and concept of democracy" are not relevant to "the order of religious creed" but to "the temporal and secular order." They are in his terms matters of "practical rather than theoretical agreement." With this I am in complete and hearty accord. It seems to me, however, that Maritain holds some other views about democracy that are oddly inconsistent with his "all-important point."

The basic tenets and practices of democracy—of the democratic faith according to Maritain—rest on simple natural "apperceptions" available to all men regardless of their religious or metaphysical persuasions, provided they are committed, again regardless of their religious and metaphysical persuasions, to the values of "truth and intelligence, human dignity, freedom, brotherly love, and the absolute value of moral good." With respect to all these—despite some ambiguities about the meaning of "brotherly love" and "absolute value," about which I shall not here cavil—once more I agree with all my heart. This "common faith" is a moral faith and I am prepared to justify democratic principles and practices in its light.

But what of this moral faith? How is it to be justified? If anyone challenges the validity of any or all of the values central to it what grounds can we offer in their support? Since we are dealing with the realm of "the practical," my position is that ultimately their validity rests upon their fruits in human experience. Moral principles cannot be derived from any principles of logic; nor from any religious or metaphysical propositions without question-begging.[2] In the realm of practice they depend upon the nature of human nature

2. Cf. my chapter on "The Justifications of Democracy" in *Political Power and Personal Freedom* (New York: Macmillan Co., 1959).

and the reflective desires based upon the assessment of alternative courses of action open to human agents. The rational or scientific approach open to any disputed policy or value is to investigate the causes and consequences of our evaluative judgments in the light of some common or shared interests. Without some common or shared interests no common or shared morality is possible. If problems of value conflict are approached piecemeal our task is always to find some common interest that will extend the area of agreement or permit us to live peacefully with our differences in a spirit of live and let live. Whether or not all creatures that are biologically defined as men do possess common interests is an empirical question, not one that is an analytical consequence of any biological definition.

Although Maritain acknowledges that this "common faith" in democracy and in the moral values constitutive of democracy is "practical," "secular," "not supernatural," he still insists that it "draws its strength . . . from beliefs which go far beyond scientific method" or anything that scientific inquiry can disclose. "In other words," he tells us, "the justification of the practical conclusions which make such a 'common faith' common to all is in each one an integral part of this very faith." This is a rather obscure saying uncharacteristic of Maritain's usual clarity. One would have thought that the justification of practical conclusions in any realm depends upon the consequences of practice, upon the fruits or issues of conduct in carrying on human affairs.

For Maritain, however, this is not the case. He removes the obscurity from his remarks by explicitly asserting that "the fact remains that democratic faith . . . cannot be *justified, nurtured, strengthened, and enriched without philosophical or religious convictions*" (my italics). Unless my logic is faulty this seems to me to represent a complete abandonment of "the all-important point" that the philosophy, concept, and faith in democracy are practical matters of the temporal and secular order. If it were true that the justification of the democratic faith rests on philosophical and religious convictions, and not on historical and practical experience, then it would follow that one could not consistently deny the philosophical and religious convictions on which democracy allegedly rests, and still affirm the validity of democracy. But Maritain had previously assured us that one could do so without inconsistency. Otherwise how could he have expressed even partial agreement with my position? Further, it is demonstrable that any philosophical or religious conviction "whether theological, metaphysical, or naturalistic" can be squared with the affirmation as well as denial of the democratic faith. At most, certain theological or metaphysical beliefs may exclude some types of social order but they cannot entail belief in the validity of democracy unless its constitutive values are already pre-supposed in the premises that serve allegedly in the argument of justification.

If Jacques Maritain believes that the democratic faith and its moral values require for their justification certain philosophical or religious convictions, whether theological or metaphysical, he is denying the autonomy of the democratic faith. And by the same logic, what is even more important, he is denying the autonomy of human morality. This, it seems to me, is the fundamental difference between us. For him and other kindred spirits, the moral order must rest ultimately on an order that transcends the natural, historical, and social order of man. This difference is reflected in the position of those today who, having abandoned "the sacral order" of medieval life, still believe that questions bearing on "the very substance and meaning of human life"—marriage, divorce, birth control, abortion, suicide and voluntary euthanasia for the hopelessly afflicted, and allied issues—cannot be decided on purely moral grounds.[3]

1945

---

3. I have discussed the differences between the moral and sacramental approach to these issues in my *The Place of Religion in a Free Society*, The Livingstone Lectures (Lincoln: University of Nebraska Press, 1963).

Chapter 21

The Autonomy of the

Democratic Faith

By religion I mean faith in the existence of some supernatural power which governs human destiny and serves as a cosmic support of human ideals. Insofar as religion functions purely as a consolation to the individual for the irremediable evils and tragedies of existence, it is too personal a matter to be anyone else's concern, and I shall not discuss it further. But the consolatory function of religious beliefs must not be proclaimed as valid evidence for their truth, since it is obvious that myths as well as truths may be consoling.

In recent years many large claims have been made for religious faith. It has been celebrated as the taproot of democracy, indeed of all morality. Its revival has been hailed as the best ground for reasonable hope in an enduring world peace. It has been urged as a specific for industrial strife, crime, poverty, and all other impediments to a just society. It has been widely asserted that we must choose between a renewed faith in religion and a faith in some totalitarian ideology which is certain to blossom wherever religion withers. A whole chorus of voices insists that the crisis of our age must ultimately be defined in these terms.

I believe all of these claims are false. The validity of democracy as a moral and political ideal does not rest upon religious doctrines. Despite the resurgence of religion during the past decade, the world is not noticeably a better place to live in. In many respects it is worse. The alternative to religion is not necessarily the brutalitarian nihilism of Hitlerism or the dictatorial, secret-police state of Stalinism or any other variety of totalitarianism. Insofar as civilization has a future, it is contingent upon the growth of ideals of a universal, democratic humanism, which embraces what is morally best in religion, fortified by reliance not on supernatural dogmas but on the instruments of enlightened, scientific intelligence. Religion has had thousands of years to unify the world into a semblance of a just and cooperative world order. It has failed. Democratic humanism may fail, too. That depends, in part, upon whether the ardor and devotion that have been expended on transcendental objects of faith can be transferred to the democratic heritage as a pattern for the reconstruction of social life.

It is an open question whether the revival of religious beliefs and institutions may not lead to the exacerbation of differences among men. For most religions make claims to being the exclusive repositories of God's truth, acceptance of which is a necessary condition of salvation. Were these claims to be abandoned, the justification for *separate* religious organizations would largely disappear. But to a militant believer religion means *the* religion—his own. When he looks to the future of religion to liberate mankind from its burden of evils, he looks primarily to his own church and its teachings.

It is hard to find a doctrine common to all religious faiths and of sufficient importance to override doctrinal differences. Belief in the Brotherhood of Man under the Fatherhood of God comes closest perhaps to being the common article of faith of all religious groups in the Western and Near Eastern worlds. It is this belief, we are told, on which the democratic philosophy rests. To accept the latter and reject the former is to be guilty of inconsistency, of sentimental and unintelligent belief in democracy.

Logically, the derivation of democracy from this belief is a complete *non sequitur*. The proposition that all men are brothers, whether taken theologically or biologically, does not entail any proposition essential to the democratic faith. No matter what the origin of man is, supernatural or natural, we cannot legitimately infer from his equality in supernatural status or natural fact that men should enjoy equality of opportunity or equality of citizenship. These democratic beliefs are compatible with many different alleged "presuppositions." Our reasons for accepting democracy rather than its ethical and political alternatives are not only independent of our reasons for accepting the theological or biological brotherhood of man; they are far more warranted in the light of experience. This is true for any moral ideal. Our grounds for belief in honesty and kindness do not depend upon belief in supernatural dogma or other "presuppositions." We would be horrified by anyone who told us that if he surrendered his belief in the existence of God or the second law of thermodynamics or what not, he would no longer regard dishonesty and cruelty as morally wrong. The same logic holds for the belief in the democratic ideal. It is in terms of its fruits and consequences in human experience that we accept or reject it: not in terms of supernatural belief, whether taken literally or metaphorically.

Historically, there is little warrant for the assertion that religious dogmas are the prime source of modern democracy. The most religious countries are notoriously not the most democratic ones. The historical record shows that organized religion has accommodated itself to all social systems and forms of government, no matter how tyrannical, which have tolerated its existence. In some countries it has actively supported social iniquities. Undeniably there have been religious movements, and still more often great religious personalities, that have aided the cause of freedom. What moved them in the main were moral insights and a complex of historical interests, shared by secular movements, too, and not special theological dogmas. For these dogmas served as identical premises in the thinking of those who opposed progressive movements. We know that Judaism countenanced slavery, while Christianity never condemned it in principle. Organized religion was one of the mainstays of feudalism. In Spain today it supports Franco. In Russia it supports Stalin—when he lets it.

The organizational structure of institutions based on supernatural dogmas and of the social systems they actively support tends toward theocracy, not democracy. Recognition of the rights of individual conscience, toleration of religious minorities, freedom of scientific inquiry, abolition of child labor, birth control, the use of anæsthetics, secular education, separation of church and state, and other liberal and humane practices have made their way in the face of opposition of organized religion.

It is sometimes maintained that nonreligious protagonists for a better world have drawn their inspiration and fire from the dying embers of a religious faith which, despite their denials, still glow within them. This is obviously question-begging, for it assumes that no validation of moral ideals is possible except in terms of supernatural belief—precisely the point at issue. It would be truer to say that religious believers who have supported the cause of social justice have been moved by the evidence of experience and not by the compelling force of theological doctrine. The evidence that men share a common lot and destiny in a world of atomic power is far stronger than the evidence that they share a common origin, and a supernatural one at that.

Those who see promise in the revival of religion overlook the significance of the fact that supernatural faith is marked by the sharpest dualism in its conception of the place of man in nature. This dualism is the root source of ambiguity in the application of religious dogmas. It denies that man is a child of nature. It endows him with an immortal soul which is essentially independent of his body and his culture. Man's soul is the most precious thing about him. He can and must keep it pure, no matter what the world, his transitory home, is like. It is as immortal souls that all men are equal before God. And this equality is essentially unaffected by any kind of social and political inequality. Consequently, it is always possible to square supernatural dogmas with societies in which democracy is absent—or present. It is never clear on religious grounds alone how its dogmas are being applied. That is why they are compatible with social policies that are mutually contradictory to each other. More important still, it is impossible within the framework of religious thought to find a *method* which will enable us to judge and negotiate conflicting interests in empirical situations. A common supernatural faith therefore provides no principle of direction for the intelligent control of social change.

Religion is sometimes understood not as involving belief in the supernatural or acceptance of doctrine, but as an attitude of ultimate concern, or in [William] James's phrase, "a man's total reaction upon life." In this sense everyone who is passionately alive to something exciting in the world or to some possibility struggling to be born, is religious; the irreligious, apparently, are those who are dead but still unburied. We possess a number of perfectly good words to designate this activity of vital emotional interest, and I prefer not to be converted to religion by definition. But if we use the term in this sense, there is a certain danger in equating religion with any large faith and then welcoming a general revival of religion. For it underestimates, when it does not ignore, the quality, content, and fruits of faith, which should be of infinitely greater concern to us than the bare act of faith, no matter how intense. Better a man of little faith in good than of great faith in evil.

A few years ago it was quite fashionable to speak of fascism as a great faith which integrated the personality of its believers, elicited a passionate devotion to objects greater than themselves, and brought a firm discipline into their emotional life. The fruits of that faith were evident even in the past to all who wished to know the truth. But in the moment of its triumph, many bowed down in vulgar worship of power, blinded by its nimbus of glory. Similarly, there are today some who have suddenly discovered that the Russian Communist faith is the only basis upon which the civilized tradition can be rebuilt. Its total reign of terror, which has grown in intensity over the years, is callously written off as a part of the costs of "progress," although the costs of Christianity, the industrial revolution, capitalism, and democracy are computed with great care and indignation. In the case of both fascism and communism, we observe a sharp dissociation between ends and means, and a substitution of unlimited faith in the future for the exercise of intelligence and humanity in the present. These faiths should be judged, not by the intensity with which they are held, but by their consequences on the lives of the human beings who accept them, on the lives of their victims, and on the lives of those on whom they are *imposed.* For in countries where such faiths are official, they are not freely selected among alternatives. In short, religious faith cannot be separated from doctrines, and from the practices to which doctrines lead or which they justify.

Some who deplore totalitarian faiths because of their degrading effects express the wish that the fanaticism with which their adherents are imbued could be harnessed to faith in democracy. This disregards the ways in which what is most typical in totalitarian faith is indissolubly bound up with its creed and practices—a union that is happily no longer true in present-day religion. A democrat cannot be fanatical in the same way as a Fascist or Communist, for whom an unanalyzed end justifies the use of *any* means. But it does not follow that because he is humane and intelligent a democrat cannot be passionate and active in his faith, that he must be a political Hamlet, irresolute before the combination of toughness and chicanery with which his totalitarian opponents confront him.

Instead of a revival of religious faith in general, we should work specifically toward a revival, or a new birth, of faith in democracy. Such a faith is the only one that can unify society without imposing uniformity upon it. It is a faith that can embrace believers and nonbelievers in a vast number of different "presuppositions"—theological, metaphysical, naturalistic. For these are all compatible with democracy. Required of those who profess them is only that they sincerely accept the democratic practices by which equality of concern for all individuals, collective participation, and freely given consent of the governed—the cardinal doctrine of democratic faith —are implemented. It excludes none but avowed totalitarians and the secret totalitarians who redefine democracy to make it synonymous with its opposite. Such a democratic faith has many fronts on which to fight: race relations, education, social, political, and economic organization. It does not fear to use power; otherwise it is at the mercy of nondemocratic faiths. It seeks to tame power by making it intelligent and responsible, that is, designed to achieve morally inclusive ends through institutions that provide for wide participation and open criticism.

As a social philosophy, the democratic faith accepts that measure of socialism which would liberate the productive forces of modern technology without curtailing the freedoms enshrined in the Bill of Rights, which would remove the blight of poverty and the threat of insecurity without making a fetish of efficiency and centralization, which would provide, as far as possible, those objective conditions of social and cultural life in whose absence "equality of opportunity for all" is a hollow phrase. It may be a tautology to say that such a form of socialism (the word is not essential—perhaps it is too late to save it from its totalitarian kidnappers) can exist only where political democracy exists. But a tautology is important when contraposed to an absurdity—such as the view that socialism can be achieved by the political dictatorship of a minority party.

The democratic faith is not only a social philosophy but a personal philosophy as well. It calls for a mode of behavior in our daily interchanges with each other that makes the inescapable occasions of differences and dispute opportunities for cooperative discussion in which all interests receive a fair hearing. It recognizes that no profound social change is possible which does not involve a change in institutions, in the impersonal relationships which govern men. But it also recognizes that institutions are even less capable than machines of running according to blueprints and plans alone. No matter how generous the declared purposes of an institution may be, unless it is operated by men and women dedicated in their own lives to these purposes, it can easily be transformed into an agency of human oppression.

There is nothing promised by a revival of religious faith, considered in terms of doctrine, which is not promised by a new growth of faith in democracy. But there are some things threatened by the revival of the first which are not threatened by the growth of the second.

How to inspire, extend, and strengthen faith in democracy, and build a mass movement of men and women personally dedicated to it, is a difficult problem which cannot be treated here. But it is clear that although devotees of the democratic faith may be found the world over, the most practical opportunities exist where democratic traditions have until now, despite all their imperfections, been strongest. In countries in which political democracy still exists, we have something to go on, a certain pattern of democratic life, and an area of freedom in which it can be enriched and deepened. If the destinies of these countries can be linked together in a common resolve not merely to preserve political democracy but to build democracy as a way of life into the very fabric of their social institutions, they will conquer the world not by force of arms but by force of example. For democracy is like love in this: It cannot be brought to life in others by command. Shared experience, sympathetic understanding, and good works are ultimately the best nourishment for democratic convictions.

1945

Index

Index